SURPRISED BY HOPE

SURPRISED BY HOPE

TOM WRIGHT

First published in Great Britain in 2007

Society for Promoting Christian Knowledge
36 Causton Street
London SW1P 4ST
www.spckpublishing.co.uk

Reprinted five times
Reissued 2011

British Library Cataloguing-in-Publication Data
A catalogue record for this book is available from the British Library

ISBN 978–0–281–06477–9

1 3 5 7 9 10 8 6 4 2

Printed in Great Britain by Ashford Colour Press

Produced on paper from sustainable forests

In grateful memory of
Stephen Neill, George Caird and Charlie Moule,
teachers, scholars, pastors and friends,
in the sure and certain hope of the resurrection
of the dead

Contents

Contents

Part 2
GOD'S FUTURE PLAN

Contents

Part 3
HOPE IN PRACTICE: RESURRECTION AND THE MISSION OF THE CHURCH

Contents

Preface

What are we waiting for? And what are we going to do about
it in the meantime?

Those are the two questions which shape this book. First, it
is about the ultimate future hope held out in the Christian
gospel: the hope, that is, for 'salvation', 'resurrection', 'eternal life'
and the cluster of other things that go with them. Second, it is
about the discovery of hope within the present world: about
the practical ways in which hope can come alive for communities and individuals who for whatever reason may lack it.
And it is about the ways in which embracing the first can and
should generate and sustain the second.

Most people, in my experience – including many Christians – don't know what the ultimate Christian hope really is.
Most people – again, sadly, including many Christians – don't
expect Christians to have much to say about hope within the
present world. Most people don't imagine that these two could
have anything to do with each other. Hence the title of the book:
hope comes as a surprise, at several levels at once.

At the first level, the book is obviously about death, and about
what can be said, from a Christian perspective, about what
lies beyond it. I am not going to attempt a physical or medical
analysis of death and its aftermath, nor yet a psychological or
anthropological description of beliefs and practices to do with
death. There are plenty of books about such things. Rather, I
approach the question as a biblical theologian, drawing on other
disciplines but hoping to supply what they usually lack, and
what I believe the church needs to recapture: the classic Christian answer to the question of death and beyond, which these
days is not so much disbelieved (in world and church alike)
as simply not known. A survey of beliefs about life after death,

conducted in Britain in 1995, indicated that, though most people believed in some kind of continuing life, only a tiny minority, even from among churchgoers, believed in the classic Christian position, that of a future bodily resurrection. Indeed, I have often found that, though Christians still use the word 'resurrection', they treat it as a synonym for 'life after death' or 'going to heaven', and that, when pressed, they often share the confusion of the wider world on the subject. And some Christian writers on the subject of death manage to marginalize resurrection and all that goes with it, without apparently supposing that any great harm is thereby done.

I should say, as a kind of disclaimer, that at one level I am not well qualified to speak on the subject of death. Now in my late 50s, I am the least bereaved middle-aged person I know. My life has been remarkably free from tragedy; almost all my relatives have lived to a good age. I am surprised and grateful for this, and I certainly don't take it for granted. Moreover, though I have been ordained for over thirty years, the fact that my vocation has led me into universities on the one hand and into cathedral and diocesan work on the other means that I have conducted fewer funerals and memorial services than most clergy manage in their first two or three years. Seldom have I stood at a deathbed. But, whereas I obviously have a lot to learn first-hand about all these matters, I think I have made up for it by soaking myself, in a way that many don't have the chance to do, in the life and thought of the early Christians.[1] As I have done that I have regularly returned with a sense that their voice has not been disbelieved, but simply not heard at all. My aim in this book is to bring their beliefs to light again, and I hope to life, in the conviction that they offer not only the best hope but the best-*grounded* hope that we have, and what's more a hope which joins up, as I have said, with the hope which ought to energize our work for God's kingdom in the present world.

At the second level, then, the book is about the groundwork of practical and even political theology – of, that is, Christian reflection on the nature of the task we face as we seek to bring God's kingdom to bear on the real and painful world in which we live. (I apologize to librarians that this may cause confusion: is the book to be catalogued with 'eschatology' (death, judgment, heaven and hell) or 'politics'?) Here, too, a disclaimer is in order. I am not a politician, though it is true that, in virtue of my office, I am a member of the British House of Lords. I have neither run for public office nor campaigned actively – in terms of the sheer hard work of speaking, writing, marching, cajoling – for many of the causes in which I believe. I have tried to put my shoulder to the wheel by other means. But the conviction has grown on me that the subjects in which I have specialized, and the pastoral situations I now face every day in a diocese several parts of which have suffered severely from the faceless cruelties of the last fifty years, challenge us to think through some at least of what a Christian should be saying and thinking about rediscovering hope in the public and political world. As I have done so, I have found that these two themes of hope have, again and again, joined themselves together. I freely hand to potential critics these two disclaimers, my inexperience in both grief and politics, and hope that nevertheless the surprise of the Christian hope in both areas will re-energize and refresh those who work, more than I have been able to do, with both the dying and the dispossessed.

One more general word of introduction. All language about the future, as any economist or politician will tell you, is simply a set of signposts pointing into a fog. We see through a glass darkly, says St Paul as he peers towards what lies ahead. All our language about future states of the world, and of ourselves, consists of complex pictures which may or may not correspond very well to the ultimate reality. But that doesn't mean it's anybody's guess, or that every opinion is as good as every other one. And – supposing someone came forwards out of the fog to meet us? That, of course, is the central, though often ignored, Christian belief.

This book grew out of lectures which were originally given in Westminster Abbey during the course of 2001. Some of these were reworked as the Stephenson Lectures in Sheffield in Spring 2003; some were given in Holy Trinity Church, Guildford, also in Spring 2003; some were reworked again into the Didsbury Lectures at the Nazarene College in Manchester in October 2005; others found their way into church study days in St Andrew's Church, Charleston, South Carolina, in January 2005; in St Mark's Episcopal Church, Jacksonville, Florida, in March 2005; in City Church, Newcastle, also in 2005; in St Mark's Theological Centre, Canberra, in April 2006; in a consortium of churches in Roanoke, Virginia, in March 2007, and (in the form of the Faraday Lecture) in Cambridge in May 2007. I am extremely grateful to all those who invited, welcomed and hosted me on all these occasions, and particularly to those who by their questions and acute comments have helped me think through the issues further and avoid at least some mistakes. I am grateful to the 'Ship of Fools' website for commissioning the piece I have included at the end, and for permission to republish a lightly emended version of it here. My thanks, too, to Dr Nick Perrin, who during his time at Westminster Abbey worked over the text as it then was and made all kinds of helpful suggestions. And my thanks, as ever and always, to Simon Kingston, Joanna Moriarty and the energetic and watchful staff at SPCK.

Tom Wright

Part 1

SETTING THE SCENE

1

All dressed up and no place to go?

1. Introduction

Five snapshots set the scene for the two questions which this book addresses.

In autumn 1997, Britain was plunged into a week of national mourning for Princess Diana, reaching its climax in the extraordinary funeral service in Westminster Abbey. All over the country, and in many parts of the world, people brought flowers, teddy bears and other objects to churches, cathedrals and town halls, and queued for hours to write touching if sometimes tacky messages in books of condolence. Similar if somewhat smaller occasions of public grief took place following such incidents as the Hillsborough disaster of 1989 (when many football supporters were crushed to death) and the Oklahoma City bombing in 1995. They showed a rich confusion of belief, half-belief, sentiment and superstition about the fate of the dead. The reaction of the churches showed how far we had come from what might once have been traditional Christian teaching on the subject.

The second scene was farce, with a serious undertone. Early in 1999 I awoke one morning to hear on the radio that a public figure had been sacked for heretical statements about the afterlife. I listened eagerly. Was this, perhaps, a radical bishop or theologian, exposed at last? Back came the answer, incredible but true: no, it was a football coach. Glenn Hoddle, the manager of the England team, declared his belief in a particular version of reincarnation, according to which sins committed in one life are punished by disabilities in the next. Groups representing disabled people objected strongly, and Hoddle was dismissed. It was commented at the time, however, that re-incarnation had become remarkably popular in our society; and that it would be very odd if Hindus (many of whom hold similar beliefs) were automatically banned from coaching a national sports team.

The third scene is not a single moment, but the snapshot will be familiar. Twenty or thirty people arrive in slow-moving cars at a shabby building on the edge of town. A tinny electronic organ plays supermarket music. A few words, the press of a button, a solemn look from the undertaker, and they file out again, go home for a cup of tea, and wonder what it was all about. Cremation, almost unknown in the United Kingdom a hundred years ago, is now the preference, actual or assumed, of the great majority. It both reflects and causes subtle but far-reaching shifts in attitudes to death and to whatever hope lies beyond.

I initially wrote those opening descriptions in early 2001. By the end of that year, of course, we had witnessed a fourth moment, too well known but also too horrible to describe or discuss in much detail. The events of September 11 of that year are etched in global memory; the thousands who died, and the tens of thousands who were bereaved, evoke our love and prayers. I shall not say much more about that day, but for many people it raised once more, very sharply, the questions which this book seeks to discuss – as did, in their different ways, the three massive so-called 'natural disasters' of 2004 and 2005: the Asian tsunami of Boxing Day 2004; the hurricanes on the Gulf Coast of America of August 2005, bringing long-lasting devastation to New Orleans in particular; and the horrifying earthquake in Pakistan and Kashmir in October of that same year.

The fifth scene is a graveyard of a different sort. If you go to the historic village of Easington in County Durham, and walk down the hill towards the sea, you come to the town called Easington Colliery. The town still bears that name, but there is no colliery there any more. Where the pit head once stood, with thousands of people at work and producing more coal, faster and more efficiently, than most other pits, there is smooth and level grass. Empty to the eye, but pregnant with bereavement. All around, despite the heroic efforts of local leaders, there are the signs of post-industrial blight, with all the human fallout of other people's power-games. And that sight stands in my mind as a symbol, or rather a symbolic question. What hope is there for communities that have lost their way, their way of life, their coherence, their *hope*?[1]

This book addresses two questions which have often been dealt with entirely separately but which, I passionately believe, belong tightly together. First, what is the ultimate Christian hope? Second, what hope is there for change, rescue, transformation, new possibilities within the world in the present? And the main answer can be put like this. As long as we see 'Christian hope' in terms of 'going to heaven', of a 'salvation' which is essentially *away from* this world, the two questions are bound to appear as unrelated. Indeed, some insist angrily that to ask the second one at all is to ignore the first one, which is the really important one. This in turn makes some others get angry when people talk of resurrection, as if this might draw attention away from the really important and pressing matters of contemporary social concern. But if the 'Christian hope' is for *God's new creation*, for 'new heavens and new earth' – and if that hope has already come to life in Jesus of Nazareth – then there is every reason to join the two questions together. And if that is so, we find that answering the one is also answering the other. I find that to many – not least many Christians – all this comes as a surprise: both that the Christian hope is surprisingly different from what they had assumed, and that this same hope offers a coherent and energizing basis for work in today's world.

In this first chapter I want to set the scene and open up the questions by looking at the contemporary confusion in our world – the wider world, beyond the churches – about life after death. Then, in the second chapter, I shall look at the churches themselves, where there seems to me a worryingly similar uncertainty. This will highlight the key questions that have to be asked, and suggest a framework for how we go about answering them.

I have become convinced that most people, including most practising Christians, are muddled and misguided on this topic, and that this muddle produces quite serious mistakes in our thinking, our praying, our liturgies, our practice, and perhaps particularly our mission to the world. What's more, as the examples at the start of this chapter indicate, the non-Christian world, not least within the contemporary West, is not just confused about what to believe on its own account; it is confused as to what Christians themselves are supposed to believe. Often people assume that Christians are simply committed to a belief in 'life after death' in the most general terms, and have no idea how the more specific notions of resurrection, judgment, the second coming of Jesus, and so on, fit together and make any sense. Let alone how they relate to the urgent concerns of today's real world.

Nor is this a matter simply of sorting out what to believe about someone who has died, or about one's own probable post-mortem destiny, important though both of those are. It's a matter of thinking straight about God and his purposes for the cosmos, and about what God is doing right now, already, as part of those purposes. From Plato to Hegel and beyond, some of the greatest philosophers have declared that what you think about death, and life beyond it, is the key to thinking seriously about everything else – and, indeed, that it provides one of the main reasons for thinking seriously about anything at all. This is something a Christian theologian should heartily endorse.

So, without further delay, we plunge into the confusion on this topic that exists in the wider world, the world outside the church door.

2. Confusion about hope: the wider world

Beliefs about death and what lies beyond come in all shapes and sorts and sizes. Even a quick glance at the classic views of the major religious traditions gives the lie to the old idea that all religions are basically the same. There is a world of difference between the Muslim who believes that a Palestinian boy killed by Israeli soldiers goes straight to heaven, and the Hindu for whom the rigorous outworking of karma means that one must return in a different body to pursue the next stage of one's destiny. There is a world of difference between the Orthodox Jew who believes that all the righteous will be raised to new individual bodily life in the resurrection, and the Buddhist who hopes after death to disappear like a drop in the ocean, losing one's own identity in the great nameless and formless Beyond.[2] And there are of course major variations between different branches or schools of thought in these great religions.

So, too, there are wide varieties of beliefs about what the dead are up to right now. In many parts of Africa the ancestors still play a large role in communal and family life, and there are widespread and complex systems for seeking their help, or at least preventing them making mischief. Nor are these – as western secularists might arrogantly assume – confined to so-called 'primitive' peoples. The anthropologist Nigel Barley tells how he met a highly trained Japanese colleague who had worked near him in Chad. Barley had been fascinated by 'the complicated form of ancestor-worship involving bones and the destruction of the skull and all sorts of exchanges between the dead and the living'. His Japanese friend had found all this quite dull. Barley comments:

He was, of course, a Buddhist who had a shrine to his departed parents in his living room, on which regular offerings were made . . . he had taken to Africa some bone from his dead father's leg, carefully wrapped in white cloth, to ensure protection during his fieldwork. For me [Barley comments], ancestor worship was something to be described and analysed. For him, it would be the *absence* of such links between the living and the dead that would require special explanation.[3]

Coming closer to home, we have seen in our own day and culture a bewildering variety not only of stated beliefs, but of telltale practices associated with death and life afterwards. I suspect there was never a period when Christian orthodoxy on the subject was the belief of even the majority of people in Britain. Certainly, already by the time of the Victorians, there was a wide variety of belief, as people wrestled with questions of faith and doubt from several angles. The famous painting by Henry Alexander Bowler entitled *The Doubt: Can These Dry Bones Live?*, painted in 1855/56, sums up the problem, as a young woman leans on the tombstone of one John Faithful, which bears the text 'I am the resurrection and the life'. On the neighbouring stone is the word RESURGAM – 'I shall arise' – which was inscribed on many tombs of the period. A horse chestnut sprouts from the tomb, and a butterfly, symbolizing the soul, sits on an exposed skull. The swirling questions and half-beliefs represented by this picture go with the similar set of questions in Tennyson's great poem *In Memoriam*. Tennyson himself, in the very last poem of his collected works, written in 1889 within three years of his death, sounds for a moment as though he is moving towards a Buddhist view of being absorbed like a drop in the ocean, but eventually comes round to a Christian note:

> Sunset and evening star,
>   And one clear call for me!
> And may there be no moaning of the bar,
>   When I put out to sea,

But such a tide as moving seems asleep,
  Too full for sound and foam,
When that which drew from out the boundless deep
  Turns again home.

Twilight and evening bell,
  And after that the dark!
And may there be no sadness of farewell,
  When I embark;

For tho' from out our bourne of Time and Place
  The flood may bear me far,
I hope to see my Pilot face to face
  When I have crost the bar.[4]

Contrast with this, however, the more robustly orthodox view of Rudyard Kipling, in a poem of 1892. How much he himself believed it, I don't know, and of course the poem is more about art than about theories of the future life; but he certainly uses, as the frame for his ideas, the Christian belief that after a period of rest there will be a new life, a new embodiment:

When Earth's last picture is painted and the tubes are twisted
  and dried,
When the oldest colours have faded, and the youngest critic
  has died,
We shall rest, and, faith, we shall need it – lie down for an
  aeon or two,
Till the Master of All Good Workmen shall put us to work anew.

And those that were good shall be happy: they shall sit in a
  golden chair;
They shall splash at a ten-league canvas with brushes of
  comets' hair.
They shall find real saints to draw from – Magdalene, Peter,
  and Paul;
They shall work for an age at a sitting and never be tired at all!

And only the Master shall praise us, and only the Master
  shall blame;

And no one shall work for money, and no one shall work for
   fame,
But each for the joy of the working, and each, in his separate
   star,
Shall draw the Thing as he sees It for the God of Things as
   They are!⁵

This variety of belief towards the end of the nineteenth century was closely reflected, as we shall see, in the hymns and prayers of the church.⁶

Going back a little further, think of Shakespeare. In *Measure for Measure*, the Duke addresses the condemned Claudio, encouraging him to face death. Life itself, he says, is not worth that much, and death may well be just as good:

The best of rest is sleep,
And that thou oft provok'st; yet grossly fears't
Thy death, which is no more. Thou art not thyself;
For thou exists on many a thousand grains
That issue out of dust. Happy thou art not;
For what thou hast not, still thou striv'st to get,
And what thou hast, forget'st . . . If thou art rich, thou'rt poor;
For, like an ass whose back with ingots bows,
Thou bear'st thy heavy riches but a journey,
And Death unloads thee . . . What's yet in this
That bears the name of life? Yet in this life
Lie hid moe thousand deaths; yet death we fear,
That makes these odds all even.

Claudio appears for the moment to be convinced by this argument:

I humbly thank you.
To sue to live, I find I seek to die;
And seeking death, find life. Let it come on.

Shortly afterwards, though, Claudio is talking with Isabella, who is offering to sacrifice her own honour to save him. He faces his dilemma: death, he says, is a fearful thing:

Ay, but to die, and go we know not where;
To lie in cold obstruction, and to rot;
This sensible warm motion to become
A kneaded clod; and the delighted spirit
To bathe in fiery floods or to reside
In thrilling region of thick-ribbed ice;
To be imprison'd in the viewless winds,
And blown with restless violence round about
The pendent world; or to be worse than worst
Of those that lawless and incertain thought
Imagine howling – 'tis too horrible.
The weariest and most loathed worldly life
That age, ache, penury, and imprisonment,
Can lay on nature is a paradise
To what we fear of death.[7]

The comfort is cold; the grim reality is still there.

Coming back towards our own time, the First World War produced not only a great deal of sudden death but much reflection on its meaning. Some historians have suggested that belief in hell, already under attack from theologians in the nineteenth century, was one of the major casualties of the Great War. There had been so much hell on earth that people couldn't believe that God would create such a place hereafter as well. But this didn't mean that people believed in Christian universalism, a Christian heaven or resurrection for all or at least most. Rather, many moved in a very different direction, already sketched by Shelley in his memorial poem for Keats:

Peace, peace! he is not dead, he doth not sleep –
He hath awakened from the dream of life –
'Tis we, who, lost in stormy visions, keep
With phantoms an unprofitable strife . . .

He is made one with Nature: there is heard
His voice in all her music, from the moan
Of thunder, to the song of night's sweet bird;
He is a presence to be felt and known

In darkness and in light, from herb and stone,
Spreading itself where'er that Power may move
Which has withdrawn his being to its own . . .

He is a portion of the loveliness
Which once he made more lovely: he doth bear
His part, while the one Spirit's plastic stress
Sweeps through the dull dense world . . .

I am borne darkly, fearfully, afar;
Whilst burning through the inmost veil of Heaven,
The soul of Adonais, like a star,
Beacons from the abode where the Eternal are.[8]

The atheist Shelley knew perfectly well that this Neoplatonic vision of a transformation of the soul into part of the beauty of the universe was a long way from traditional Christian teaching. Today's irony is that many express similar sentiments and imagine them to be Christian, and expect the church to allow them to be read out during Christian funerals. But more of that anon. We find a similar position taken by Rupert Brooke, commanding his friends in 1914:

If I should die, think only this of me:
That there's some corner of a foreign field
That is for ever England. There shall be
In that rich earth a richer dust concealed;
A dust whom England bore, shaped, made aware,
Gave, once, her flowers to love, her ways to roam,
A body of England's, breathing English air,
Washed by the rivers, blest by suns of home.

And think, this heart, all evil shed away,
A pulse in the eternal mind, no less
Gives somewhere back the thoughts by England given;
Her sights and sounds; dreams happy as her day;
And laughter, learnt of friends; and gentleness,
In hearts at peace, under an English heaven.[9]

An English heaven, perhaps, but scarcely the heaven of Christian tradition or of the New Testament. Similar views are familiar from such writers as George Eliot, who spoke of 'the immortal dead who live again / in minds made better by their presence'.[10]

The most obvious anticipation of the outpouring of grief over Princess Diana was the funeral of the Unknown Warrior in November 1920. There, millions who had lost family members, many blown to bits or never recovered, were able to grieve as though this unknown were in fact their own son or husband. So much death affected so many at that time, and again less than a generation later in the second war, that my own reading of our twentieth-century British attitudes to death is that there was simply too much to cope with. I grew up in a culture of near-silence about death; children in the 1950s were insulated from it. I didn't attend a funeral until I was nearly twenty. This may have been, I suspect, a reaction against perceived melodramatic Victorian deathbed and funeral practices. It may also have been a strategy whereby adults might protect themselves from their own enormous and still-buried grief, which could all too clearly be reflected, and brought to the surface, in the innocent reactions of a child.

But if death, and life beyond, was the great unmentionable in the 1950s, it certainly isn't now. Films, plays and novels have explored it from all kinds of angles. Films like *Four Weddings and a Funeral* and *Perchance to Dream* have reflected the interest, even the fascination, of a new generation with the question they had not asked and to which they knew no satisfying answers. The darker end of the market wallows in death, not only in screened violence but in 'snuff' movies where death becomes the ultimate thrill. The nihilism to which secularism has given birth leaves many with no reason for living, and death is once again in the cultural air. The most brilliant play I saw when we lived in London was the Pulitzer prize-winning play *Wit*, by Margaret Edson, a schoolteacher from Atlanta, Georgia.[11] The heroine, Vivian Bearing, is a renowned specialist in the Holy Sonnets of John Donne, and the entire play takes place in the cancer ward where she is herself dying, reflecting as she does so on Donne's great sonnet 'Death be not proud', to which I shall presently return. The play was more successful in New York than in London; perhaps Britain is not yet as ready for a full exploration of mid-life death as are our American cousins. But the questions are around us all the time. At the time I was writing the lectures on which this book was based, the columnist John Diamond was nationally famous for writing with stoic and laconic wit about his terminal throat cancer, and about his robust atheism which refused all comfort, all offers of some kind of salvation beyond the grave. He has since died. The interest in his column, and the correspondence which went to and fro around it, indicate well enough the strong, renewed interest that exists in our world for everything to do with the subject of death and what lies, or does not lie, beyond it.

So where does all this leave us? Not long ago Ruth Gledhill, the religious affairs correspondent of *The Times*, published an article arguing that a gulf has opened up between the mainline churches on the one hand and the 'magic' of various New Age philosophies, cults and superstitions on the other. One reader wrote back to say that, from the outside, the mainstream churches seemed themselves committed to believing in magic. 'To non-Christians,' he wrote, 'C of E members apparently believe in a reanimated corpse' – the implication being that if that isn't magic, he doesn't know what is.

Well, is it or isn't it? What *do* people believe in when they talk about Easter? And how is that related to what the mainstream creeds declare about our own future destiny, when they say, 'I believe in the resurrection of the body'? What did this language mean when the first Christians used it, and what might it mean today? What do we now hope for after death? What answer might we get to this question if we took a straw poll on the street in our towns and villages? And, since good theology is never a matter of majority voting, what is the teaching of the Bible on this subject? Of Jesus and the apostles?

3. Varieties of belief

The main beliefs that emerge in the present climate seem to me of three types, none of which corresponds to Christian orthodoxy. There are still attempts at restating a more traditional view; I think, for instance, of William Golding's dark but stunning *Pincher Martin*. But in general the mood has been that traditional beliefs, both in judgment and hell on the one hand and in resurrection on the other, are offensive to modern sensibilities.[12]

First, some believe in complete annihilation; that is at least clean and tidy, however unsatisfying it may be as an account of human destiny. This, presumably, is what lies underneath Dylan Thomas's angry outburst at the death of his father:

> Do not go gentle into that good night.
> Rage, rage, against the dying of the light.[13]

But not many can sustain complete denial of any future life. Look at the 'religion' sections of the average bookshops, and you will find that more and more people today seem to believe in some form of reincarnation. This is not confined to practising Hindus and half-converts like Glenn Hoddle. In the gruesome but fascinating novel by Will Self, *How the Dead Live*, his central character, a grumpy London woman recently deceased, living in a ghostly parody of London, discovers that she will be condemned to regular reincarnation unless she manages to grasp at what her underworld guide calls 'the hooks and eyes of grace', through which, it seems, she will be able to escape the continual circle:

Still one last chance to get off the go-round, girl . . . Still time
to attach you to the hooks and eyes of grace. If you want it.
If you can just – even for a few instants – achieve a one-
pointedness of thought.[14]

But she doesn't, and is reborn – as an unhappy baby, destined
to a short and brutal life. Will Self seems to envisage a kind
of Hinduism, where the mental achievement of brief focused
thought, replacing the wandering and distracted mind or soul,
is the key to escaping the cycle, the ever-rotating wheel, of death
and birth. A different twist to this is provided by the many for
whom, again to judge from the literature available, reincarnation has become a way of pursuing psychoanalysis by other
means, discovering aspects of your personality which come
from who you were, or what happened to you, in a previous
life. It thus flows into the larger New Age culture in which bits
and pieces of esoteric beliefs are mixed with dreams of self-help
and self-fulfilment.

Also on the fringe of various New Age ideas we find a
revival of the views we discovered in Shelley, a sort of low-
grade popular nature-religion with elements of Buddhism.
At death one is absorbed into the wider world, into the wind
and the trees. The anonymous poem left by a soldier going to
Northern Ireland, in case of his death, expresses it well:

> Do not stand at my grave and weep;
> I am not there. I do not sleep.
> I am a thousand winds that blow,
> I am the diamond glints on snow.
> I am the sunlight on ripened grain,
> I am the gentle autumn rain . . .
> Do not stand at my grave and cry,
> I am not there. I do not die.[15]

After Diana's death one message left in London spoke as in the
Princess's own voice: 'I did not leave you at all. I am still with
you. I am in the sun and in the wind. I am even in the rain. I

did not die, I am with you all.'[16] Many funerals, memorial services, and even funerary inscriptions, now give voice to this kind of belief. Many would-be Christians try to persuade themselves and others that this kind of ongoing life is really what is meant by traditional teaching either about the immortality of the soul or the resurrection of the dead. Others, however, like the highly successful children's writer Philip Pullman, who takes something like this line, make it pretty clear that he is thereby attacking and deconstructing traditional Christian belief and offering something else instead.[17]

A striking, sharply delineated example comes unexpectedly in Nick Hornby's book *Fever Pitch*, a passionate and funny account of his love affair with football (the English variety), and with Arsenal in particular. Coming upon a dead football supporter lying in the street, he muses on death and football. Wouldn't it be awful, he thinks, to die in mid-season and not to know how it all ended? But that's how it is:

> Maybe we will die the night before our team appears at Wembley, or the day after a European Cup first-leg match, or in the middle of a promotion campaign or a relegation battle, and there is every prospect, according to many theories about the afterlife, that we will not be able to discover the eventual outcome. The whole *point* about death, metaphorically speaking, is that it is almost bound to occur before the major trophies have been awarded.[18]

But this is highly unsatisfactory, and leads Hornby to speculate on what possibilities there may be after all for an afterlife in which (of course) football will still play a central role. Cremation offers one possibility:

> I am one of those who would, I think, be happy to have my ashes scattered over the Highbury pitch (although I understand that there are restrictions: too many widows contact the club, and there are fears that the turf would not respond kindly to the contents of urn after urn) ... Certainly I'd rather be

sprinkled over the East Stand than dumped into the Atlantic or left up some mountain.

And this might just give rise to a different sort of 'survival', he muses:

> It would be nice to think that I could hang around inside the stadium in some form, and watch the first team one Saturday, the reserves the next; I would like to feel that my children and grandchildren will be Arsenal fans and that I could watch with them. It doesn't seem a bad way to spend eternity . . . I want to float around Highbury as a ghost watching reserve games for the rest of time.[19]

Here we see the current complete confusion about life after death, played out, so to speak, on the ground of a monomaniacal obsession (Hornby's own self-description) with one particular area of life.

The funeral practices that have grown up, or reappeared, in our own day exhibit the same kind of confusion. The practice of putting objects in coffins along with the dead, to comfort or help them in the life to come, was until recently described by students of culture as an interesting practice now abandoned in the modern West; but gifts for the dead are making a comeback, with photographs, jewellery, teddy bears and the like being placed in coffins.[20] Nigel Barley relates stories, told by a crematorium official, of widows placing in the coffin a packet of digestive biscuits, or the deceased's spare glasses and false teeth. On one occasion a widow put into her husband's coffin two cans of the spray adhesive that the dead man had used to paste on his toupee, causing an explosion that bent the furnace door.[21] What sort of belief, if any, does all this reflect?

Finally, at the popular level, belief in ghosts, and the possibility of spiritualistic contact with the dead, has resisted all the inroads of a century of secularism. When this book was originally given as a series of lectures in Westminster Abbey, the weekly newsletter that advertised the first lecture also announced that one of the Abbey's very own seventeenth-century ghosts might make his annual appearance around the same time. And there are of course numerous popular phenomena on both sides of the Atlantic, such as the continuing Elvis cult in the USA, which would need categories of their own to describe.

I take it that I am describing a world my readers will recognize. My aim is not to catalogue it exhaustively, but to draw attention to certain features of it, and to the striking fact that not only is it quite unlike anything that can be called orthodox Christian belief, but that, so far as I can tell, *most people simply don't know what orthodox Christian belief might be.* It is assumed that Christians believe in life after death, as opposed to a straightforward denial of any 'survival', and that any and every sort of 'life after death' must therefore be much the same kind of (Christian) thing. The idea that within the general idea of 'life after death' there might be variations, embodying significantly different beliefs about God and the world, and significantly different agendas for how people might live in the present, has simply never occurred to most modern western people. In particular, most people have little or no idea what the word 'resurrection' actually means, or why Christians say they believe it.

What is more worrying, this multiple ignorance seems often to be true in the churches as well. This is the subject of the next chapter.

2

Puzzled about paradise?

1. Christian confusion about hope

One of the most frequently quoted Anglican sermons of the twentieth century is also, alas, one of the most misleading. In a widely used guide to arranging secular funerals, words by Canon Henry Scott Holland of St Paul's are quoted as the preface, and thousands of people request that they be read at funerals and memorial services:

> Death is nothing at all. It does not count. I have only slipped away into the next room. Nothing has happened. Everything remains exactly as it was. I am I and you are you, and the old life we lived so fondly together is untouched, unchanged. Whatever we were to each other, that we still are. Call me by the old familiar name. Speak of me in the easy way which you always used. Put no difference into your tone. Wear no forced air of solemnity or sorrow . . . Life means all that it ever meant. It is the same as it ever was. There is absolute and unbroken continuity. What is this death but a negligible accident? Why should I be out of mind because I am out of sight? I am waiting for you, for an interval, somewhere very near, just around the corner. All is well. Nothing is hurt; nothing is lost. One brief moment and all will be as it was before. How we shall laugh at the trouble of parting when we meet again![1]

What nobody usually points out is that this was not the view that Scott Holland himself was advocating. It was simply what, he suggested, came to mind as we 'look down upon the quiet face' of 'one who has been very near and dear to us'. Elsewhere in the same sermon, preached in 1910 upon the death of King Edward VII, he spoke of the other feelings which belong as well with death, which seems

> so inexplicable, so ruthless, so blundering . . . the cruel ambush into which we are snared . . . it makes its horrible breach in our gladness with careless and inhuman disregard of us . . . beyond the darkness hides its impenetrable secret . . . Dumb as the night, that terrifying silence!

Scott Holland went on to attempt something of a reconciliation between these two views of death. The Christian has, according to the New Testament, 'already passed from death to life', so that the further transition of actual death ought not to be as terrifying as it appears. In addition, we should (he suggests) think of the life beyond death in terms of a continuation of that growth in the knowledge of God, and in personal holiness, which has already begun here. That raises questions which we cannot address at this stage of the book; but it is already clear that to take the paragraph so frequently quoted out of the context of the sermon in which it was originally spoken does serious violence to the author's intention. We can only wonder at the extraordinary denial which is going on when this is done. It amounts to a resolute refusal to tell the truth about the real and savage break, the horrible denial of the goodness of human life, which every death involves. I would love to think that one of the effects of the present book would be to challenge the use of the Scott Holland piece in Christian funerals. It offers hollow comfort. By itself, without comment, it simply tells lies. It is not even a parody of Christian hope. Instead, it simply denies that there is any problem, any need for hope in the first place.

Contrast with that well-known piece the robust attitude of a classic Christian theology, stated by the sometime Dean of St Paul's, John Donne:

Death be not proud, though some have callèd thee
    Mighty and dreadful, for thou art not so;
    For those who thou think'st thou dost overthrow
Die not, poore Death, nor yet canst thou kill me.
From rest and sleep, which but thy pictures be,
    Much pleasure – then, from thee much more must flow;
    And soonest our best men with thee do go,
Rest of their bones, and soul's delivery.
Thou'rt slave to fate, chance, kings, and desperate men,
    And dost with poison, war, and sickness dwell,
    And poppy or charms can make us sleep as well,
And better than thy stroke. Why swell'st thou then?
    One short sleep past, we wake eternally,
    And death shall be no more. Death, thou shalt die.[2]

At first sight this might seem rather close to Scott Holland. Death is nothing at all? Death is not after all mighty and dreadful? But no: the last two lines say it all. Death is a great enemy, but it has been conquered and will at the last be conquered fully. 'One short sleep past, we wake eternally, / And death shall be no more. Death, thou shalt die.' In the Scott Holland passage, there is nothing to be conquered. For John Donne, death is important; it is an enemy; but, for the Christian, it is a *beaten* enemy. In line with much classic Christian thought, and indeed with the Kipling poem we noted earlier, Donne sees life after death in two stages: first, a short sleep, then an eternal waking.[3] *And death shall be no more*. Donne had grasped what we shall discover to be the central New Testament belief: that, at the last, death will not simply be redefined, but defeated. God's intention is not to let death have its way with us. If the promised final future is simply that immortal souls will have left behind their mortal bodies, why then death still rules – since that is a description, not of the *defeat* of death, but simply of death itself, seen from one angle.[4]

But I am running too far ahead of myself. The classic Christian position is stated in the early creeds, themselves dependent on the New Testament in ways we shall explore later in the book. In my church, we declare every day and every week that we believe in 'the resurrection of the body'. But do we? Many Christian teachers and theologians in recent decades have questioned the appropriateness of this language. One recent lavishly illustrated coffee-table book on the subject of death and the afterlife, devoting a bare four pages to the apparently odd idea of resurrection, declares blandly that 'current orthodox Christianity no longer holds to the belief in physical resurrection, preferring the concept of the eternal existence of the soul, although some creeds still cling to the old ideas'.[5] Let us again be quite clear. If this is true, then death is not conquered, but redescribed: no longer an enemy, it is simply the means by which, as in *Hamlet*, the immortal soul shuffles off its mortal coil.[6]

2. Exploring the options

There has been, in fact, an oscillation between two poles, which you can see by walking around any old church and looking at the monuments. Some envisage death as a horrid enemy, stalking its prey. This is often combined with the firm proclamation that, though an enemy, death will finally be defeated: the tradition of inscribing RESURGAM, 'I shall arise', which we noted in the previous chapter, means that, like Donne and Kipling, the deceased believes in an intermediate sleep to be followed by a new bodily life at some future point. That was why people were buried facing east, so as to rise to meet the Lord at his coming – though one of the most recent painters to depict the resurrection, Stanley Spencer, ignores that detail in favour of the semi-realism of corpses coming out of their tombs in all directions in the Cookham churchyard. We shall come back to this in the tenth chapter in particular.

The other pole of belief is represented by St Francis's hymn 'All creatures of our God and King', with its remarkable in-vocation of 'And thou, most dear and kindly death, waiting to hush our latest breath'. Many hymns, prayers and sermons have attempted to soften the blow by presenting death as a friend, coming to take us to a better place; this was a familiar theme in the nineteenth century, and has its secular echo in the modern movements towards voluntary euthanasia. Thus Christian thought has oscillated between seeing death as a vile enemy and as a welcome friend.

Traditionally, of course, we have supposed that Christianity teaches about a heaven above, to which the saved or blessed go, and a hell below, for the wicked and impenitent. This is still assumed by many both inside and outside the church to be the official line, which they may or may not accept.

A remarkable example arrived in the mail not long ago: a book, apparently a best-seller, by Maria Shriver, the wife of Arnold Schwarzenegger and niece of John F. Kennedy, called *What's Heaven?*[7] The book is aimed at children, and has lots of large pictures of fluffy clouds in blue skies. Each page of text has one sentence in extra large type, making the basic message of the book crystal clear. Heaven, says Shriver,

> is somewhere you believe in . . . it's a beautiful place where you can sit on soft clouds and talk to other people who are there. At night you can sit next to the stars, which are the brightest of anywhere in the universe . . . If you're good throughout your life, then you get to go to heaven . . . when your life is finished here on earth, God sends angels down to take you up to Heaven to be with him . . . [And Grandma is] alive in me . . . Most important, she taught me to believe in myself . . . She's in a safe place, with the stars, with God and the angels . . . she is watching over us from up there . . .
>
> 'I want you to know' [says the heroine to her great-Grandma] 'that even though you are no longer here, your spirit will always be alive in me.'[8]

This is undoubtedly more or less exactly what millions of people in the western world have come to believe, to accept as truth and to teach to their children. The book was sent to me by a friend who works with grieving children, and who described this as 'one of the worst books for children' and said, 'I hope you find this awful book helpful in what not to say'! It is indeed a prime example of that genre. The truth of what the Bible teaches is very, very different at several levels.

It comes as something of a shock when people are told what is in fact the case: that there is very little in the Bible about 'going to heaven when you die', and not a lot about a post-mortem hell either. The medieval pictures of heaven and hell, boosted though not created by Dante's classic work, have exercised a huge influence on western Christian imagination. Many Christians grow up assuming that whenever the New Testament speaks of 'heaven' it refers to the place to which the saved will go after death. In Matthew's gospel, Jesus' sayings about the 'kingdom of God' in the other gospels are rendered as 'kingdom of heaven'; since many read Matthew first, when they find Jesus talking about 'entering the kingdom of heaven', they have their assumptions confirmed, and suppose that he is indeed talking about 'how to go to heaven when you die', which is certainly not what either Jesus or Matthew has in mind. Many mental pictures have grown up around this which are now assumed to be 'what the Bible teaches' or 'what Christians believe'.[9]

But the language of heaven in the New Testament doesn't work that way. 'God's kingdom' in the preaching of Jesus refers, not to post-mortem destiny, not to our escape from this world into another one, but about God's sovereign rule coming 'on earth as it is in heaven'.[10] The roots of the misunderstanding go very deep, not least into the residual Platonism that has infected whole swathes of Christian thinking and has misled people into supposing that Christians are meant to devalue this present world, and our present bodies, and regard them as shabby or shameful.

Likewise, the pictures of heaven in the book of Revelation have been much misunderstood. The wonderful description in Revelation 4 and 5 of the twenty-four elders casting their crowns before the throne of God and the Lamb, beside the sea of glass, is not, despite one of Charles Wesley's great hymns, a picture of the last day, with all the redeemed in heaven at last.[11] It is a picture of *present* reality, the heavenly dimension of our present life. Heaven, in the Bible, is regularly not a future destiny, but the other, hidden dimension of our ordinary life – God's dimension, if you like. God made heaven and earth; at the last, he will remake both, and join them together for ever. And when we come to the picture of the actual End in Revelation 21—22, we find, not ransomed souls making their way to a disembodied heaven, but rather the new Jerusalem coming down from heaven to earth, uniting the two in a lasting embrace.[12]

Most Christians today, I fear, never think about this from one year to the next. They remain satisfied with what is at best a truncated and distorted version of the great biblical hope. Indeed, the popular picture is reinforced again and again in hymns, prayers, monuments and even quite serious works of theology and history. It is simply assumed that the word 'heaven' is the appropriate term with which to designate the *ultimate* destination, the final 'home', and that the language of 'resurrection', and of the new earth as well as the new heavens, must somehow be fitted into that.[13]

What we see in today's church is, I think, a confused combination of several things. On the one hand, the old heaven-and-hell view has been under attack. Many now refuse to believe in hell at all; but we have found over the last century, as this denial has developed, that paradoxically it leads to a diminution of the promise of heaven, since if everybody is on the same track it would seem unfair to allow some to go directly to the destination rather than continue the long post-mortem journey. The idea of such a 'journey' after death is itself now frequent, though again it has virtually no warrant in the Bible or early Christian thought. We have seen, too, the rehabilitation of a modern, sanitized, version of the old theory of purgatory: since at death we are all still quite unready to meet our Maker, we will need (it is suggested) a period of refinement, of growing towards the light. (People who today think like this tend to prefer to put it that way, rather than emphasizing 'purging' or other uncomfortable things.[14]) Many have embraced a universalism in which God will endlessly offer to the unrepentant the choice of faith, until at last all succumb to the wooing of divine love.[15] Some have declared that heaven as traditionally pictured looks insufferably boring – sitting on clouds playing harps all the time – and that they either don't believe it or don't want to go there. Others have declared, rather sniffily, that a God who simply wants people to adore him all the time is not a figure they would respect. Those of us who protest that the orthodox picture is of a vibrant and active human life, reflecting God's image in the new heavens and new earth, are sometimes accused of projecting our go-getting contemporary life on to the screen of the future.

3. The effects of confusion

This many-sided confusion plays out in the hymns we sing, in the way we celebrate the Christian year, and in the type of funerals or cremations we have. A few words about each of these will show what I mean.

First, hymns. A glance through the average hymn book reveals that a good many references to the future life beyond death are closer to Tennyson, or even to Shelley, than they are to orthodox Christianity:

> Till in the ocean of thy love
> We lose ourselves in heaven above

– the words are those of the devout John Keble, but it was he who was for a moment lost here, not in Christianity, but in a drop-in-the-ocean Buddhist eschatology.[16] And what about his

Oxford Movement colleague, John Henry Newman, with his almost gnostic line:

> So long thy power hath blest me, sure it still
>> Will lead me on,
> O'er moor and fen, o'er crag and torrent, till
>> The night is gone.
> And with the morn those angel faces smile
>> Which I have loved long since, and lost awhile.

Did Newman *really* believe that he had had a previous life with the angels, whether before his conception or in early childhood, and that he would return there in due course? And – though of course the idea of the lonely pilgrim following the 'kindly light' across the moors and fens is a powerful, romantic idea – did he really think that the present world, and the present life, could be described simply as 'night'?[17]

Or what about the blatant Platonism of the hymn 'Abide with me', still a favourite in some circles:

> Heaven's morning breaks, and earth's vain shadows flee.

There are entire hymns and anthems which embody this train of thought: think, for instance, of Vaughan's 'My soul, there is a country', or of Isaac Watts's 'There is a land of pure delight'. I prefer Watts: he is after all using the biblical typology of crossing the Jordan and entry into the Promised Land, whereas Vaughan offers us a flagrantly Platonic upstairs/downstairs world with, to my mind, little actual Christian content deeper than the surface. In a quick flip through the hymn book I noted dozens of other examples, not all explicable by the process of selection at a time when the prevailing theology wanted to say that sort of thing.

Or what about the Christmas hymn 'It came upon the midnight clear', which declares in the final verse that

> For lo! the days are hastening on
> By prophet bards foretold,

When, with the ever-circling years
Comes round the age of gold.
When peace shall over all the earth
Its ancient splendours fling,
And the whole world give back the song
Which now the angels sing.

It's a well-loved Christmas carol, but the idea of cycles of history eventually returning to a golden age is neither Christian nor Jewish, but decidedly pagan. While we're on Christmas carols, consider 'Away in a manger', which prays, 'and fit us for heaven, to live with thee there'. No resurrection; no new creation; no marriage of heaven and earth. And when we find in the hymn book the blatant romantic nature-religion and universalism of Paul Gerhardt, in his poem 'The duteous day now closeth', we may be forgiven for thinking that whoever compiled the hymn book only looked at the first verse, and didn't bother to check the theology of the rest. Otherwise, surely, someone might have raised an eyebrow at the suggestion that a life without faith, in the present created world, might lead to a future of salvation in a Platonic escape from creation:

Awhile his mortal blindness
May miss God's loving kindness
And grope in faithless strife;
But when life's day is over
Shall death's fair night discover
The fields of everlasting life.

Death in the New Testament is never a 'fair night'. It is an enemy, conquered by Jesus but still awaiting its final defeat.

Some of the hymns in the revivalist and charismatic traditions slip into the easy mistake, cognate as we shall see with misleading views of the 'second coming', of suggesting that Jesus will return to take his people away from earth and 'home' to heaven. Thus that wonderful hymn, 'How great thou art', in its final stanza, declares:

When Christ shall come, with shout of acclamation,
And take me home, what joy shall fill my heart.

The second line (to anticipate our later argument) might better read 'And heal this world . . .'. Actually, the original Swedish version of the hymn doesn't talk about Christ coming to take me home; that is the adaptation by the translator. Rather, it speaks of the veils of time falling, faith being changed into clear sight, and the bells of eternity summoning us to our sabbath rest, all of which has a lot more to recommend it.[18]

There are, of course, some hymns which stand out against this trend. 'Jerusalem the golden' draws attention to the decisive final chapters of Revelation. A few hymns speak of being 'woken by the last dread call', or of 'rising glorious at the last day'. One great hymn speaks of God working his purpose out, so that 'the earth shall be filled with the glory of God as the waters cover the sea'. But, towering over all these, is the great All Saints' Day hymn, 'For all the saints', whose sequence of thought catches the New Testament emphasis exactly right. After celebrating the life of the saints in the opening verses, our communion with them in the fourth, and their strengthening of us in the fifth, the sixth verse speaks of our joining them in their present abode, which is *not* the final resting place but rather the intermediate place of rest, joy and refreshment, for which one name is paradise:

The golden evening brightens in the west;
Soon, soon, to faithful warriors cometh rest:
Sweet is the calm of Paradise the blest. Alleluia! Alleluia!

Only *after* that does the resurrection occur:

But lo! there breaks a yet more glorious day;
The Saints triumphant rise in bright array:
The King of glory passes on his way. Alleluia! Alleluia!

– which leads in to the triumphant final verse, arriving at last in the new Jerusalem.[19]

If our hymns reveal the confusion we have got ourselves into, the way we keep the Christian year shows much the same thing. I have written elsewhere about the sheer muddle which has, in recent years, allowed a two-day festival, if you can call it that, of All Saints and All Souls, preceded yet more confusingly by Hallowe'en. Few who keep this double (or triple) event, I think, believe the medieval theology that made at least some sense of it. It reflects, rather, the confusion of a church that no longer quite believes in heaven, probably doesn't really believe in hell, and prefers a gentle sort of purgatory to either, but has no place at all for the resurrection of the body, the new creation, the new Jerusalem coming down from heaven to earth.[20]

But this is only part of the muddle. In some recent Anglican schemes one entire section of the Christian year has become fudged. Advent, the four Sundays before Christmas, used to focus on the doctrines of the second coming, of God's judgment, and of the final destiny of human beings. Today, the lectionaries have changed all that, and various aspects of preparation for Christmas have taken over instead. The month or so before Advent – more or less the whole of November – was for a while (in the 1990s) relabelled as the 'Kingdom Season', making various peculiar and inconsistent assumptions about death and what lies beyond. Though that particular label has now been withdrawn, the confusion remains, reflected in various liturgical prayers which speak of 'the light of the kingdom which the saints enjoy', as though – despite what the New Testament says – God's 'kingdom' is a place called 'heaven' where some of the Christian dead, not all, have already arrived.

Christmas itself has now far outstripped Easter as the real celebratory centre of the Christian year – a move which completely reverses the New Testament's emphasis. We sometimes try, in hymns, prayers and sermons, to build a whole theology on Christmas, but it can't in fact sustain such a thing. We then keep Lent, Holy Week and Good Friday so thoroughly that we have hardly any energy left for Easter, except for the first night and day. Easter, however, should be the centre. Take that away and there is, almost literally, nothing left.

The same confusions are apparent in the ways we do funerals. There have been many new funeral rites penned and published in recent years, often after lengthy debates. But before we get to them, a word about the implicit theology held by many of those who opt for cremation rather than burial. Of course there were reasons of hygiene and overcrowding which led reformers towards the end of the last century to propose this step – which, as not all western Christians know, is still firmly opposed by the Eastern Orthodox (despite the shortage of land in Greece at least) as well as orthodox Jews and Muslims. But cremation has tended, classically, to belong more with a Hindu or Buddhist theology; and that, at a low-grade and popular level, is as we have already seen where we as a culture are rapidly moving. When people ask for their ashes to be scattered on a favourite hillside, or in a well-loved river or shoreline, we can sympathize with the feeling (though not, perhaps, with denying the bereaved a specific spot to visit in their grief). But the underlying implication, of a desire simply to be merged back into the created world, without any affirmation of a future life of new embodiment, flies in the face of classic Christian theology.

I am not of course saying that cremation is heretical. I shall speak in due course about its relation to the resurrection body. I am merely noting that the huge swing towards it in the last century reflects at least in part some of the confusions, both in the church and in the world, which we have observed. I also note, in passing, that a ceremony in a building which is used for nothing else is a very different event from a funeral, whether or not followed by cremation, in a building which is used daily and weekly for prayer, eucharist, celebration, for baptisms and weddings, for the whole worshipping life of a community. Or, to look at it another way, there is something wonderful and profound about entering church through the churchyard where there lie buried those who have worshipped there in centuries past. But all that, too, is another story.

When it comes to funerals themselves, the confusion elsewhere is reflected quite faithfully (if that's the right word). So much has gone on in different churches that I can only comment very selectively and in relation to my own church (the Church of England). Spot checks elsewhere indicate that it is not untypical. When the new Church of England funeral liturgies emerged at the end of the twentieth century, there were several helpful resources published to enable clergy to make the best of the sensitive and often tricky pastoral opportunities. One such book, published by the Church's official publishing house and with prefatory commendations by senior church figures, offers a wonderful guide to everything one could want to know and do – except for the fact that, throughout the book, resurrection is never mentioned.[21] This is perhaps not so surprising when we examine the new services themselves. Thankfully, resurrection has not disappeared from them, but it is muted, and the general tenor is to support the increasingly prevalent view of a single-stage post-mortem destination ('turn the darkness of death into the dawn of new life, and the sorrow of parting into the joy of heaven', as one prayer puts it[22]). One could put it like this: if someone came to these funeral services with no idea of what the classic Jewish and Christian teaching on the subject was, this funeral service itself would do little to enlighten them, and plenty to mislead them or confirm them in the muddle they already had.

The 'prayers of entrusting and commending' would not help much at this point, either:

> . . . we commend *N* into your arms of mercy,
> believing that, with sins forgiven,

he/she will share a place of happiness, light and peace
in the kingdom of your glory for ever.

. . . God now welcomes *him/her* to his table in heaven
To share in eternal life with all the saints.

We commend *N* to your mercy
and pray that as you gather *him/her* to yourself,
you will give to us your blessing of peace . . .

We entrust *him/her* to your mercy,
and pray that you will show us the path of life,
and the fullness of joy in your presence
through all eternity.[23]

In the middle of this sequence, there is one prayer which
stands out by its ringing affirmation of what all the early
Christians would have wanted to say:

Trusting in your faithfulness,
we commend *N* to your mercy
as we await that great day
when you raise us with *him/her* to life in triumph
and we shall stand before you,
with all your whole creation made new in him,
in the glory of your heavenly kingdom.

– though we may be excused for wondering whether the last
line takes back with the left hand what had just been given with
the right, since the point of the final new creation, and the
resurrection itself, is that this is the moment when, fully and
finally, the 'heavenly kingdom' *arrives on earth*.

The main new Church of England funeral service, then,
would give little indication of the classic Christian belief. Nor
would the 'burial of ashes', which ends with three prayers:

Heavenly Father,
we thank you for all those whom we love but see no longer.
As we remember *N* in this place,

hold before us our beginning and our ending,
the dust from which we come
and the death to which we move,
with a firm hope in your eternal love and purposes for us,
[this is the point at which the older services would have said
'in the sure and certain hope of the resurrection', or words to
that effect],
in Jesus Christ our Lord. Amen.

God of hope,
grant that we, with all who have believed in you,
may be united in the full knowledge of your love
and the unclouded vision of your glory;
through Jesus Christ our Lord. Amen.

May the infinite and glorious Trinity,
the Father, the Son, and the Holy Spirit,
direct our life in good works,
and after our journey through this world
grant us eternal rest with all the saints. Amen.[24]

These are moving, humble and gentle prayers. But they make
no mention of the distinctive Christian hope. I hope that those
who take seriously the argument of this present book will
examine the current practice of the church, from its official
liturgies to all the unofficial bits and pieces that surround
them, and try to discover fresh ways of expressing, embodying
and teaching what the New Testament actually teaches, rather
than the mangled, half-understood and vaguely held theories
and opinions we are meeting in these first two chapters.
Frankly, what we have at the moment isn't, as the old liturgies
used to say, 'the sure and certain hope of the resurrection
of the dead', but the vague and fuzzy optimism that somehow
things may work out in the end.

There are various recent discussions of contemporary funeral liturgies.[25] There is no space here for detailed debate with
them. I simply note that we now find, again and again, what

has become the classic fudge for those who have not thought through what 'resurrection' actually means, namely the collapsing of 'resurrection' language into 'going to heaven' language. Thus, for instance, Paul Sheppy offers this as 'The Word of Resurrection':

> Lord, you renew the face of the earth;
> gather to yourself *N* whom we have loved,
> and grant to *her* those things
> which eye has not seen, nor ear heard,
> nor the human heart imagined.[26]

But this, again, is not 'the sure and certain hope of the resurrection of the body', rooted in the resurrection of Jesus himself, and located within the promise of new heavens and new earth; it is, rather, the generalized and pious hope for a blessed immortality starting more or less at once and continuing in an undifferentiated future. What's more, this failure to distinguish between the blessed but temporary state upon which God's people enter at death and the final resurrection for which the whole creation is still longing has made its way into collects, eucharistic prayers and much other liturgical and devotional material. As the argument of this book develops, it will become clear that we cannot simply regard this as the kind of problem at which one can simply shrug one's shoulders and say 'well, there are different views on these topics'. What we say about death and resurrection gives shape and colour to everything else. If we are not careful, we will offer merely a 'hope' that is no longer a surprise, no longer able to transform lives and communities in the present, no longer generated by the resurrection of Jesus himself and looking forward to the promised new heavens and new earth.

Hymns, the Christian year and ceremonies of death all tell a similar story. Perhaps equally important is the larger theology, and the wider worldview, which go with the contemporary muddle.

4. Wider implications of confusion

What role does a belief in life beyond the grave play within the larger issues which face us in Christian life and thought?

Karl Marx famously spoke of religion as the opium of the people. He supposed that oppressive rulers would use the promise of a joyful future life to try to stop the masses from rising in revolt. That has indeed often been the case. But my impression is that this is what happens when the 'religion' in question includes the Platonic downgrading of bodies and of the created order in general, regarding them as the 'vain shadows' of earth, which we shall happily leave behind at death. Why try to improve the present prison if release is at hand? Why oil the wheels of a machine that will soon plunge over a cliff? That is precisely the effect created to this day by some devout Christians who genuinely believe that 'salvation' has nothing to do with the way the present world is ordered.

By contrast, it has often been observed that the robust Jewish and Christian doctrine of the resurrection, as part of God's new creation, gives more value, not less, to the present world, and to our present bodies. What these doctrines give, both in classic Judaism and in classic Christianity, is a sense of continuity as well as discontinuity between the present world (and the present state) and the future, whatever it shall be, with the result that what we do in the present is seen to matter enormously. Paul speaks of the future resurrection as a major motive for treating our bodies properly in the present time (1 Corinthians 6.14), and as the reason, not for sitting back and waiting for it all to happen, but for working hard in the present, knowing that nothing done in the Lord, in the power of the Spirit, in the present time will be wasted in God's future (1 Corinthians 15.58). To this we shall return.

The classic Christian doctrine, therefore, is actually far more powerful and revolutionary than the Platonized one. It was people who believed robustly in the resurrection, not people who compromised and went in for a mere spiritualized survival, who stood up against Caesar in the first centuries of the Christian era. A piety which sees death as the moment of 'going home at last', the time when we are 'called to God's eternal peace', has no quarrel with those who want to carve up the world to suit their own ends. Resurrection, by contrast, has always gone with a strong view of God's justice, and of God as the good creator. Those twin beliefs give rise, not to a meek acquiescence in injustice in the world, but to a robust determination to oppose it. It is telling that English evangelicals gave up believing in the urgent imperative to improve society (such as we find with Wilberforce in the late eighteenth and early nineteenth centuries) about the same time that they gave up believing robustly in resurrection and settled for a disembodied heaven instead. We shall come back to this crucial theme towards the end of the book.

5. The key questions

I hope the brief survey offered in these first two chapters is enough to give at least a flavour of the very confusing picture that meets us at every turn today in world and church alike. We must now list the key questions which lie underneath the whole book, and glance ahead to the discussions, and indeed to the solutions, that I shall offer in the coming chapters.

The first two questions are presupposed throughout, without having a particular chapter devoted to them. First, how do we know about all this? My own church, the Church of England, part of the worldwide Anglican Communion, declares that it finds its doctrine in scripture, tradition and reason, taken together in their proper blend.[27] I suggest that a good deal of our current view of death and the life beyond has come from none of these, but from impulses in the culture which have created at best semi-Christian informal traditions that now need proper re-examination in the clear light of scripture.

Scripture, in fact, teaches things about the future life which most Christians, and almost all non-Christians, have never heard of. Of course, the evidence of parapsychology and similar studies, and of so-called 'near-death' experiences, are not unimportant, but they quite easily blend with the accumulation of folk wisdom. What we are here concerned with is to go beyond that, and investigate the often forgotten riches of the Christian tradition itself, with scripture at its heart.

Second, do we have immortal souls, and if so what are they? Again, much Christian and sub-Christian tradition has assumed that we all do indeed have 'souls' that need 'saving', and that the 'soul', if 'saved', will be the 'part' of us that 'goes to heaven when we die'. All this, however, finds minimal support in the New Testament, including the teaching of Jesus, where the word 'soul', though rare, reflects when it does occur underlying Hebrew or Aramaic words that refer, not to a disembodied entity hidden within the outer shell of the disposable body, but rather to what we would call the whole 'person' or 'personality', seen as being confronted by God. As to immortality, 1 Timothy 6.16 declares that only God himself has immortality, and 2 Timothy 1.10 declares that immortality has only come to light, and hence is presumably only available, through the gospel. In other words, the idea that every human possesses an immortal soul, which is the 'real' part of them, finds little support in the Bible.

Third, the starting point for all Christian thinking about this whole topic must be Jesus' own resurrection. But to understand this, and what it meant to the first disciples, and why they drew from it the conclusions they did, we must look at issues of life after death in Jesus' own world, the world of first-century Judaism, with its Old Testament roots and its surrounding context in the world of Greece and Rome. So the third chapter will examine what the ancient world believed about life after death, and the radical and revolutionary nature of the Jewish belief in resurrection which flourished at Jesus' time; and the fourth chapter will address, in that context, the question: what can we say about the resurrection of Jesus himself?

This will project us forward into the second and central part of the book, in which I shall ask: what then is the ultimate Christian hope, for the whole world and for ourselves? This divides into three separate topics, each with its own further divisions of material: first, what can we say about the future of the whole cosmos; second, what do we mean when we speak of Jesus 'coming again to judge the living and the dead'; and, third, what should we mean by, and what should we believe about, 'the resurrection of the body and the life ever-lasting'? There is a further question which goes with all this, but which I believed was so important that I turned it into a separate small book on its own:[28] where are the dead now, especially the Christian dead? What can we say in the present time about them? Should we pray for them, or even *to* them? Is any contact permissible? What is the Communion of Saints? And, not least, how can Christians grieve appropriately? In the present book I have summarized these topics into a single chapter, together with a section on the prospect of final loss.

Then, in the third and final part of the book, we come back from the past (Part 1) and the future (Part 2) to the present, and ask, how can we appropriately celebrate and live by this very specific hope in our own day and culture? What will it mean, in particular, in terms of the church's mission and work in the world? What might 'hope' look like, not just in the ultim-ate future, but nearer at hand? What surprises might there be in store there?

The whole book thus attempts to reflect the Lord's Prayer itself when it says, 'thy kingdom come, on earth as in heaven'. That remains one of the most powerful and revolutionary sentences we can ever say. As I see it, the prayer was powerfully answered at the first Easter, and will finally be answered fully when heaven and earth are joined in the new Jerusalem. Easter was when Hope in person surprised the whole world by coming forward from the future into the present. The ultimate future hope remains a surprise, partly because we don't know when it will arrive, and partly because at present we only have images and metaphors for it, leaving us to guess that the reality will be far greater, and more surprising, still. And the intermediate hope – the things which happen in the present time which implement Easter and anticipate the final day – is always surprising, because, left to ourselves, we lapse into a kind of collusion with entropy, acquiescing in the general belief that things may be getting worse but that there's nothing much we can do about them. And we are wrong. Our task in the present – of which this book, God willing, may form part – is to live as resurrection people in between Easter and the final day, with our Christian life, corporate and individual, in both worship and mission, as a sign of the first and a foretaste of the second.

3

Early Christian hope
in its historical setting

1. Introduction

On Friday 25 October 1946, at 8.30 p.m., in a large room in King's College, Cambridge, two of the greatest philosophers of the twentieth century came face to face for the first and last time. It was not a happy occasion. Afterwards, when those present compared notes, nobody could quite agree what exactly had happened.

The two philosophers were Ludwig Wittgenstein and Karl Popper. Wittgenstein had already established a reputation for brilliance; many were under the spell of his revolutionary ideas. He was the chairman of the Cambridge Moral Science Club (in Cambridge, 'Moral Science' means 'philosophy'.) Many other philosophers, though, including Popper, regarded him with deep distrust. Popper was just making his name, having recently published the English translation of his masterpiece, *The Open Society and its Enemies*.[1] Both men had been brought up, as assimilated Jews, in pre-war Vienna: Wittgenstein in a wealthy family with the world at his feet, Popper in a much more ordinary setting. Popper had longed for a chance to demonstrate the folly of Wittgenstein's ways, and now here it was. He had come to Cambridge to give a paper in which he would attack the great man head on. It was a chilly evening; the fire was lit in the grate; and Wittgenstein was sitting beside it. Many of those present were, or would become, household names in philosophy: Bertrand Russell, Peter Geach, Stephen Toulmin, Richard Braithwaite. Others went into other professions, such as the law. Many of them are still alive and remember the occasion well. Or so they say.

Popper was not to know that Wittgenstein was not in the habit of listening to papers all the way through, or that he had a reputation for arrogance and rudeness, or that he frequently left meetings well before the end. Before long, that evening – and this is where the accounts start to diverge – Wittgenstein had interrupted Popper, and the two men had begun a brief acrimonious exchange. At one point Wittgenstein picked up the poker from the fireplace and waved it around. Shortly after that he left the room and did not return.

Within a short time rumours had gone literally around the world. Popper got a letter from New Zealand asking if it was true that Wittgenstein had threatened him with a red-hot poker. From that day to this the great minds present cannot agree as to what precisely happened. Some say the poker was red-hot, others that it was cool. Some say Wittgenstein waved it around to make his point (which wouldn't have been unusual); others, including Popper, say he seemed to threaten his opponent with it. Some say that Wittgenstein left after an angry exchange with Russell, and that after he'd gone Popper suggested, as an example of an obvious moral principle, 'Not to threaten visiting speakers with pokers'. Others, including Popper, say that he left when Popper said that to his face. Some say he slammed the door; others, that he left quietly. It's a fascinating story, and has recently been written up as an enterprising book.[2] The main conclusion the book draws is that Wittgenstein probably left before Popper's remark. Popper's memory had probably played him false; he had so much at stake, personally and professionally, that he badly wanted to tell the story as the story of his famous victory over Wittgenstein. So, quite soon, he did; and so, before too long, he believed his own account.

Everybody disagrees on the precise details. But nobody doubts that the meeting took place. Nobody doubts that

Wittgenstein and Popper were the two main adversaries, with Russell as a kind of senior umpire. Nobody doubts that Wittgenstein did at least wave a poker around, and that he left quite abruptly.

I begin with this story for an obvious reason. It is a commonplace among lawyers that eyewitnesses disagree, but that this doesn't mean that nothing happened. It is the more remarkable that disagreement happens when the witnesses are all extremely erudite and professionally concerned with knowledge and truth. But there it is. And the Christian gospel affirms, as the central fact without which there would be no gospel at all, something that happened perhaps fifty years before our most detailed records of it, and about which those records don't match exactly. Some have said that this casts doubt on whether anything happened at all on the first Easter day. We have in the four gospels, together with Acts and Paul, a first-century equivalent of the varying accounts of Wittgenstein's poker, and my question now is clear: what sort of an event was it? Just how empty was the tomb on Easter morning?

With this we dive, of course, right into the middle of one of the debates that has bothered the mainstream western church for well over a century. William Temple, subsequently to become Archbishop of Canterbury, did not get ordained until he had made up his mind that he really did believe in the bodily resurrection of Jesus. Subsequent clergy, including many bishops, have not taken the same line, and David Jenkins famously whipped up a storm of controversy with his remarks about the empty tomb, Jesus' bones, and conjuring tricks – though his words, like the exchange between Popper and Wittgenstein, have had an interesting subsequent career in oral and written tradition. What should we believe about Jesus' resurrection, and why?

This question has been muddled up with several other related but distinct questions, and it's often now difficult to clear people's minds sufficiently to concentrate on the real issues. The issue is not whether the Bible is true or not. The issue is not whether miracles occur or not. The issue is not whether we believe in something called 'the supernatural' or not. The issue is not whether Jesus is alive today and we can get to know him for ourselves. If we treat the question of Easter simply as a test case in any of those discussions, we are missing the point.

Nor can we say, though many have tried to, that because we know the laws of nature, whereas first-century people didn't, we now know that Jesus can't have risen from the dead. As I have shown in considerable detail elsewhere, the ancient world – with the exception of the Jews – was adamant that dead people did not rise again; and the Jews did not believe that anyone *had* done so, or that anyone *would* do so all by themselves in advance of the general resurrection.[3] But even when we've cleared away those misunderstandings, deep questions remain. What precisely was it that the early Christians believed? Why did they use the language of resurrection to express that belief? Is it possible to mount a historical case for or against the empty tomb and the bodily resurrection, or will it always be a matter of take-it-or-leave-it? How far can history take us, what role does faith have, and how do they work together? The question is not simply *what* we can know, but also *how* we can know; and at this point all our knowing is called into question.

Edmonds and Eidinow advance their investigation of the Popper/Wittgenstein encounter by two principal methods. First, they interrogate the eyewitnesses to make sure the apparent first-hand evidence is on the table. Second, they painstakingly reconstruct the background to the meeting in terms of the complex lives and agendas of the two main characters. They then draw their conclusions in terms of a connected historical narrative, claiming not that it is absolutely true but that it is the most likely way of reconciling the various claims.

We must do something similar in looking at the empty tomb, and at the event of Easter itself. The eyewitnesses – if that is what they are – are well known. We have them in front of us in the New Testament. We can reconstruct the background quite fully in terms of Jewish beliefs and expectations, and of Jesus' own public career and his followers' beliefs and hopes. But there is a third element, without a real parallel in the 1946 Cambridge debate. The philosophical issues there discussed, and the heat they generated, were of their time and have passed away. Popper is increasingly 'old hat'; Wittgenstein's more brilliant legacy is deeply ambiguous. We can't tell, by looking at subsequent philosophy, who if anybody 'won' the debate that evening. Even if one or other man's achievement was now seen as superior, that might well have nothing to do with ten minutes of heated Cambridge rhetoric. But with Easter it's different. What happened then, whatever it was, generated something quite new: something that grew and developed in particular ways, but always with this moment as its supposed point of origin. A major part of our enquiry, then, must be to look at the emerging Christian movement, and to ask: what caused it? Even if our eyewitnesses disagree in detail, something must have happened.

Since I have written about all this extensively elsewhere, we can now cut straight to the heart of the issue. In the present chapter, I shall locate the early Christian beliefs about life beyond death on the map of ancient views, both pagan and Jewish. The striking results of this will send us back, in the next chapter, to the Easter narratives themselves for a fresh investigation as to their character and provenance, and to reflect on the options open to the historian.

2. Resurrection and life after death in ancient paganism and Judaism

To begin with, then, what did the ancient world believe about life beyond the grave? I am here summarizing the mass of evidence I have set out elsewhere.

As far as the ancient pagan world was concerned, the road to the underworld ran only one way. Death was all-powerful; one could neither escape it in the first place nor break its power once it had come. Everybody knew there was in fact no answer to death. The ancient pagan world then divided broadly into those who, like Homer's shades, might have wanted a new body but knew they couldn't have one, and those who, like Plato's philosophers, didn't want one because being a disembodied soul was far better.

Within this world, the word 'resurrection' in its Greek, Latin or other equivalents was never used to mean 'life after death'. 'Resurrection' was used to denote new bodily life *after* whatever sort of 'life after death' there might be. When the ancients spoke of resurrection, whether to deny it (as all pagans did) or to affirm it (as some Jews did), they were referring to a two-step narrative in which resurrection, meaning new bodily life, would be preceded by an interim period of bodily death. 'Resurrection' wasn't, then, a dramatic or vivid way of talking about the state people went into immediately after death. It denoted something that might happen (though almost everyone thought it wouldn't) some time *after* that. This meaning is constant throughout the ancient world until the post-Christian coinages of second-century gnosticism. Most of the ancients believed in life after death; some of them developed complex and fascinating beliefs about it, which we have only just touched on; but, outside Judaism and Christianity (and perhaps Zoroastrianism, though the dating of that is controversial), they did not believe in resurrection.

In content, 'resurrection' referred specifically to something that happened to the body; hence the later debates about how God would do this, whether he would start with the existing bones or make new ones, or whatever. One would only have debates like that if it was quite clear that what you ended up with was something, as we would say, tangible and physical. Everybody knew about ghosts, spirits, visions, hallucinations and so on. Most people in the ancient world believed in some such things. They were quite clear that that wasn't what they meant by 'resurrection'. When Herod is reported to have thought Jesus might have been John the Baptist raised from the dead, he didn't think he was a ghost.[4] Resurrection meant bodies. We cannot emphasize this too strongly, not least because much modern writing continues, most misleadingly, to use the word 'resurrection' as a virtual synonym for 'life after death' in the popular sense.

An important conclusion follows from all this, before we look at the Jewish material. When the early Christians said that Jesus had risen from the dead they knew that they were saying that something had happened to him which had happened to nobody else, and which nobody had expected to happen. They were not talking about Jesus' soul going into heavenly bliss. Nor were they saying, confusedly, that Jesus had now become divine. That is simply not what the words meant; there was no implicit connection for either Jews or pagans between resurrection and divinization. When the ancient Romans declared that the recently departed emperor had gone to heaven and become divine, nobody dreamed of saying that he had been raised from the dead. The exception proves the rule: those who believed that Nero had come back to life (a group, we may suppose, not unlike those who think Elvis has come back to life, despite his well-known and much-visited grave) precisely did *not* think that he was now in heaven.

What then about the ancient *Jewish* world? Some Jews agreed with those pagans who denied any kind of future life, especially a re-embodied one. The Sadducees are famous for taking this position. Others agreed with those pagans who thought in terms of a glorious though disembodied future for the soul. Here the obvious example is the philosopher Philo. But most Jews of the day believed in an eventual resurrection: that is, that God would look after the soul after death until, at the last day, God would give his people new bodies at the time when he judged and remade the whole world. That is what Martha assumed Jesus was talking about in their conversation beside the tomb of Lazarus: 'I know he will rise again in the resurrection on the last day.'[5] That is what 'resurrection' meant.[6]

Jesus' own teaching, during his brief public career, simply reinforced the Jewish picture. He redefined a lot of ideas that were current at the time – notably, of course, 'kingdom of God' itself, explaining in many coded parables and symbolic actions that God's sovereign, saving rule *was* now breaking in, even though it didn't look like what his contemporaries had imagined and wanted. But he hardly even tried to redefine the notion of resurrection. When he did, briefly and cryptically, his closest followers, as we shall see presently, didn't have a clue what he was talking about.

In the one head-on discussion of the topic – the time when the Sadducees asked him a trick question designed to make the idea of resurrection look silly – he answered in quite a traditional fashion, doing better with the question than the Pharisees would have done, but not moving significantly beyond the then standard Jewish view.[7] He spoke of 'the resurrection' as a complete event in the future, when all the righteous would be raised; and he seems to have indicated that in this resurrection state certain things would be different, so that there would be no problem about who had been married to whom in the present life – the point on which the Sadducees had tried to nail him down. (Contrary to what people sometimes suggest, by the way, he didn't say that in the resurrection God's people would *become* angels, but that they would in certain respects be *like* angels (Matthew, Mark) or *equal to* angels (Luke).) Apart from this discussion, almost the only reference to 'the resurrection' as a whole within the gospels occurs at Matthew 13.43, when Jesus declares that on the last day the righteous will shine like the sun in the kingdom of their father. The echo of Daniel 12.3 would ensure that this would be taken as a reference to the resurrection. When Jesus speaks of the reward awaiting God's people, he can simply refer to 'the resurrection of the righteous' in the normal Jewish way (Luke 14.14). In one isolated Johannine saying (John 5.29) he speaks of a coming resurrection of both the righteous and the wicked. Thus far he is exactly on the map of first-century Jewish belief. Unlike his redefinitions of kingdom and messiahship, he seems to have little or nothing new to say.

Except that he then begins to tell his followers that he himself is going to be killed, and then raised again three days later. Many scholars have thought, of course, that these are pseudo-'prophecies', read back on to Jesus' lips by the later church. I have argued at length for the opposite view: that someone doing what Jesus was doing, thinking as he must have been thinking, was highly likely to foresee his own death, to speak of it in apocalyptic imagery and metaphor, and to invest it, as the Maccabean martyrs were thought to have done in respect of their own deaths, with some kind of saving significance. In that world, someone thinking that sort of thing would be almost bound to say, in addition: 'And God will vindicate me after my death.' And the kind of vindication they would have expected, as 2 Maccabees again bears witness, would of course be resurrection.

But the disciples, as the gospels insist over and over, simply couldn't understand what Jesus was saying. His dark saying was in any case couched in the apocalyptic metaphor about the son of man, and they clearly thought they were meant to decode it but didn't know how. The last thing they imagined was that this kingdom-bringer, this Jesus they were coming to believe might be God's Messiah, would die at the hands of the pagan occupying forces. At no point do we get even a hint of anyone saying, 'Well, that's all right – he's got to go and die to save us, and then he'll rise again soon after.' Thus the one time that Jesus really does seem to have been trying to redefine the Jewish belief in resurrection, by hinting that it was going to happen to him in the first place all by himself, they had no idea what he was talking about. When he told them not to breathe a word about the transfiguration 'until the son of man is raised from the dead', they discussed among themselves, in some puzzlement, what this 'rising from the dead' might mean.[8] It wasn't that they didn't know about resurrection. It was, rather, that they had never thought – despite Herod's supposed remark about John the Baptist – that, as Jesus seemed to be implying, it was something that would happen to one person ahead of everybody else. This scenario is completely credible both for Jesus and for the disciples. It fits with everything else we know about their context, their understanding and their motivations.

And it shows, of course, that the crucifixion of Jesus was the end of all their hopes. Nobody dreamed of saying, 'Oh, that's all right – he'll be back again in a few days.'[9] Nor did anybody say, 'Well, at least he's now in heaven with God.' They were not looking for that sort of 'kingdom'. After all, Jesus himself had taught them to pray that God's kingdom would come 'on earth as in heaven'. What they said – and again this has the ring of first-century truth – was things like 'We had hoped that he was the one who would redeem Israel' (Luke 24.21), with the implication, 'but they crucified him, so he can't have been'. The cross, we note, already had a symbolic meaning throughout the Roman world, long before it had a new one for the Christians. It meant: we Romans run this place, and if you get in our way we'll obliterate you, and do it pretty nastily too. Crucifixion meant that the kingdom hadn't come, not that it had. Crucifixion of a would-be Messiah meant that he wasn't the Messiah, not that he was. When Jesus was crucified, every single disciple knew what it meant: we backed the wrong horse. The game is over. Whatever their expectations, and however Jesus had been trying to redefine those expectations, as far as they were concerned hope had crumbled into ashes. They knew they were lucky to escape with their own lives.

51

That is the world within which early Christianity burst upon the scene as a new thing, and yet not new. What happens when we locate this sudden movement on the map of ancient Judaism, within its wider pagan context?

3. The surprising character of early Christian hope

The answer, put simply, is that the early Christian belief in hope beyond death belongs demonstrably on the Jewish, not the pagan, map, but that in seven significant ways this Jewish hope has undergone remarkable modifications, which can be plotted with remarkable consistency in writers from Paul in the middle of the first century to Tertullian and Origen at the end of the second, and beyond.

To begin with, then, the early Christian future hope centred firmly on resurrection. The first Christians did not simply believe in 'life after death'; they virtually never speak simply of 'going to heaven when they died' (as I have often said, alluding to the title of a good popular book on this subject, heaven is important but it's not the end of the world[10]); and when they do speak of heaven as a post-mortem destination they seem to regard this 'heavenly' life as a temporary stage on the way to the eventual resurrection of the body. When Jesus tells the brigand that he will join him in paradise that very day, 'paradise' clearly cannot be their ultimate destination, as Luke's next chapter makes clear. 'Paradise' is, rather, the blissful garden where God's people rest prior to the resurrection. When Jesus declares that there are many dwelling-places in his father's house, the word for 'dwelling-place' is *monē*, which denotes a temporary lodging. When Paul says that his desire is 'to depart and be with Christ, which is far better', he is indeed thinking of a blissful life with his Lord immediately after death, but this is only the prelude to the resurrection itself.[11] In terms of the discussion in the previous chapter, the early Christians hold firmly to a two-step belief about the future: first, death and what-ever lies immediately beyond; second, a new bodily existence in a newly remade world.

There is nothing remotely like this in paganism. This belief is as Jewish as you can get. But within this Jewish belief there are seven early Christian modifications, each of which crops up in writers as diverse as Paul and John the Seer, as Luke and Justin Martyr, as Matthew and Irenaeus. This is highly significant, because what people believe about life beyond death tends to be very conservative. Faced with bereavement, people lurch back for the safety of what they heard or learnt before. But the early Christians all articulate a belief which is, in these seven ways, quite new; and the historian has to ask, why?

(1) The first of these modifications is that within early Christianity there is virtually no spectrum of belief about life beyond death. What people believe about life beyond death, and the social and cultural ways in which these beliefs find expression, is notoriously one of the most conservative features of a culture. Yet, whereas the early Christians were drawn from many strands of Judaism and from widely differing back-grounds within paganism, and hence from circles which must have held very different beliefs about life beyond death, they have all modified that belief to focus on one point on the spectrum. Christianity looks, to this extent, like a variety of Pharisaic Judaism. There is no trace of a Sadducean view, or of that of Philo.

The Corinthians, muddled ex-pagans that they were, had some people, apparently, who denied the resurrection; well, they would, but that didn't last long.[12] Two teachers mentioned in the Pastorals claim that the resurrection is past already.[13] That was a misunderstanding likely to occur, anticipating perhaps the later gnostic rethinking of the whole question, but it doesn't alter the overwhelming impression of unanimity. And, to anticipate a later argument, let us not imagine, as some do today, that the reason for the apparent unanimity is that the heavy-handed orthodox obliterated all trace of a more poly-morphous early period. We have plenty of evidence of debates about all sorts of things, and the virtual unanimity on resurrection stands out. Only in the late second century, a good 150 years after the time of Jesus, do we find people using the word 'resurrection' to mean something quite different from what it meant in Judaism and early Christianity, namely a 'spiritual experience' in the present leading to a disembodied hope in the future.[14] For almost all the first two centuries resurrection, in the traditional sense, holds not only centre stage but the whole stage.

(2) This leads to the second mutation. In second-Temple Judaism, resurrection is important but not that important. There are lots of lengthy works which never mention the question, let alone this answer. It is still difficult to be sure what the authors of the Dead Sea Scrolls thought on the topic. Apart from occasional highlights like 2 Maccabees 7, resurrection is a peripheral topic. But in early Christianity resurrection has moved from the circumference to the centre. You can't imagine Paul's thought without it. You shouldn't imagine John's thought without it, though some have tried. It is enormously important in Clement and Ignatius, in Justin and Irenaeus. It is one of the key beliefs which infuriated the pagans in Lyons in AD 177 and drove them to butcher several Christians, including the bishop who preceded the great Irenaeus. Belief in bodily resurrection was one of the two central things that the pagan doctor Galen noted about the Christians (the other being their remarkable sexual restraint). Take away the stories of Jesus' birth, and all you lose is two chapters of Matthew and two of Luke. Take away the resurrection and you lose the entire New Testament, and most of the second-century fathers as well.

(3) These first two mutations have to do with the new place that resurrection has taken within early Christianity, as opposed to the place it held within its native Judaism. The next

mutation has to do with something more organic about what precisely resurrection *means*. In Judaism it is almost always left quite vague as to what sort of a body the resurrected will possess. The Maccabean martyrs assume it will be a body more or less exactly like the present one. Most of the Jewish texts that glance at the question have little to say beyond this, apart from occasional references to 'glory', perhaps in the sense of light. But from the start within early Christianity it was built in as part of the belief in resurrection that the new body, though it would certainly *be* a body in the sense of a physical object occupying space and time, will be a *transformed* body, a body whose material, created from the old material, will have new properties. There has been a dramatic sharpening-up of what 'resurrection' itself actually entailed.

It is of course Paul, in a much misunderstood passage in 1 Corinthians 15, who sets this out most clearly and to whom many, though not all, subsequent writers look back. He speaks of two sorts of body, the present one and the future one. He uses two key adjectives to describe these two bodies. Unfortunately, many translations have got him radically wrong at this point, leading to the widespread supposition that for Paul the new body would be a 'spiritual' body in the sense of a 'non-material' body, a body which in Jesus' case wouldn't have left an empty tomb behind it. It can be demonstrated in great detail, philologically and exegetically, that this is precisely not what Paul meant. The contrast he is making is not between what we would mean by a present 'physical' body and what we would mean by a future 'spiritual' one, but between a present body animated by the normal human soul and a future body animated by God's spirit.[15]

And the point about the future body is that it will be incorruptible. The present flesh and blood is corruptible, doomed to decay and die. That's why Paul says that 'flesh and blood cannot inherit God's kingdom'. The new body will be incorruptible. The entire chapter, one of Paul's longest sustained discussions and the vital climax of the whole letter, is about new creation, about the creator God remaking the creation, not abandoning it as Platonists of all sorts, including gnostics, would have wanted.

But this transformed physicality (or, as I have called it in *The Resurrection of the Son of God*, 'transphysicality') does not involve being transformed into luminosity. Here again many go wrong, misunderstanding the word 'glory' to imply a physical shining rather than a status within God's world. This is the more remarkable in that the best-known of the biblical resurrection texts, Daniel 12, speaks of the resurrected righteous shining like stars. Surprisingly, this text is never quoted in the New Testament about the resurrection body except in the interpretation of one parable.[16] When we do find it, it is used metaphorically of present Christian witness in the world.[17] What we find, then, throughout early Christian resurrection belief, is the view that the new body, when it is given, will possess a transformed physicality, but not transformed in the one way the central biblical text might have suggested.

(4) The fourth surprising mutation evidenced by the early Christian resurrection belief is that 'the resurrection', as an event, has split into two. The first letter to the Corinthians 15 is again central for this, but it is assumed right across the first two centuries. No first-century Jew, prior to Easter, expected 'the resurrection' to be anything other than a large-scale event happening to all God's people, or perhaps to the entire human race, as part of the sudden event in which God's kingdom would finally come on earth as in heaven. There is no suggestion that one person will rise from the dead in advance of all the rest. The 'exceptions' sometimes quoted (Enoch and Elijah) do not count, precisely because (a) they were held not to have died, and so 'resurrection' (new life after bodily death) would not be relevant, and (b) they were in heaven, not in a new body on earth.[18] 'Resurrection', we must never cease to remind ourselves, did not mean 'going to heaven' or 'escaping death' or

'having a glorious and noble post-mortem existence' but 'coming to bodily life again after bodily death'. This is why, when after the transfiguration Jesus tells the disciples not to mention the vision until the son of man has been raised from the dead, they are (as we saw a few moments ago) puzzled, and wonder what this 'rising from the dead' can mean, if it is to be an event that will leave them in a position to be telling people about details of Jesus' life, rather than an event in which God's whole new world will be born.

There were, of course, other Jewish movements roughly contemporary with early Christianity which also held some kind of inaugurated eschatology (i.e., the belief that 'the end' had already, in some sense, begun). The Essenes, as represented in the Scrolls, believed that the covenant had been secretly re-established with them, in advance of the final denouement. But outside Christianity we never find what becomes a central feature within it: the belief that the mode of this inauguration consisted in the resurrection itself happening to one person in the middle of history in advance of its great, final occurrence, anticipating and guaranteeing the final resurrection of God's people at the end of history.

(5) I am indebted to Dominic Crossan for highlighting what I now list as the fifth mutation in Jewish resurrection belief. In a public debate in New Orleans in March 2005, Crossan designated this mutation as 'collaborative eschatology'. My understanding of this, in line with what I believe Crossan intended, is this. Because the early Christians believed that 'resurrection' had begun with Jesus, and would be completed in the great final resurrection on the last day, they believed that God had called them to work with him, in the power of the Spirit, to implement the achievement of Jesus and thereby to anticipate the final resurrection, in personal and political life, in mission and holiness. It was not merely that God had inaugurated the 'end'; if Jesus, the Messiah, was the End in person, God's-future-arrived-in-the-present, then those who belonged

to Jesus and followed him and were empowered by his Spirit were charged with transforming the present, as far as they were able, in the light of that future.

(6) The sixth remarkable mutation within the Jewish belief is the quite different metaphorical use of 'resurrection'. Within Judaism, resurrection could function both as metaphor and as metonymy for the return from exile. For Ezekiel himself, in chapter 37, it is pretty clearly metaphor; by the time the rabbis come to the idea, and indeed already in 2 Maccabees, 4 Ezra and elsewhere, and also in the gospels,[19] it is metonymy, one part of the great eschatological whole which can stand for the whole. And the concrete referent of this Jewish metaphor is the national, ethnic, geographical restoration of Israel. So when 'resurrection' is used metaphorically in Judaism, it refers to the restoration of Israel; but from the earliest days of Christianity, all the more remarkably when we consider how it began as a Jewish messianic movement, this meaning has disappeared, making perhaps its only fleeting appearance in the disciples' puzzled question at the start of Acts ('Lord, will you at this time restore the kingdom to Israel?').[20]

In its place, equally remarkably, we have a new metaphorical meaning of resurrection, which has already taken firm root by the time of Paul: resurrection as referring metaphorically to baptism as a dying and rising with Christ, and resurrection as referring to the new life of strenuous ethical obedience, enabled by the Holy Spirit, to which the believer is committed. We should note that these metaphorical meanings are regularly found right alongside passages in which the literal meaning, of a future actual bodily resurrection, is also emphasized, as for instance in Romans; in other words, this is not the beginning of a slide into a non-physical meaning. And we should also note that this metaphorical meaning still has a concrete referent – baptism and ethics – rather than the abstract or 'spiritual' one beloved of the later gnostics.

This, then, is the sixth modification of the Jewish belief: re-surrection, while still being embraced as literal language about a future embodied existence, has shed its powerful earlier meta-phorical meaning about the renewal of ethnic Israel and has acquired a new one, about the renewal of human beings in general. In fact, within early Christianity we begin to discover the language of return from exile, of the ethnic and territorial renewal of Israel, now itself used metaphorically to refer both to the present renewal of human beings and to their eventual bodily resurrection. Once more, all these meanings only make sense within the Jewish world of thought; no pagan ever dreamed of anything like this; but until Christianity no Jew had come this route either. We are faced with a further remarkable mutation from within.

(7) The seventh and last mutation from within the Jewish resurrection belief was its association with messiahship. No-body in Judaism had expected the Messiah to die, and there-fore naturally nobody had imagined the Messiah rising from the dead. This leads to a remarkable modification not just of resurrection belief but of messianic belief itself. Where mes-sianic speculations existed (again, by no means all Jewish texts spoke of a Messiah, but the notion became central in early Christianity), the Messiah was supposed to fight God's victor-ious battle against the wicked pagans; to rebuild or cleanse the Temple; and to bring God's justice to the world. Jesus, it appeared, had done none of these things. He had suffered the typical injustice of the world; he had mounted a strange and apparently ineffectual demonstration in the Temple; and he had died at the hands of the pagans, rather than defeating them gloriously in battle. No Jew with any idea of how the language of messiahship worked at the time could have possibly im-agined, after his crucifixion, that Jesus of Nazareth was indeed the Lord's anointed. But from very early on, as witnessed by what may be pre-Pauline fragments of early credal belief, the

Christians affirmed that Jesus was indeed the Messiah, precisely because of his resurrection.

We may note at this point, as an aside but an important one, how impossible it is to account for the early Christian belief in Jesus as Messiah without the resurrection. We have evidence of several other Jewish movements, messianic movements, prophetic movements, during the one or two centuries either side of Jesus' public career. Routinely they ended with the violent death of the central figure. Members of the movement (always supposing they got away with their own skins) then faced a choice: either give up the struggle, or find a new Messiah. Had the early Christians wanted to go the latter route, they had an obvious candidate: James, the Lord's brother, a great and devout teacher, the central figure in the early Jerusalem church. But nobody ever imagined that James might be the Messiah. Josephus describes him, somewhat contemptuously but echoing the language people must have used of him, as 'the brother of the so-called Messiah'.[21]

This means we can already rule out the revisionist positions on Jesus' resurrection that have been offered by so many writers in recent years. Many have suggested that the early disciples were so overwhelmed with grief at Jesus' death that they picked up the idea of resurrection from their surrounding culture and clung on to it, persuading themselves that Jesus had been raised from the dead though of course they knew he hadn't been. Some have suggested that the earliest Christians believed that Jesus, after his death, had been exalted to heaven; or that they had a strange sense that his mission, to bring in God's kingdom, was now going ahead in a new way; and that this kind of belief led them to say he'd been raised from the dead.

But would this make any sense? We can test it out with a little thought experiment. In AD 70, the Romans conquered Jerusalem, and they led thousands of Jews captive back to Rome, including the man they regarded as the leader of the

Jewish revolt, 'the king of the Jews', a man called Simon bar Giora. He was led into Rome at the back of the triumphal procession, and the end of the spectacle was Simon being flogged and then killed.[22]

Now: suppose we imagine a few Jewish revolutionaries, three days or three weeks later. The first one says, 'You know, I think Simon really was the Messiah – and he still is!'

The others would be puzzled. Of course he isn't; the Romans got him, as they always do. If you want a Messiah, you'd better find another one.

'Ah,' says the first, 'but I believe he's been raised from the dead.'

'What d'you mean?' his friends ask. 'He's dead and buried.'

'Oh no,' replies the first, 'I believe he's been exalted to heaven.'

The others look puzzled. All the righteous martyrs are with God, everybody knows that; their souls are in God's hand; that doesn't mean they've *already* been raised from the dead. Anyway, the resurrection will happen to us all at the end of time, not to one person in the middle of continuing history.

'No,' replies the first, 'you don't understand. I've had a strong sense of God's love surrounding me. I have felt God forgiving me – forgiving us all. I've had my heart strangely warmed. What's more, last night, I saw Simon; he was there with me . . .'

The others interrupt, now angry. We can all have visions. Plenty of people dream about recently dead friends. Sometimes it's very vivid. That doesn't mean they've been raised from the dead. It certainly doesn't mean that one of them is the Messiah. And if your heart has been warmed, then sing a psalm, don't make wild claims about Simon.

That is what they would have said to anyone offering the kind of statement which, according to the revisionists, someone must have come up with as the beginning of the idea of Jesus' resurrection. But this solution isn't just incredible; it's impossible. Had anyone said what the revisionists suggest, some such conversation as the above would have ensued. A little bit of disciplined historical imagination is all it takes to blow away enormous piles of so-called historical criticism.

What is more (to round off this final mutation from within the Jewish belief), because of the early Christian belief in Jesus as Messiah, we find the development of the very early belief that Jesus is Lord and that therefore Caesar is not. This is a whole other topic for another occasion. But already in Paul the resurrection, both of Jesus and then, in the future, of his people, is the foundation of the Christian stance of allegiance to a different king, a different Lord.[23] Death is the last weapon of the tyrant; and the point of the resurrection, despite much misunderstanding, is that death has been defeated. Resurrection is not the redescription of death; it is its overthrow, and with that the overthrow of those whose power depends on it. Despite the sneers and slurs of some contemporary scholars, it was those who believed in the bodily resurrection who were burned at the stake and thrown to the lions. Resurrection was never a way of settling down and becoming respectable; the Pharisees could have told you that. It was the gnostics, who translated the language of resurrection into a private spirituality and a dualistic cosmology, thereby more or less altering its meaning into its opposite, who escaped persecution. Which emperor would have sleepless nights worrying that his subjects were reading *The Gospel of Thomas*? Resurrection was always bound to get you into trouble, and regularly did.[24]

We have thus noted seven major mutations within the Jewish resurrection belief, each of which became central within the Christianity of the first two centuries. The early Christian belief in resurrection remains emphatically on the map of first-century Judaism rather than paganism; but, from within the Jewish theology of monotheism, election and eschatology, it has opened up a whole new way of seeing history, hope and hermeneutics. *And this demands a historical explanation.* Why did the early Christians modify the Jewish resurrection-language in these seven ways, and do it with such consistency? When we ask them, they of course reply that they did it because of what they believed had happened to Jesus on the third day after he died. This projects us on into the next chapter, to ask: what then must we say about the very strange stories which they tell as they describe the events of that first Easter day?

4

The strange story of Easter

1. Stories without precedent

When we plunge in to the stories of the first Easter day – the accounts we find in the closing chapters of the four canonical gospels – we find ourselves back with Wittgenstein's poker. Notoriously, the accounts of Easter do not fit snugly together.[1] How many women went to the tomb, and how many angels or men did they meet there? Did the disciples meet Jesus in Jerusalem or Galilee or both? And so on. But, as with Cambridge in 1946, so with Jerusalem in AD 30 (or whenever it was): surface discrepancies do not mean that nothing happened. Indeed, they are a reasonable indication that something remarkable happened, so remarkable that the first witnesses were bewildered into telling different stories about it.

As part of the larger argument that I have advanced elsewhere, I here draw attention to four strange features shared by the accounts in the four canonical gospels. These features, I suggest, compel us to take them seriously as very early accounts, not, as is often suggested, later inventions.[2]

(1) First, we note the strange silence of the Bible in the stories. Up to this point, all four evangelists have drawn heavily upon biblical quotation, allusion and echo to make it clear that Jesus' death was 'according to the scriptures'. Even the burial narrative has biblical echoes. But the resurrection narratives are almost entirely innocent of them, with only a couple of small exceptions. This is the more remarkable, in that from as early as Paul the common credal formula declared that the resurrection, too, was 'according to the scriptures', and Paul himself

joins the rest of the early church in ransacking psalms and prophets to find texts that will explain what has just happened and set it within, and as the climax to, the long story of God and Israel. Why do the gospel resurrection narratives not do the same? It would have been easy for Matthew to refer to one or two scriptural prophecies which were being fulfilled, but he doesn't. John tells us that the disciples didn't yet know the scriptural teaching that the Messiah would rise again, but he doesn't quote the texts he has in mind.

We could say, of course, that whoever wrote the stories in the form we now have them had gone through, cunningly, and taken material out *to make them look as if they were very old*, rather like someone deliberately taking all the electric fittings out of a house to make it look like it might have done a century or more ago. The normal assumption among many scholars, that the stories grew up in the second generation, as late (say) as the 80s or 90s, would require us to say that, though they interestingly embody (as we shall see) the theology of Paul, they have carefully extracted from that theology all the biblical allusions which are already so plentiful in a passage like 1 Corinthians 15.

That might be marginally plausible if we had just one account, or if the four accounts were obviously derived from one another. We don't, and they aren't.[3] You either have to imagine four very different writers each deciding to write up an Easter narrative, based on the theology of the early church, but removing all the biblical echoes, and managing to do so in four very different though theologically consistent ways; or you have to say, which I think is infinitely more probable, that the stories, even if they were written down a lot later, go back to very, very early oral tradition which had been formed, and set firmly in the memory of different storytellers, before there had been any time for biblical reflection.

(2) The second strange feature of the stories is more often remarked upon: the presence of the women as the principal

witnesses. Whether we like it or not, women were not re-garded as credible witnesses within the ancient world. When the tradition had time to sort itself out, and acquire the fixed form we already find in Paul's quotation of it in 1 Corinthians 15, the women have been quietly dropped; they are apologetically embarrassing. But there they are in all four gospel stories, front and centre, the first witnesses, the first apostles. Nobody would have made them up. Had the tradition started in the male-only form we find in 1 Corinthians 15, it would never have developed, in such different ways as well, into the female-first stories we find in the gospels.

(3) The third strange feature is the portrait of Jesus himself. If, as many revisionists have tried to make out, the gospel stories developed either from people mulling over the scriptures or from an experience of inner subjective illumination, the one thing you would expect to find is the risen Jesus shining like a star. That's what Daniel says will happen; that's what an experience of inner illumination might have generated. We have such an account in the transfiguration. But none of the gospels say this about Jesus at Easter. Indeed, he appears as a human being with a body that in some ways is quite normal, and can be mistaken for a gardener, or a fellow-traveller on the road. Yet the stories also contain – and this marks them out as among the most mysterious stories ever written – definite signs that this body has been transformed. It is clearly physical: it uses up (so to speak) the matter of the crucified body; hence the empty tomb. But, equally, it comes and goes through locked doors; it is not always recognized; and in the end it disappears into God's space, i.e., 'heaven', through the thin curtain which in much Jewish thought separates God's space from human space. This kind of account is without precedent. No biblical texts predict that the resurrection will involve this kind of body. No speculative theology had laid this trail for the evangelists to follow – and to follow, we note once more, in interestingly different ways.

In particular, this should put a stop to the old nonsense that Luke's and John's accounts, which are the most apparently 'physical', were written late in the first century in an attempt to combat docetism (the view that Jesus wasn't a real human being but only 'seemed' to be so).[4] Granted, if all you had was Jesus eating broiled fish (Luke), and inviting Thomas to touch him (John), such an account might have some initial plausibility. But if Luke and John were simply constructing narratives to combat docetism, they have surely shot themselves in the foot with both barrels when they speak of the risen Jesus appearing through locked doors, disappearing again, sometimes being recognized, sometimes not, and finally ascending into heaven.

(4) The fourth strange feature of the resurrection accounts is the fact that they never mention the future Christian hope. Almost everywhere else in the New Testament, the resurrection of Jesus is spoken of in connection with the final hope that those who belong to Jesus will one day be raised as he has been, and with the note that this must be anticipated in the present in baptism and behaviour. Despite a thousand Easter hymns and a million Easter sermons, the resurrection narratives in the gospels never, ever say anything like 'Jesus is raised, therefore there is a life after death', let alone 'Jesus is raised, therefore we shall go to heaven when we die'. Nor even, in a more authentic first-century Christian way, do they say 'Jesus is raised, therefore we shall be raised from the dead after the sleep of death'. No. In so far as the event is interpreted, Easter has a very this-worldly, present-age meaning: Jesus is raised, so he is the Messiah, and therefore he is the world's true Lord; Jesus is raised, so God's new creation has begun – and we, his followers, have a job to do! Jesus is raised, so we must act as his heralds, announcing his lordship to the entire world, making his kingdom come on earth as in heaven! To be sure, as early as Paul the resurrection of Jesus is firmly linked to the final resurrection of all God's people. Had the stories been invented

towards the end of the first century, they would certainly have included a mention of the final resurrection of all God's people. They don't, because they weren't.

There is much more to say about the gospel resurrection narratives. But I conclude this first section of the chapter with the proposal that it is far, far easier to believe that the stories are essentially very early, pre-Pauline, and have not been substantially altered, except for light personal polishing, in subsequent transmission or editing. Yes, they show signs of the theological interests of the different evangelists: Matthew's story of the resurrection emphasizes typically Matthean themes, and so on. But this is like what you get when different artists paint portraits of the same person. This painting is certainly a Rembrandt; that is indubitably a Holbein. The touch of the individual artist is unmistakable. And yet the sitter is fully recognizable. The artists have not changed the colour of her hair, the shape of her nose, the particular half-smile. And when we ask why such stories, so different in many ways and yet so interestingly consistent in these and other features, could have come into existence so early, all the early Christians give the obvious answer: something like this is what happened, even though it was hard to describe at the time and remains mindboggling thereafter. The stories, though lightly edited and written down later, are basically very, very early. They are not, as has so often been suggested, legends written up much later to give a pseudo-historical basis for what had essentially been a private, interior experience.

This, then, is the more or less universal witness of the early Christians: that they are who they are, they do what they do, they tell the stories they tell, not because of a new religious experience or insight but because of something that had happened; something that had happened to the crucified Jesus; something that they at once interpreted as meaning that he was after all the Messiah, that God's new age had after all broken into the present time, and that they were charged with a new commission; something which made them reaffirm the Jewish belief in resurrection, not swap it for a pagan alternative, but introduce several distinctive but consistent modifications within it. It is now time to ask, in the second section of this chapter: what can the historian say about all this?

2. Easter and history

I begin with what I regard as fixed historical points. The only way we can explain the phenomena we have been examining is by proposing a two-pronged hypothesis: first, Jesus' tomb really was empty; second, the disciples really did encounter him in ways which convinced them that he was not simply a ghost or hallucination. A brief word about each of these.

If the disciples had simply seen, or thought they had seen, someone they took to be Jesus, that would not by itself have generated the stories we have. Everyone in the ancient world took it for granted that people sometimes had strange experiences involving encounters with the dead, particularly the recently dead. They knew at least as much as we do about such visions, about ghosts and dreams – and the fact that such things often occurred within the context of bereavement or grief. They had language for this, and it wasn't 'resurrection'. However many such visions they had had, they wouldn't have said Jesus was raised from the dead; they weren't expecting such a resurrection.

In any case – a point people often ignore or conveniently forget – Jesus was buried according to a particular Jewish tradition, which was designed to occur in two stages. First, you carefully wrapped up the body with spices and linen and placed it on a shelf in a cave. Then, when the flesh had decomposed – hence the spices, because of the smell, since the cave would be used for more than one corpse – you would collect the bones, fold them up reverently, and store them in a bone-box (an 'ossuary'). If Jesus had not been raised, then sooner or later someone would have had to go and collect his bones, fold them up and store them. Even if anyone had been suggesting that he had been raised from the dead, that would be enough to disprove the suggestion. Nobody in the Jewish world would have spoken of such a person being already raised from the dead.

Thus, without the empty tomb, the disciples would have been as quick to say 'hallucination' as we would. Apparent 'meetings' with Jesus would have been dismissed: you've obviously seen a ghost.

Equally, an empty tomb by itself proves almost nothing. It might (as many have suggested) have been the wrong tomb, though a quick check would have sorted that one out. Some- one – the soldiers, the gardeners, the chief priests, other dis- ciples or someone else – might have taken away the body for some reason or other. Grave-robbery was well known. That was the conclusion Mary drew in John's gospel: they've taken him away – and perhaps it was the gardener that did it. That was the conclusion the Jewish leaders put about according to Matthew: his disciples took him away. All sorts of similar explanations could have been offered, and would have been, had not the empty tomb been accompanied by sightings of, and meetings with, Jesus himself. No: in order to explain, histor- ically, how all the early Christians came to the belief they held, that Jesus had been raised, we have to say at least this: that the tomb was empty, except for some graveclothes, and that they really did see and talk with someone who gave every appear- ance of being a solidly physical Jesus, though a Jesus who was strangely changed, more strangely than they were able fully to describe.

The meetings on the one hand, and the empty tomb on the other, are therefore each necessary if we are to explain the rise of the belief, and the writing of the stories as we have them. Neither by itself would be sufficient; put them together, though, and they provide a complete and coherent explanation for the rise of the early Christian belief.

Is there an alternative explanation, one which would get us off the hook of saying that the ancient pagan view (resurrection is impossible) was wrong, along with its modern equivalents? No. Like everything else in this chapter, the answer could be spelled out at much greater length; but we must at least note that the main alternative accounts, the revisionist proposals, lack all explanatory power.

Take the phenomenon of 'cognitive dissonance', about which much has been written in the last half-century or so. 'Cognitive dissonance' is what happens when people who badly want something to be true, but are faced with strong evidence to the contrary, manage to leap over the data that point the wrong way, and become even more strident in announcing their claims. This theory has some initial plausibility. There are some interesting examples of people behaving in this way. But theories like this will not serve as an explanation of the early Christian phenomena. In fact, the research on which the theory was originally based was already deeply flawed, as I have shown elsewhere.[5]

But, more particularly, it simply doesn't fit the state of affairs at Easter. The disciples were emphatically not expecting Jesus to be raised from the dead, all by himself in the middle of history. The fact that they were second-Temple Jews, and that resurrection was, as some have said, an idea that was 'in the air', simply won't account for the radical modifications we noted above within the Jewish belief, or for the astonishing features of the Easter stories themselves.

In the same way, some have suggested that the early disciples had a new experience of grace, that they felt forgiven in a new way, that they had come to a new faith in the power of God, a new conviction that God's kingdom-project was still going ahead despite Jesus' death.[6] But this, too, simply won't work. As we saw earlier, to say one had had a new experience of grace or anything like that doesn't take you one step nearer saying that the leader you had followed had been raised from the dead.

The resurrection did indeed function as metaphor, but not as metaphor for a new religious experience. Judaism already had a rich language for that. Saying 'he's been raised from the dead', if he hadn't been, is simply inexplicable historically. I am reminded of John Updike's trenchant poem:

> Let us not mock God with metaphor,
> analogy, sidestepping, transcendence;
> making of the event a parable, a sign painted in the
>   faded credulity of earlier ages:
> let us walk through the door.
>
> Let us not seek to make it less monstrous,
> for our own convenience, our own sense of beauty,
> lest, awakened in one unthinkable hour, we are
>   embarrassed by the miracle,
> and crushed by remonstrance.[7]

There are many smaller arguments which might be brought in at this point, but which we can only summarize. To begin with, the other proposals that are regularly advanced as rival explanations to the early Christian one:

1 Jesus didn't really die; someone gave him a drug which made him look like dead, and he revived in the tomb. Answer: Roman soldiers knew how to kill people, and no disciple would have been fooled by a half-drugged, beat-up Jesus into thinking he'd defeated death and inaugurated the kingdom.
2 When the women went to the tomb they met someone else (perhaps James, Jesus' brother, who looked like him), and in the half-light they thought it was Jesus himself. Answer: they would have noticed soon enough.
3 Jesus only appeared to people who believed in him. Answer: the accounts make it clear that Thomas and Paul do not come into this category; and actually none of Jesus' followers believed, after his death, that he really was the Messiah, let alone that he was in any sense divine.

4 The accounts we have are biased. Answer: so is all history, all journalism. Every photo is taken by somebody from some angle.

5 They began by saying 'he will be raised', as people had done of the martyrs, and this quickly passed into saying 'he has been raised' which was functionally equivalent. Answer: no, it wasn't.[8]

6 Lots of people have visions of someone they love who has just died; this was what happened to the disciples. Answer: they knew perfectly well about things like that, and they had language for it; they would say 'it's his angel' or 'it's his spirit' or 'his ghost'.[9] They wouldn't say 'he's been raised from the dead'.

7 Perhaps the most popular: what actually happened was that they had some kind of rich 'spiritual' experience, which they interpreted through Jewish categories. Jesus after all really was alive, spiritually, and they were still in touch with him. Answer: that is simply a description of a noble death followed by a Platonic immortality. Resurrection was and is the *defeat* of death, not simply a nicer *description* of it; and it's something that happens some while *after* the moment of death, not immediately.

Equally, we may just notice three of the numerous small-scale arguments which are often, and quite rightly, advanced to support the belief that Jesus did indeed rise from the dead:

1 Jewish tombs, especially those of martyrs, were venerated and often became shrines. There is no sign whatever of that having happened with Jesus' grave.

2 The early church's emphasis on the first day of the week as their special day is very hard to explain unless something striking really did happen then. A gradual or even sudden dawning of faith is hardly sufficient to explain it.

3 The disciples were hardly likely to go out and suffer and die for a belief that wasn't firmly anchored in fact. This is an

important point, though subject to the weakness that they might have been genuinely mistaken: they believed the resurrection of Jesus to be a fact, and acted on that belief, but we know (so it would be said) that they were wrong.

All this brings us face to face with the ultimate question. The empty tomb and the meetings with Jesus are as well established, by the arguments I have advanced, as any historical data could expect to be. They are, in combination, the only possible explanation for the stories and beliefs that grew up so quickly among Jesus' followers. How, in turn, do we explain *them*?

In any other historical enquiry, the answer would be so obvious that it would hardly need saying. Here, of course, this obvious answer ('well, it actually happened') is so shocking, so earth-shattering, that we rightly pause before leaping into the unknown. And here, indeed, as some sceptical friends have cheerfully pointed out to me, it is always possible for anyone to follow the argument so far and to say, simply, 'I don't have a good explanation for what happened to cause the empty tomb and the appearances, but I choose to maintain my belief that dead people don't rise and therefore conclude that something else must have happened, even though we can't tell what it was.' That is fine; I respect that position; but I simply note that it is indeed then a matter of choice, not a matter of saying that something called 'scientific historiography' itself forces us to take that route.

But at this moment in the argument all the signposts are pointing in one direction. I and others have studied quite extensively all the alternative explanations, ancient and modern, for the rise of the early church and the shape of its belief.[10] Far and away the best historical explanation is that Jesus of Nazareth, having been thoroughly dead and buried, really was raised to life on the third day with a renewed body (not a mere 'resuscitated corpse', as people sometimes dismissively say), a new *kind* of physical body which left an empty tomb behind it because it had 'used up' the material of Jesus' original body, and which possessed new properties which nobody had expected or imagined but which generated significant mutations in the thinking of those who encountered it. If something like this happened, it would perfectly explain why Christianity began and why it took the shape it did.

But this is where I want to heed carefully the warnings of those theologians who have cautioned against any attempt to stand on the ground of rationalism and to attempt to 'prove', in some 'mathematical' fashion, something which, if it happened, ought itself to be regarded as the centre not only of history but also of epistemology, not only of *what* we know but of *how* we know it. I do not claim, in other words, that I have hereby 'proved' the resurrection in terms of some neutral standpoint. I am offering, rather, a historical challenge to other explanations, and to the worldviews within which they gain their meaning. Precisely because at this point we are faced with worldview-level issues, there is no neutral ground, no island in the middle of the epistemological ocean as yet uncolonized by any of the warring continents. Historical argument alone cannot force anyone to believe that Jesus was raised from the dead; but historical argument is remarkably good at clearing away the undergrowth behind which scepticisms of various sorts have long been hiding. The proposal that Jesus was bodily raised from the dead possesses unrivalled power to explain the historical data at the heart of early Christianity. The obvious fact that this remains hugely challenging at the personal and corporate level ought not to put us off from taking it seriously. Or were we only playing when we entertained the question in the first place?

There are, after all, different types of 'knowing'. Science studies the repeatable; history studies the unrepeatable. Caesar only crossed the Rubicon once, and if he'd crossed it again it would have meant something different the second time. There was, and could be, only one first landing on the moon. The fall of the second Jerusalem Temple took place in AD 70 and never happened again. Historians don't of course see this as a problem, and are usually not shy about declaring that these events certainly took place, even though we can't repeat them in the laboratory.

But when people say 'but that can't have happened, because we know that *that sort of thing* doesn't actually happen', they are appealing to a kind of would-be scientific principle of history, namely the principle of *analogy*. The problem with analogy is that it never quite gets you far enough. History is full of unlikely things that happened once and once only, with the result that the analogies are often at best partial. In any case, if someone declares that certain kinds of events 'don't normally happen', that merely invites the retort, 'who says?' And indeed, in the case in point, we should note as an obvious but often overlooked point the fact that the early Christians did *not* think that Jesus' resurrection was one instance of something that happened from time to time elsewhere. Granted, they saw it as the first, advance instance of something that would eventually happen to everyone else. But they didn't employ that future hope as an analogy from which to argue backwards that it had happened already in this one instance ('it's going to happen to everyone eventually, so that shows it's all right for it to have happened this once, in advance').

So how does the historian work when the evidence points towards things which we do not normally expect? The resurrection is such a prime example of this that it's hard to produce, at this meta-level, analogies for the question itself. But, sooner or later, questions of worldview begin to loom up in the background, and the question of what kinds of material the historian will allow on stage is inevitably affected by the worldview within which he or she lives. And at that point we are back to the question of the scientist who, faced with the thoroughly repeatable experiment of what happens to dead bodies, what has always, it seems, happened and what seems likely always to go on happening, declares that the evidence is so massive that it is impossible to believe in the resurrection without ceasing to be a scientist altogether.

But how far does that 'scientific' position go? When we ask 'what can a scientist believe?' about something we are asking a two-level question. First, we are asking about what sort of things the 'scientific method' can explore, and how it can know or believe certain things. Second, we are asking about the kind of commitment someone wedded to scientific knowing is expected to have in all other areas of his or her life. Is a scientist, for example, expected to have a 'scientific' approach to listening to music? To watching a football game? To falling in love? The question of whether a scientist can believe in Jesus' resurrection assumes, I think, that 'the resurrection', and perhaps particularly 'the resurrection of Jesus', is something that might be expected to impinge on the scientist's area of concern, somewhat as if one were to say 'can a scientist believe that the sun could rise twice in a day?', or 'can a scientist believe that a moth could fly to the moon?'.[11] This is different, in other words, from saying, 'can a scientist believe that Schubert's music is beautiful?' or 'can a scientist believe that her husband loves her?'; and there are those, of course, who by redefining the resurrection to make it simply a spiritual experience in the inner hearts and minds of the disciples, have pulled the question towards the latter pair and away from the former. But that is ruled out by what, as we shall see, all first-century users of the language of resurrection meant by the word. 'Resurrection' in the first century meant that someone who was physically thoroughly dead had become physically thoroughly alive again, not simply 'surviving' or entering a 'purely spiritual' world, whatever that might be. 'Resurrection' therefore necessarily impinges on the public world.

But at this point we meet a third element in 'knowing', a puzzling area beyond science (which 'knows' that which it can in principle repeat in a laboratory) and the kind of 'history' which claims to 'know' that which makes sense by analogy with our own experience. Sometimes human beings – individuals or communities – are confronted with something which they must either reject outright or which, if they accept it, will demand the remaking of their worldview.

To make this point, I once imagined a fantasy Oxbridge scenario. A rich old member gives to a college a wonderful, glorious painting which simply won't fit any of the spaces available in college, and which is so magnificent that eventually the college decides to pull itself down and rebuild itself around this great and unexpected gift, discovering as it does so that all the best things about the college are thereby enhanced within the new structure, and all the problems of which people had been aware are thereby dealt with. And the key thing about that illustration, inadequate though it is, is that there must be some point at which the painting is received by the existing college, some epistemological overlap-point to enable the college officers to make their momentous decision. The donor doesn't just come along, pull down the college unasked, present the painting, and then say 'now figure out what to do'. My point is that the resurrection of Jesus, presenting itself as the obvious answer to the question of 'how do you explain the rise of early Christianity?', has that kind of purchase on serious historical enquiry, and therefore poses that kind of challenge to the larger worldview of both the historian and the scientist.

The challenge is in fact the challenge of *new creation*. To put it at its most basic: the resurrection of Jesus offers itself, to the student of history or science no less than the Christian or the theologian, not as a very odd event within the world as it is, but as the utterly characteristic, prototypical and foundational event within the world as it has begun to be. It is not an absurd event within the old world, but the symbol and starting point of the new world.[12] The claim advanced in Christianity is of that magnitude: that with Jesus of Nazareth there is not simply a new religious possibility, not simply a new ethic or a new way of salvation, but a new creation.

Now that might seem to be an epistemological, as well as a theological, pre-emptive strike. If there really is a new creation on the loose, the historian wouldn't have any analogies for it, and the scientist wouldn't be able to rank its characteristic events with other events that might otherwise have been open to inspection. What are we to do?

History alone, certainly as conceived within the modern western world, and placed on the Procrustean bed of the science which (rightly) observes the world as it is, appears to leave us like the children of Israel waiting in fear on the shore of the Red Sea. Behind are the forces of scepticism: Pharaoh's hordes, mocking and shouting that they're coming to get us. Ahead is the sea, representing chaos and death, forces which nobody else has ever really supposed have been beaten. What are we to do? There is no way back. No other explanations have been offered, in two thousand years of sneering scepticism against the Christian witness, that can satisfactorily account for how the tomb came to be empty, how the disciples came to see Jesus, and how their lives and worldviews were transformed. The alternative accounts are actually remarkably thin; I've read most of the current ones, and many of them are laughable. History appears to leave us shivering on the shore. It can press the question to which Christian faith is the answer. But, if someone chooses to stay between Pharaoh and the deep sea, history itself cannot force them further.[13]

Everything then depends on the context within which the history is done. The most important decisions we make in life are not taken by post-Enlightenment left-brain rationality alone. I would not suggest that one can argue right up to the central truth of Christian faith by pure human reason building on simple observation of the world. Indeed, it should be obvious that that is impossible. Equally, I would not suggest that historical investigation of this sort has therefore no part to play, and that all that is required is a blind leap of faith. God has given us minds to think; the question has been appropriately raised; Christianity appeals to history, and to history it must go. And the question of Jesus' resurrection, though it may in some senses burst the boundaries of history, also remains within them; that is precisely why it is so important, so disturbing, so life-and-death. We could cope – the world could cope – with a Jesus who ultimately remains a wonderful idea inside his disciples' minds and hearts. The world cannot cope with a Jesus who comes out of the tomb, who inaugurates God's new creation right within the middle of the old one.

That is why, for a complete approach to the question, we need to locate our study of history within a larger complex of human, personal and corporate contexts. This of course forms a challenge not only to the historian, not only to the scientist, but to all humans in whatever worldview they habitually live. Worldview issues are at stake here, and are not to be dealt with by the old liberal strategy of pretending (as some reviewers of my earlier work have suggested) that to believe in the resurrection of Jesus is impossible for those who accept what one writer has called 'current paradigms of reality'. If this means capitulating before the worldview of Hume and other Enlightenment thinkers, I reply that precisely now, in the early twenty-first century, there are all kinds of reasons for questioning current paradigms. In any case, it is as we have seen wrong to imply that the choice is between an ancient worldview and a modern (or even a postmodern) one. The ancient worldview of Homer, Plato, Cicero and the rest had no room for resurrection either. What is at stake is the clash between a worldview which allows for a God of creation and justice and worldviews which don't.

I am aware that for many people still today it is assumed that faith lives in a private sphere, shutting itself off from history lest history make unwelcome inroads. Meanwhile, for many others, history consists simply of a closed chain of visible cause and effect, which is never open to anything new ever happening. What the Easter stories do – and what, I have argued, the whole existence of the church does, from the very first days onwards – is to pose a huge question. We need to set our asking of that question, ultimately, in dialogue at least with the life of the community that believes the gospel and seeks by its life to live out its truth. We need to set it within the reading of the scriptures which, by their whole narrative, lay out the worldview within which it makes sense. We need to think it through within a context of personal openness to the God of whom the Bible speaks – the creator of the world, not simply a divine presence within it, the God of justice and truth. These are not substitutes for historical enquiry, nor lame supplements to it. They are ways of opening the windows of mind and heart to see what really, after all, might be possible in God's world, the world not only of creation as it is but also of new creation. History, I believe, brings us to the point where we are bound to say: there really was an empty tomb, and there really were sightings of Jesus, the same and yet transformed. History then says: so how do you explain that?

It offers us no easy escapes at that point, no quick side-exits to the question. They've all been tried, and they none of them work. History poses the question. And, when Christian faith answers it, a sober, humble, questioning history (as opposed to an arrogant rationalism that has decided the issue in advance) may find itself saying, 'that sounds good to me'.

The story of Thomas in John 20 will serve as a parable for all of this. Thomas, like a good historian, wants to see and touch. Jesus presents himself to his sight, and invites him to touch; but Thomas doesn't. He transcends the type of knowing he had intended to use, and passes into a higher and richer one. In the image I used before, of Israel at the Red Sea, this is how it looks, in words from the *Easter Oratorio*.[14] Thomas begins with doubt:

The sea is too deep
The heaven's too high
I cannot swim
I cannot fly;
I must stay here
I must stay here
Here where I know
How I can know
Here where I know
What I can know.

Jesus then reappears, and invites Thomas to see and touch. Suddenly the new, giddying possibility appears before him:

The sea has parted. Pharaoh's hosts –
Despair, and doubt, and fear, and pride –
No longer frighten us. We must
Cross over to the other side.

The heaven bows down. With wounded hands
Our exiled God, our Lord of shame
Before us, living, breathing, stands;
The Word is near, and calls our name.

New knowing for the doubting mind,
New seeing out of blindness grows;
New trusting may the sceptic find
New hope through that which faith now knows.

And with that, Thomas takes a deep breath, and brings history and faith together in a rush. 'My Lord', he says, 'and my God.'

That is not an anti-historical statement. The 'Lord' in question is precisely the one who is the climax of Israel's history and the launch of a new history. Once you grasp the resurrection, you see that Israel's history is full of partial and preparatory analogies for this moment. The epistemological weight is borne, not simply by the promise of ultimate resurrection and new creation alone, but by the narrative of God's mighty actions in the past.

Nor is it an anti-scientific statement. The world of new creation is precisely the world of new *creation*; as such, it is open to, and indeed eager for, the work of human beings – not to manipulate it with magic tricks, nor to be subservient to it as though the world of creation were itself divine, but to be its stewards. And stewards need to pay close, minute attention to that of which they are stewards, in order the better to serve it and to enable it to attain its intended fruitfulness.

What I am suggesting is that faith in Jesus risen from the dead *transcends but includes* what we call history and what we call science. Faith of this sort is not blind belief which rejects all history and science. Nor is it simply – which would be much 'safer'! – a belief which inhabits a totally different sphere, discontinuous from either, in a separate watertight compartment. Rather, this kind of faith, which like all modes of knowledge is defined by the nature of its object, is faith in the creator God, the God who has promised to put all things to rights at the last, the God who (as the sharp point where those two come together) has raised Jesus from the dead *within* history, leaving evidence which demands an explanation from the scientist as well as anybody else. In so far as I understand scientific method, when something turns up which doesn't fit the paradigm you're working with, one option at least, perhaps when all others have failed, is to change the paradigm – not to exclude everything you've known to that point, but to include it within a larger whole. That is, if you like, the Thomas challenge.

If Thomas represents an epistemology of faith, which transcends but also includes historical and scientific knowing, we might suggest that Paul represents at this point an epistemology of hope. In 1 Corinthians 15 he sketches his argument that there will be a future resurrection, as part of God's new creation, the redemption of the entire cosmos as in Romans 8. Hope, for the Christian, is not wishful thinking or mere blind optimism. It is a mode of knowing, a mode within which new things are possible, options are not shut down, new creation can happen. There is more to be said about this, but not here.

All of which brings us to Peter. Epistemologies of faith and hope, both transcending but including historical and scientific knowing, point on to an epistemology of love – an idea I first met in Bernard Lonergan, but which was hardly new with him. The story of John 21 sharpens it up. Peter, famously, has denied Jesus. He has chosen to live within the normal world, where the tyrants win in the end, and where it's better to dissociate yourself from people who get on the wrong side of them. But now, with Easter, Peter is called to live in a new and different world. Where Thomas is called to a new kind of faith, and Paul to a radically renewed hope, Peter is called to a new kind of love.[15]

Here I go back to Wittgenstein once more, not now for a poker but for a famous and haunting aphorism: 'It is *love* that believes the resurrection.'[16] 'Simon, son of John,' says Jesus, 'do you love me?' There is a whole world in that question, a world of personal invitation and challenge, of the remaking of a human being after disloyalty and disaster, of the refashioning of epistemology itself, the question of how we know things, to correspond to the new ontology, the question of what reality consists of. The reality which is the resurrection cannot simply be 'known' from within the old world of decay and denial, of tyrants and torture, of disobedience and death. But that's the point. To repeat: the resurrection is not, as it were, a highly peculiar event within the *present* world (though it is that as well); it is, principally, the defining event of the *new* creation, the world which is being born with Jesus. If we are even to glimpse this new world, let alone enter it, we will need a different kind of knowing, a knowing which involves us in new ways, an epistemology which draws out from us not just the cool appraisal of detached quasi-scientific research, but that whole-person engagement and involvement for which the best shorthand is 'love', in the full Johannine sense of *agapē*. My sense, from talking to some scientific colleagues, is that, though it's hard to describe, something like this is already at work when the scientist devotes him- or herself to the subject matter so completely that the birth of new hypotheses seems to come about, not so much through an abstract brain (a computer made of meat?) crunching data from elsewhere, but more through a soft and mysterious symbiosis of knower and known, of lover and beloved.[17]

The sceptic will at once suggest that this is a way of collapsing the truth of Easter once more into mere subjectivism. Not so. Just because it takes *agapē* to believe the resurrection, that doesn't mean that all that happened was that Peter and the others felt their hearts strangely warmed. Precisely because it is *love* we are talking about, it must have a correlative reality in the world outside the lover. Love is the deepest mode of knowing, because it is love that, while completely engaging with reality other than itself, affirms and celebrates that other-than-self reality. This is the point at which much modernist epistemology breaks down. The sterile antithesis of 'objective' and 'subjective', where we say that things are either objectively true (and can be perceived as such by a dispassionate observer) or subjectively true (and so of no use as an account of the real, public world), is overcome by the epistemology of love which is called into being as the necessary mode of knowing for those who will live in the new public world, the world launched at Easter, the world in which Jesus is Lord and Caesar isn't.

That is why, though the historical arguments for Jesus' bodily resurrection are truly strong, we must never suppose that they will do more than bring people to the questions faced by Thomas, Paul and Peter, the questions of faith, hope and love. We cannot use a supposedly 'objective' historical epistemology as the ultimate ground for the truth of Easter. To do so would be like lighting a candle to see whether the sun had risen. What the candles of historical scholarship will do is to show that the room has been disturbed, that it doesn't look like it did last night, and that would-be 'normal' explanations for this won't do. Maybe, we think after the historical arguments have done their work, maybe morning has come and the world has woken up. But to investigate whether this is so we must take the risk and open the curtains to the rising sun. When we do so, we won't rely on the candles any more, not because we don't believe in evidence and argument but because they will have been overtaken by the larger reality from which they borrow, to which they point, and in which they will find a new and larger home. All knowing is a gift from God, historical and scientific knowing no less than that of faith, hope and love; but the greatest of these is love.

3. Conclusion

One final note. I have become convinced that the climate of scepticism which has, for the last two hundred years, made it unfashionable and even embarrassing to suggest that Jesus' resurrection really happened, was never, and is not now, itself a neutral thing, sociologically or politically. The intellectual *coup d'état* by which the Enlightenment convinced so many that 'we now know that dead people don't rise', as though this was a modern discovery rather than simply the reaffirmation of what Homer and Aeschylus had taken for granted, goes hand in hand with the Enlightenment's other proposals, not least that we have now come of age, that God can be kicked upstairs, that we can get on running the world however we want to, carving it up to our advantage without outside interference. To that extent, the totalitarianisms of the last century were simply among the varied manifestations of a larger totalitarianism of thought and culture against which postmodernity has now, and rightly in my view, rebelled. Who, after all, was it who didn't want the dead to be raised? Not simply the intellectually timid or the rationalists. It was, and is, those in power, the social and intellectual tyrants and bullies; the Caesars who would be threatened by a Lord of the world who had defeated the tyrant's last weapon, death itself; the Herods who would be horrified at the post-mortem validation of the true King of the Jews.[18] *And this is the point where believing in the resurrection of Jesus suddenly ceases to be a matter of enquiring about an odd event in the first century and becomes a matter of rediscovering hope in the twenty-first century.* Hope is what you get when you suddenly realize that a different worldview is possible, a worldview in which the rich, the powerful and the unscrupulous do not after all have the last word. The same worldview shift which is demanded by the resurrection of Jesus is the shift that will enable us to transform the world.

Think of Oscar Wilde's wonderful scene, in his play *Salome*, when Herod hears reports that Jesus of Nazareth has been raising the dead.

'I do not wish him to do that,' says Herod. 'I forbid him to do that. I allow no man to raise the dead. This man must be found and told that I forbid him to raise the dead.'

There is the bluster of the tyrant who knows his power is threatened, and I hear the same tone of voice not just in the politicians who want to carve up the world to their advantage, but in the intellectual traditions that have gone along for the ride.

But Wilde's next, haunting line is the real crunch, for us as for Herod. 'Where is this man?' demands Herod. 'He is in every place, my lord,' replies the courtier, 'but it is hard to find him.'[19]

Part 2

GOD'S FUTURE PLAN

5

Cosmic future: progress or despair?

1. Introduction

I suggested in the first part of the book that when we look at the contemporary world and church, we discover great confusion about future hope, but that when we look at the early Christians we find not just faith, but a very precise and specific faith, both about Jesus and his resurrection and about the future life which God had promised to all his people.

This isn't a matter of ancient people being credulous and modern people being sceptical. There is a great deal of credulity in our present world, and there was a great deal of scepticism in the ancient world. It is, rather, something to do with the very specific worldview which was generated by the events concerning Jesus, and supremely the event of Easter itself.

The early Christians looked back with joy to that great event. But precisely because of their very Jewish belief in God as the creator and redeemer, and because they had seen this belief confirmed in the totally unexpected event of Jesus' resurrection, they also looked forward eagerly to an event yet to come in which what began at Easter would be completed. This larger picture of a still-future renewal is the subject of the present Part of the book.

It would be possible at this point to jump right in and to speak of the personal hope which the gospel provides for each believer. What God did for Jesus on the first Easter day, he has promised to do for each one who is in Christ, each one indwelt by the Spirit of Christ. That is the biblical and historic

Christian expectation, in terms of ourselves as human beings. We shall come to this in due course.

But there are good reasons for not starting there. In the last two hundred years western thought has overemphasized the individual at the expense of the larger picture of God's creation. What is more, in much western piety, at least since the Middle Ages, the influence of Greek philosophy has been very marked, resulting in a future expectation that bears far more resemblance to Plato's vision of souls entering into disembodied bliss than to the biblical picture of new heavens and new earth. If we start with the future hope of the individual, there is always the risk that we will, at least by implication, understand that as the real centre of everything, and treat the hope of creation as mere embroidery around the edges. That has happened often enough. I am keen to rule it out by the structure of the argument, as well as through the detailed exposition.

The order of the discussion is therefore determined by what seems to me the appropriate arrangement of the material. Instead of looking first at the promise to the individual, and working up from that to the renewal of creation, we begin with the biblical vision of the future world – a vision of the present cosmos renewed from top to bottom by the God who is both creator and redeemer. That is the context within which we will then be able to speak of the 'second coming' of Jesus, and then of the bodily resurrection.[1]

We turn, then, to the large-scale hope of the whole cosmos, the great drama within which our little dramas are, as it were, the play within the play. What is God's purpose for the world as a whole?

To answer this, we must first look, in the present chapter, at two very popular options, before, in the next chapter, exploring the alternative which (though you'd never know it from much contemporary Christianity) is the one offered by the New Testament itself.[2]

2. Option 1: evolutionary optimism

At the risk of gross oversimplification, we may suggest that there have been two quite different ways of looking at the future of the world. Both of these ways have sometimes been confused with the Christian hope, and indeed both have made use of some elements of the Christian hope in telling their grand stories. But neither comes anywhere near the picture we have in the New Testament, and indeed, in flashes, in the Old. The Christian answer lies not so much half-way in between as in a biblical answer which combines the strengths, and eliminates the weaknesses, of both.

The first position is the myth of progress. Many people, particularly politicians and secular commentators in the press and elsewhere, still live by this myth, appeal to it, and encourage us to believe it. Indeed (if I may digress for a moment), one might suggest that the demise of serious political discourse today consists not least in this, that the politicians are still trying to whip up enthusiasm for their versions of this myth – it's the only discourse they know, poor things – while the rest of us have moved on. They are, to that extent, like people trying to row a boat towards the shore while the strong tide pulls them further and further out to sea. Because they face the wrong way they can't see that their efforts are in vain, and they call out to other boats to join them in their splendid shorebound voyage. That is why the relentlessly modernist and progressivist projects that the politicians feel obliged to offer us ('vote for us and things will get better!') have to be dressed up with the relentlessly postmodernist techniques of spin and hype: in the absence of real hope, all that is left is feelings. Persuasion will not work, because we're never going to believe it. What we appear to need, and therefore what people give us, is entertainment. As a journalist said recently, our politicians demand to be treated like rock stars, while our rock stars are pretending to be politicians. Sorting out this mess – which the Christian hope, despite current opinion, is well suited to do – should mean, among many other things, a renewal of genuine political discourse, which God knows we badly need.

But to return to our main theme. The myth of progress has deep roots in contemporary western culture, and some of those roots are Christian.[3] The idea that the human project, and indeed the cosmic project, could and would continue to grow and develop, producing unlimited human improvement and marching towards a Utopia, goes back to the Renaissance, and was given its decisive push by the eighteenth-century European Enlightenment. The full flowering of this belief took place in Europe in the nineteenth century, when the combination of scientific and economic advances on the one hand, and democratic freedoms and wider education on the other, produced a strong sense that history was accelerating towards a wonderful goal. El Dorado was just round the corner, the millennium in which the world would live at peace. Prosperity would spread out from enlightened Europe and America, and embrace the world. By no means all thinkers a hundred years ago fitted into this mould, but many, including some of enormous influence such as Hegel, did so enthusiastically. This, again, is precisely where some of our politicians still gain their inspiration.

This Utopian dream is in fact a parody of the Christian vision. The kingdom of God and the kingdoms of the world come together to produce a vision of history moving forwards towards its goal, a goal which will emerge from within rather than being a new gift from elsewhere. Humans can be made perfect, and are indeed evolving inexorably towards that point. The world is ours to discover, exploit and enjoy. Instead of dependence on God's grace, we will become what we have the potential to be by education and hard work. Instead of creation and new creation, science and technology will turn the raw material of this world into the stuff of Utopia. Like the mythical Prometheus, defying the gods and attempting to run the world his own way, liberal modernism has supposed that the world can become everything we could want it to be by working a bit harder and helping forward the great march into the glorious future.

I leave to one side in this brief sketch the role played by Charles Darwin, whose iconic figure continues to haunt several quite different contemporary discussions. One of the strange and perhaps poetically appropriate twists in that story is our increasing recognition that Darwin was himself not so much the great new thinker, coming from nowhere to his radical new idea, but rather the exact product of his times, one particular high-water mark in the onward rush of liberal modernist optimism, himself the product of a particular evolution in western thought. The eagerness with which his ideas were embraced and reapplied, not only in the narrow biological sphere in which they belonged but in far wider areas such as society and politics, indicates well enough the mood of the times. The world in general, and humankind in particular, were marching onwards and upwards, in an immanent process which couldn't be stopped and which would result in the great future that lay just around the corner. Evolution, in this more general sense of progress, was already widely believed; it was a deeply convenient philosophy for those who wanted to justify their own massive industrial and imperial expansion; Darwin gave it some apparent scientific legitimacy, which was quickly seized upon and which, within half a century, had been used to justify everything from eugenics to war. The same could be said, of course, *mutatis mutandis*, of Karl Marx.[4]

Many Christian thinkers went along for the ride on this apparently incoming tide of progress. Many embraced Darwin's ideas as a way of solving (for instance) some of the problems they had felt about the Old Testament. Many eagerly expounded social Darwinism as the way forward for the world, with some even encouraging the pursuit of war as the proper way to test who among the human species was the fittest and hence the most deserving of survival. Many Christians embraced what they called the 'social gospel', attempting to put into practice in society the promises of the Christian message. An enormous amount of good work was done by this means, though after a century of it we now all know that it isn't the full answer.

But the best-known Christian development of the myth of progress was that of Pierre Teilhard de Chardin. This French Jesuit, born in 1881, was a distinguished scientist of human origins, and a fervent Christian mystic who believed that the presence of God was to be discovered anywhere and everywhere in the natural world. He believed that the living world disclosed itself as an all-encompassing 'cosmic, christic and divine milieu'; despite the turmoil and suffering of the world, he believed that it was being 'animated and drawn up towards God'. The divine spirit, he believed, is involved in the evolutionary process at every stage, so that 'cosmic and human evolution are moving onwards to an ever fuller disclosure of the Spirit, culminating in "Christ-Omega".'[5] All history had been moving towards the Omega-point of the emergence of the Christ, and was now moving towards the climax and goal in which all creation would find its fulfilment in him. Teilhard de Chardin's most famous book, *The Phenomenon of Man*, written before World War II but only published after his death in 1955, became a best-seller and has influenced a whole generation of those who have wanted to combine Christian spirituality with scientific thought. One recent enthusiastic writer suggests that 'his powerful affirmation of the Incarnation and his vision of the universal, cosmic Christ within an evolutionary perspective' can now 'reaffirm the core of the Christian faith for our scientific age'.[6] The influence of Teilhard de Chardin may lie behind the recent popularity of a prayer which speaks of 'all things returning to perfection through him from whom they took their origin'.[7]

Teilhard de Chardin's thinking is many-sided and subtle, and this isn't the place to launch an exposition, let alone a critique. It is a caricature to say, as some have done, that he is simply an advance prophet of New Age spirituality. Likewise, though there appear to be pantheistic elements in his thought, Teilhard de Chardin was not himself a pantheist as such. However, he does share the weaknesses of the evolutionary optimism of his times, not least, as we shall see, an inability to factor into his thinking the fact of radical evil (it was, interestingly, an early work on original sin, or rather its absence, that first brought him critical attention in his own church). Teilhard and his supporters have appealed to the Pauline idea of the 'cosmic Christ', as in Colossians 1.15–20; but Paul's thinking, there and elsewhere, hardly supports the structure Teilhard wishes to erect. In the long run – and of course it was to the long run that he appealed – he may appear as one of the great flowerings, in Christian form, of that evolutionary optimism of which our post-scientific age is now increasingly sceptical. But more of that anon.

The real problem with the myth of progress is, as I just hinted, that it cannot deal with evil. And when I say 'deal with', I don't just mean intellectually, though that is true as well; I mean in practice. It can't develop a strategy which addresses the severe problems of evil in the world. This is why all the evolutionary optimism of the last two hundred years remains helpless before world war, drug crime, Auschwitz, apartheid, child pornography and the other interesting sidelines that evolution has thrown up for our entertainment in the twentieth century. We not only can't explain them, given the myth of progress; we can't eradicate them. Marx's own agenda, not to explain the world but to change it, remains unfulfilled. Of course, the twentieth century provides a quite full answer to the myth of progress, as many people (such as Karl Barth) saw during the First World War; but it's remarkable how many others have continued to believe and propagate it none the less. Teilhard himself was a stretcher-bearer during the Great War, and the experience was influential, not in leading him away from evolution, but in his attempt to factor human suffering into his equation. Part of the problem in our contemporary debates about asylum-seekers, or about the Middle East, is that our politicians still want to present us with the dream of progress, the steady forward advance of the golden dream of 'freedom'; and when the tide of human misery washes up on our beaches, or when people in cultures very different from our own seem not to want the kind of 'freedom' we had in mind, it is not just socially but ideologically untidy and inconvenient. It reminds the politicians that there is a gap in their thinking. The world is still a sad and wicked place, not a happy upward progress towards the light.[8]

The myth, then, cannot deal with evil, for three reasons. First, it can't stop it: if evolution gave us Hiroshima and the Gulag it can't be all good. There is no observable reason, in science, philosophy, art or anywhere else to suppose that if we simply plough ahead with the Enlightenment dream these glitches will be ironed out and we'll get to Utopia eventually. What's more, today's cutting-edge science is quite clear that, whatever may and may not be true about specifically biological evolution, the cosmos as a whole is simply not evolving towards a golden future. The world that began with the Big Bang is heading either for the Big Cool-Down, as energy gradually runs out and the universe expands into the cold, dark beyond, or for the Big Crunch, as gravity reasserts itself and everything slows down, stops and then rushes back together again. It is quite possible that, before either of these worrying possibilities takes place, a giant meteorite such as most likely wiped out the dinosaurs could strike the earth with similar devastating effects. None of these scenarios makes any sense within the myth of progress.[9]

Second, even if 'progress' brought us to Utopia after all, that wouldn't address the *moral* problem of all the evil that's happened to date in the world. Suppose the golden age arrived tomorrow morning; what would that say to those who are being tortured to death today? How would that be a satisfactory solution to the huge and indescribable evils of the last century, let alone all of world history? If, akin to Teilhard de Chardin, we were to make God part of the process of it all, what sort of a god would it be who builds his kingdom on the bones and ashes of those who have suffered along the way? The picture reminds me of the story of the old Oxford don who, whenever the paper on his desk got quite out of control, would simply spread a copy of *The Times* over the lot and start again. After his death they found several layers, like an archaeologist's tell, of matters that had never been dealt with. And after the construction of an evolutionist's kingdom of God, God would be left with precisely the same problem. It was because of this that the ancient Jews began to speak of the resurrection.

The myth of progress fails because it doesn't in fact work; because it would never solve evil retrospectively; and, thirdly, because it underestimates the nature and power of evil itself, and thus fails to see the vital importance of the cross, God's No to evil which then opens the door to his Yes to creation. Only in the Christian story itself – certainly not in the secular stories of modernity – do we find any sense that the problems of the world are solved, not by a straightforward upward movement into the light, but by the creator God going down into the dark, to rescue humankind and the world from its plight.

The myth of progress, then, has been enormously powerful in our culture. In fact, it still is, not least as an implicit belief that can be appealed to to justify any and every 'development' in a supposed liberalizing, humanizing, freedom-bringing direction. ('Don't you believe in *progress?*' people ask scornfully when someone objects to a new 'moral' proposal. They used to say that when people objected to cutting down ancient trees to build a new road; but we have begun to realize that 'progress' in that sense wasn't always all it was cracked up to be.) Christians have often gone along with the general idea of 'progress', but, though it sometimes runs on parallel lines to Christian hope, it comes from a different origin and veers off towards a very different destination – just as the trains that run from London to Manchester coincide for a stretch with those that run from Southampton to Newcastle, but start and finish somewhere very different. Politicians and the media plug into the myth constantly, though the appliances they run off it frequently subvert it, like someone using a power drill to cut into the very socket where the tool is getting its electricity. No wonder we live in a world of flying sparks, of self-defeating energy. But before we look at the truly Christian alternative we must examine, more briefly, the other myth, the negative myth, the story that tells us the world is a wicked place and we'd do better to escape it altogether.

3. Option 2: souls in transit

Plato remains the most influential thinker in the history of the western world. For Plato, as for the Buddha, the present world of space, time and matter is a world of illusion, of flickering shadows in a cave, and the most appropriate human task is to get in touch with the true reality, which is beyond space, time and matter. For Plato, this was the eternal Forms; for the Buddha, the eternal Nothingness.

To oversimplify once more, we may say that Plato's picture was based on a rejection of the phenomena of matter and transience. The mess and muddle of the space-time-matter world was an offence to the tidy, clean philosophical mind, which dwelt upon eternal realities. It wasn't just evil that was wrong with the world; it was change and decay, the transitoriness of matter: the fact that spring and summer are followed by autumn and winter, that the sunset tails off into darkness, that human blossoming and flourishing are the prelude to suffering and death.

Here worldviews diverge radically. The optimist, the pantheist, the evolutionist, the myth-of-progress school, will all say that these are just the growing pains of something bigger and better. The Platonist, the Buddhist, the Hindu – and, following the

Platonic line, the gnostic, the Manichaean and countless others within variants of the Christian and Jewish traditions – will all say that these are the signs that we are made for something quite different, a world not made of space, time and matter, a world of pure spiritual existence where we shall happily have got rid of the shackles of mortality once and for all. And the way you get rid of mortality, within this worldview, is to get rid of the thing which can decay and die, namely our material selves.

The Platonic strain entered Christian thinking early on, not least with the phenomenon known as gnosticism. Since the gnostics have been making something of a comeback recently, a word about them is appropriate.[10] The gnostics believed, like Plato, that the material world was an inferior and dark place, evil in its very existence, but that within this world were to be found certain people who were meant for something else. These children of light were like fallen stars, tiny pinpricks of light currently hidden within a gross material body. Once they had realized who they were, though, this 'knowledge' (Greek *gnosis*) would enable them to enter into a spiritual existence in which the material world would no longer count. Having entered upon that spiritual existence, they would then live by it, through death and into the infinite world beyond space, time and matter. 'We are stardust,' sang Joni Mitchell, plugging in to this millennia-old mythology, 'we are golden; and we've got to get ourselves back to the garden.'[11] The gnostic myth often suggests that the way out of our mess is to return to our primeval state, before the creation of the world. In this view, creation itself is the 'fall', producing matter, which is the real evil. I hope it is clear both how closely this view parodies some aspects of Christianity and how deeply and thoroughly it diverges from it.

Though most people in today's world have probably only a sketchy idea of what gnosticism might be, assuming they've heard of it at all, it has been argued with some plausibility that some elements of it at least – and gnosticism is always a very eclectic phenomenon – are to be found in some of the seminal thinkers and writers of the last two hundred years in our culture. The writer and playwright Stuart Holroyd, himself an unashamed apologist for gnosticism, lists Blake, Goethe, Melville, Yeats and Jung among others as representing this stream in the modern West, and though their insights have often been cross-fertilized with other different types he has a point which should not be ignored. Basically, if you move away from materialistic optimism but without embracing Judaism or Christianity, you are quite likely to land up with some kind of gnosticism. It should be no surprise that certain elements of the Romantic movement, and some of their more recent heirs, have been prone to this.[12] The discovery of the Nag Hammadi scrolls (a library of gnostic texts found in Upper Egypt) has in our day fuelled a desire to reinterpret Christianity itself in terms of a supposedly original gnostic spirituality which contrasts sharply with the very concrete kingdom-of-God-on-earth announced by the Jesus of the canonical gospels. Travel far enough down that road, and you will end up with the blatant and outrageous conspiracy theories of a book like *The Da Vinci Code*. But there are many who, without going that far, have come to assume that some kind of gnosticism is what genuine Christianity was supposed to be about.

Most western Christians – and most western non-Christians, for that matter – have in fact supposed that Christianity was committed to at least a soft version of Plato's position. A good many Christian hymns and poems wander off unthinkingly in the direction of gnosticism. The 'just passing through' spirituality (as in the spiritual 'This world is not my home, / I'm just a'passin' through'), though it has of course some affinities with classical Christianity, encourages precisely a gnostic attitude: the created world is at best an irrelevance, at worst a dark, evil, gloomy place, and we immortal souls, who existed originally in a different sphere, are looking forward to returning to it as soon as we're allowed to. There has been such a massive assumption made in western Christianity that the purpose of being a Christian is simply, or at least mainly, to 'go to heaven when you die', that texts which don't say that, but which mention heaven, are read as if they did say it, and that texts which say the opposite, like Romans 8.18–25 and Revelation 21—22, are simply screened out as if they didn't exist.[13]

The results are all around us in the western church and in the worldviews which western Christianity has generated. Secularists often criticize Christians for having contributed to ecological disaster, and there's more than a grain of truth in the charge. I have heard it seriously argued in North America that since God intends to destroy the present space-time universe, and moreover since he intends to do so quite soon now, it really doesn't matter whether we emit twice as many greenhouse gases as we do now, whether we destroy the rain forests and the Arctic tundra, whether we fill our skies with acid rain. That is a peculiarly modern form of would-be Christian negativity about the world, and of course its skin-deep 'spiritual' viewpoint is entirely in thrall to the heart-deep materialism of the business interests that will be served, in however short a term, by such hazardous practices.

I shall come to that sort of thing in more detail later on. My point for now is to notice that in many parts of the world an appeal to a Christian view of the future is taken to mean an appeal to the eventual demise of the created order and to a destiny which is purely 'spiritual' in the sense of being completely non-material. That remains the popular perception, both from inside and outside the church, of what we Christians are supposed to believe when we speak of 'heaven', and when we talk of the hope that is ours in Christ.

Over against both these popular and mistaken views, the central Christian affirmation is that what the creator God has done in Jesus Christ, and supremely in his resurrection, is what he intends to do for the whole world – meaning, by 'world', the entire cosmos with all its history. It is to this hope that I turn in the next chapter.

6

What the whole world's waiting for

1. Introduction

The early Christians did not believe in 'progress'. They did not think the world was getting better and better under its own steam – or even under the steady influence of God. They knew God had to do something fresh to put it to rights.

But nor did they believe that the world was getting worse and worse and that their task was to escape it altogether. They were not dualists.

Since most people who think about these things today tend towards one or other of those two points of view, it comes as something of a surprise to discover that the early Christians held a quite different view. They believed that God was going to do for the whole cosmos what he had done for Jesus at Easter. This is such a surprising belief, and so little reflected on even in Christian circles, still less outside the church, that we must set it out step by step and show how the different early writers developed different images which together add up to a stunning picture of a future for which, so they insisted, the whole world was waiting on tiptoe.

2. Fundamental structures of hope

The clearest statements of the large-scale Christian hope are to be found in the New Testament, in Paul and in the book of Revelation. I want to explore these now, drawing out as we do so the ways in which they answer the two opposite views I have sketched. We need to notice, in particular, the way in which three themes come out.

First, the *goodness of creation*. Granted the swirling currents of alternative worldviews available in the first century, it is a remarkable feature of the earliest Christianity known to us that it refused to lapse at any point into a cosmological dualism in which the created world is regarded as less than good and God-given. But it is good as *creation*, not as an independent or self-sufficient 'nature'. There is no suggestion of pantheism, or even panentheism. God and the world are not the same thing; nor is everything simply held within something called 'god'. Within biblical theology it remains the case that the one living God created a world that is other than himself, not contained within himself. Creation was from the beginning an act of love, of affirming the goodness of the other. God saw all that he had made, and it was very good; but it was not itself divine. At its height, which according to Genesis 1 is the creation of humans, it was designed to *reflect* God, both to reflect God back to God in worship and to reflect God into the rest of creation in stewardship. But this image-bearing capacity of humankind is not in itself the same thing as divinity. Collapsing this distinction means taking a large step towards a pantheism within which there is no way of understanding, let alone addressing, the problem of evil.

Second, then, the *nature of evil*. Evil is real and powerful, within biblical theology, but it consists neither in the fact of being created, nor in the fact of being other than God (since being loved into life by the one God is quite good enough!), nor yet in the fact that it's made of physical matter and belongs within space and time, instead of being pure spirit in an eternal heaven. Nor – and this is crucial – does evil consist in being transient, made to decay. There is nothing wrong with the tree dropping its leaves in the autumn. There is nothing wrong with the sunset fading away into darkness. Evil consists in none of those things; indeed, it is precisely the transience of the good creation that serves as a pointer to its larger purpose. Creation was good, but it always had a forward look. Transience acts as a god-given signpost, pointing not from the material world to a non-material world, but from the world *as it is* to the world *as it is meant one day to be*; pointing, in other words, from the present to the future which God has in store. The human project, of bringing wise order to the garden, is not yet complete, and without transience we might the more easily be led into idolatry, treating the creature as though it was the creator – which, goodness knows, is all too easy as it is. This harks back to what I said in the first two chapters. What matters is eschatological duality (the present age and the age to come), not ontological dualism (an evil 'earth' and a good 'heaven').

Evil then consists, not in being created, but in the rebellious idolatry by which humans worship and honour elements of the natural world rather than the God who made them. The result is that the cosmos is out of joint. Instead of humans being God's wise vice-regents over creation, they ignore the creator and try to worship something less demanding, something which will give them a short-term fix of power or pleasure. The result is that death, which was always part of the natural transience of the good creation, gains a second dimension, which the Bible sometimes calls 'spiritual death'. In Genesis, and indeed for much of the Old Testament, the controlling image for death is exile. Adam and Eve were told that they would die on the day they ate the fruit; what actually happened was that they were expelled from the garden. Turning away from the worship of the living God is turning towards that which has no life in itself. Worship that which is transient, and it can only give you death. But when you do commit that idolatry, evil is unleashed into the world, setting off chain reactions with incalculable consequences. Mysteriously, this out-of-jointness seems to become entangled with the transience and decay necessary within the good-but-incomplete creation, so that what we perhaps misleadingly call 'natural evil' can be seen as, among other things, the advance signs of that final 'shaking' of heaven and earth which the prophets understood to be necessary if God's eventual new world was to be born.[1]

Third, the *plan of redemption*. Precisely because creation is the work of God's love, redemption is not something alien to the creator, but something he will undertake with delight and glad self-giving. The point about redemption is that it doesn't mean scrapping what's there and starting again from a clean slate, but rather liberating what has come to be enslaved. And, because of the analysis of evil not as materiality but as rebellion, the slavery of humans and of the world does not consist in embodiment, redemption from which would mean the death of the body and the consequent release of the soul or spirit. The slavery consists, rather, in sin, redemption from which must ultimately involve not just goodness of soul or spirit but a newly embodied life.

This is the plan which, throughout the Bible, is articulated in terms of God's choice of Israel as the means of redemption, and then, after the long and chequered story of God and Israel, God's sending of his son, Jesus. Incarnation – already adumbrated in the Jewish tradition in terms not least of the Temple as the place where God chooses to live on earth – is not a category mistake, as Platonists ancient and modern imagine. It is the centre and fulfilment of the long-term plan of the good and wise creator.

If you tell this story from the point of view of the good creation, the coming of Jesus emerges as the moment all creation had been waiting for. Humans were made to be God's stewards over creation; so the one through whom all things were made, the eternal son, the eternal wisdom, becomes human, so that he might truly become God's steward, ruler over all his world. Equally, if you tell the story from the point of view of human rebellion and the consequent sin and death which has engulfed the whole world, this again emerges as the moment all creation had been waiting for: the eternal expression of the father's love became the incarnate expression of the father's love, so that by his self-giving to death, even the death of the cross, the whole creation can be reconciled to God. If you put these two ways of telling the story together, and cast them into poetry, you will find you have rewritten Colossians 1.15–20. This is the real 'cosmic Christology' of the New Testament: not a kind of pantheism, running under its own steam, and cut off from the real Jesus, but a retelling of the Jewish story of wisdom in terms of Jesus himself, focusing on the cross itself as the act whereby the good creation is brought back into harmony with the wise creator.

The balance of the clauses in the poem in Colossians 1 shows the extent to which Paul has insisted on holding together creation and redemption.[2] Redemption is not simply making creation a bit better, as the optimistic evolutionist would try to suggest. Nor is it rescuing spirits and souls from an evil material world, as the gnostic would want to say. It is the remaking of creation, having dealt with the evil which is defacing and distorting it. And it is accomplished by the same God, now known in Jesus Christ, through whom it was made in the first place. It is highly significant that in the passage just after the great poem of 1.15–20, Paul declares that the gospel has already been announced to every creature under heaven (1.23). What has happened in the death and resurrection of Jesus Christ, in other words, is by no means limited to its effects on those human beings who believe the gospel and thereby find new life here and hereafter. It resonates out, in ways that we can't fully see or understand, into the vast recesses of the universe.

Creation; evil; and the plan of redemption, revealed in action in Jesus Christ. These are the constant themes which the New Testament writers, particularly Paul and the author of Revelation, struggle to express. I now want to explore the key New Testament texts which speak of the cosmic dimension of

Christian hope. There are six main themes to be explored; several of these are themselves powerful images taken from the world of creation. If you're going to speak of God doing something new which nevertheless affirms the old, what better way than to speak of seedtime and harvest, of birth and new life, and of marriage. We begin with the first of these, seedtime and harvest.

3. Seedtime and harvest

In 1 Corinthians 15 Paul uses the image of the 'first fruits'.[3] This goes back to the Jewish festivals of Passover and Pentecost, which in their developed forms at least were both agricultural and salvation-historical festivals. Passover was the time when the first crop of barley was presented before the Lord. Pentecost, seven weeks later, was the time when the first fruits of the wheat harvest were presented. The offering of the first fruits signifies the great harvest still to come. At the salvation-historical level, of course, Passover commemorated Israel coming out of Egypt, while Pentecost, seven weeks later, commemorated the arrival at Sinai and the giving of Torah. The two strands were woven together, since part of God's promise in liberating Israel and giving it the Law was that Israel would inherit the land and that the land would be fruitful.

Paul applies this Passover image to Jesus. He is the first fruits, the first to rise from the dead. But this isn't an isolated instance. The point of the first fruits is that there will be many, many more. Jesus' Passover, that is, Calvary and Easter, which occurred of course at Passover time and was from very early on interpreted in the light of that festival, indicated that the great slavemaster, the great Egypt, sin and death themselves, had been defeated when Jesus came through the Red Sea of death and out the other side. And Paul goes on, later in the chapter, to expound the nature of the Christian's resurrection body on the basis of the new body of Jesus. Please note, over against any

move towards gnosticism, how this imagery indicates continuity as well as discontinuity. Note too, over against any kind of
evolutionary optimism, that moving from seed sown to crop
harvested involves discontinuity as well as continuity, and in
particular that the Exodus from Egypt, symbolized by this story,
could only be seen as an act of pure grace. 'Progress', left to itself,
could never have brought it about.[4]

4. The victorious battle

The first letter to the Corinthians then continues with a quite
different image, one not so organically related to the natural
order of creation, but with many biblical antecedents: that
of a king establishing his kingdom by subduing all possible
enemies.

Paul is careful to stress both that Jesus will rule until every
single power in the cosmos has been subjected to him, and that
God the father is not included in that category. Whatever
we say about the implied Christology of this passage, Paul is
clearly articulating a theology of *new creation*. Every force,
every authority in the whole cosmos will be subjected to the
Messiah; and finally death itself will give up its power. In other
words, that which we are tempted to regard as the permanent
state of the cosmos – entropy, threatening chaos and dissolu-
tion – will be transformed by the Messiah, acting as the agent
of the creator God. If evolutionary optimism is squelched by,
among other things, the sober estimates of the scientists that
the universe as we know it today is running out of steam and
cannot last for ever, the gospel of Jesus Christ announces that
what God did for Jesus at Easter he will do, not only for all those
who are 'in Christ', but for the entire cosmos. It will be an act
of new creation, parallel to and derived from the act of new
creation when God raised Jesus from the dead.

Here we find, coming into full view, one of the direct results
of saying that Jesus was raised bodily from the dead, rather than

saying that upon his death he began to exist in a new, non-bodily mode. As I have argued elsewhere, if after his death he had gone into some kind of non-bodily existence, death would not be defeated. It would remain intact; it would merely be redescribed. Jesus, humankind and the world itself could not look forward to any future within a created and embodied mode such as we now know. But this is precisely what Paul is denying. Death is the last enemy, not a good part of the good creation; and therefore death must be defeated if the life-giving God is to be honoured as the true Lord of the world.[5] When this has happened, and only then, Jesus the Messiah, the Lord of the world, will hand over the rule of the kingdom to his father, and God will be all in all. We shall return to this presently.

5. Citizens of heaven – colonizing the earth

Before we get to that, we look across to another royal image, found in Philippians 3.20–21. It is very close in theme to 1 Corinthians 15, quoting in fact at the crucial point from the same Psalm (Psalm 8), emphasizing Jesus' authority over all other powers.

Philippi was a Roman colony. Augustus had settled his veterans there after the battles of Philippi (42 BC) and Actium (31 BC). Not all residents of Philippi were Roman citizens, but all would know what citizenship meant. The point of creating colonies was twofold. First, it was aimed at extending Roman influence around the Mediterranean world, creating cells and networks of people loyal to Caesar in the wider culture. Second, it was one way of avoiding the problems of overcrowding in the capital itself. The emperor certainly did not want retired soldiers, with time (and blood) on their hands, hanging around Rome ready to cause trouble. Much better for them to be establishing farms and businesses elsewhere.

So when Paul says 'we are citizens of heaven', he doesn't at all mean that when we're done with this life we'll be going off to live in heaven.[6] What he means is that the saviour, the Lord, Jesus the King – all of those were of course imperial titles – will come *from* heaven *to* earth, to change the present situation and state of his people. The key word here is 'transform': 'he will transform our present humble bodies to be like his glorious body'. Jesus will not declare that present physicality is redundant and can be scrapped. Nor will he simply improve it, perhaps by speeding up its evolutionary cycle. In a great act of power – the same power that accomplished Jesus' own resurrection, as Paul says in Ephesians 1.19–20 – he will *change* the present body into the one that corresponds in kind to his own, as part of his work of bringing all things into subjection to himself. Philippians 3, though it is primarily speaking of human resurrection, indicates that this will take place within the context of God's victorious transformation of the whole cosmos.[7]

6. God will be all in all

Turning back to 1 Corinthians 15, we find Paul declaring that, as the goal of all history, God will be 'everything in everything', or if you like 'all in all' (15.28). This is one of the clearest statements of the very centre of the future-orientated New Testament worldview.

At this level, the problem with a Teilhardian evolutionary optimism, as well as with any form of actual pantheism, is that it collapses the entire future into the present, and indeed into the past. God *will be* all in all. The tense is future. Until the final victory over evil, and particularly over death, this moment has not arrived. To suggest that it has is to collude with evil, and with death itself.

How then can we think wisely about God's present relation to the created order? If God is indeed the creator of the world, it matters that creation is other than God. This is not a moral problem, as has sometimes been thought (if a good God makes something that is not himself, it must be less than good, and therefore he is not a good God for making it). Nor is it a logical one (if, in the beginning, God is all that there is, how can there be ontological room for anything or anyone else?). As we said earlier, if creation was a work of love, it must have involved the creation of something other than God. That same love then allows creation to be itself, sustaining it in providence and wisdom but not overpowering it. Logic cannot comprehend love; so much the worse for logic.

That, though, is not the end of the story. God intends, in the end, to fill all creation with his own presence and love. This is part at least of an answer to Jürgen Moltmann's proposal to revive the rabbinic doctrine of *zimzum*, in which God as it were retreats, creates space within himself, so that there is ontological space for there to be something else other than him.[8] If I am right, it works the other way round. God's creative love, precisely by being love, creates *new* space for there to be things which are genuinely other than God.

The New Testament develops the doctrine of the Spirit in just this direction, but the future glimpse is already provided in Isaiah. In chapter 11, anticipating the 'new creation' passage in chapters 65 and 66, the prophet declares that 'the earth will be full of the knowledge of the Lord as the waters cover the sea'.[9] As it stands that is a remarkable statement. How can the waters cover the sea? They *are* the sea. It looks as though God intends to flood the universe with himself; as though the universe, the entire cosmos, was designed as a receptacle for his love. We might even suggest, as part of a Christian aesthetic, that the world is beautiful, not just because it hauntingly reminds us of its creator, but because it is pointing forwards: it is designed to be filled, flooded, drenched in God; as a chalice is beautiful not least because of what we know it is designed to contain, or as a violin is beautiful not least because we know the music of which it is capable. I shall return to this later.

The answer to the pantheism of the evolutionary or progressive optimist on the one hand, and to the dualism of the gnostic or Manichee on the other, now begins to come into full view in the form of the cosmic eschatology offered in the New Testament. The world is created good *but incomplete.* One day, when all forces of rebellion have been defeated, and the creation responds freely and gladly to the love of its creator, God will fill it with himself, so that it will *both* remain an independent being, other than God, *and also* will be flooded with God's own life. This is part of the paradox of love, in which love freely given creates a context for love to be freely returned, and so on in a cycle where complete freedom and complete union do not cancel each other out, but rather celebrate each other and make one another whole.

7. New birth

This brings us to Romans 8, where we find a further image deeply embedded within the created order itself: that of new birth. This passage has routinely been marginalized for centuries by exegetes and theologians who have tried to turn Romans into a book simply about how individual sinners get individually saved. But it is in fact one of the great climaxes of the letter, and indeed of all Paul's thought.

In this passage, Paul again uses the imagery of the Exodus from Egypt, but this time in relation not to Jesus, nor even to ourselves, but to creation as a whole. Creation, he says (v. 21) is in slavery at the moment, like the children of Israel. God's design was to rule creation in life-giving wisdom through his image-bearing human creatures. But this was always a promise for the future, a promise that one day the true human being, the Image of God himself, God's incarnate son, would come to lead the human race into their true identity. Meanwhile, the creation was subjected to futility, to transience and decay, until the time when God's children are glorified, when what happened to Jesus at Easter happens to all Jesus' people. This is where Romans 8 dovetails with 1 Corinthians 15. The whole creation, as he says in verse 19, is on tiptoe with expectation, longing for the day when God's children are revealed, when their resurrection will herald its own new life.

Paul then uses the image of birth pangs – a well-known Jewish metaphor for the emergence of God's new age – not only of the church in verse 23, and of the Spirit a couple of verses later, but here in verse 22 of creation itself. Once again this highlights both continuity and discontinuity. This is no smooth evolutionary transition, in which creation simply moves up another gear into a higher mode of life. This is traumatic, involving convulsions and contractions and the radical discontinuity in which mother and child are parted and become not one being but two. But nor is this a dualistic rejection of physicality as though, because the present creation is transient and full of decay and death, God must throw it away and start again from scratch. The very metaphor which Paul chooses for this decisive moment in his argument shows that what he has in mind is not the unmaking of creation, nor simply its steady development, but the drastic and dramatic birth of new creation from the womb of the old.

8. The marriage of heaven and earth

We thus arrive at the last and perhaps the greatest image of new creation, of cosmic renewal, in the whole Bible. This scene, set out in Revelation 21—22, is not well enough known or pondered (perhaps because, in order to earn the right to read it, one should really read the rest of the Revelation of St John first, which proves too daunting for many). This time the image is that of marriage. The new Jerusalem comes down out of heaven like a bride adorned for her husband.

We notice right away how drastically different this is from all those would-be Christian scenarios in which the end of the story is the Christian going off to heaven as a soul, naked and unadorned, to meet its maker in fear and trembling. As in Philippians 3, it is not we who go to heaven; it is heaven that comes to earth; indeed, it is the church itself, the heavenly Jerusalem,[10] that comes down to earth. This is the ultimate rejection of all types of gnosticism, of every worldview that sees the final goal as the separation of the world from God, of the physical from the spiritual, of earth from heaven. It is the final answer to the Lord's Prayer, that God's kingdom would come and his will be done on earth as in heaven. It is what Paul is talking about in Ephesians 1.10, that God's design and promise was to sum up all things in Christ, things both in heaven and on earth. It is the final fulfilment, in richly symbolic imagery, of the promise of Genesis 1, that the creation of male and female would together reflect God's image into the world. And it is the final accomplishment of God's great design, to defeat and abolish death for ever – which can only mean the rescue of creation from its present plight of decay.

Heaven and earth, it seems, are not after all poles apart, needing to be separated for ever when all the children of heaven have been rescued from this wicked earth. Nor are they simply different ways of looking at the same thing, as would be implied by some kinds of pantheism. No: they are different, radically different; but they are made for each other in the same way (Revelation is suggesting) as male and female. And, when they finally come together, that will be cause for rejoicing in the same way that a wedding is: a creational sign that God's project is going forwards; that opposite poles within creation are made for union, not competition; that love and not hate have the last word in the universe; that fruitfulness and not sterility is God's will for creation.

What is promised in this passage, then, is what Isaiah foresaw: a new heaven and a new earth, replacing the old heaven and the old earth, which were bound to decay. This doesn't mean, as I have stressed throughout, that God will wipe the slate

clean and start again. If that were so, there would be no celebration, no conquest of death, no long preparation now at last
complete. As the chapter develops, the Bride, the wife of the
Lamb, is described lovingly: she is the new Jerusalem promised
by the prophets of the Exile, especially Ezekiel. But, unlike in
Ezekiel's vision, where the rebuilt Temple takes eventual centre
stage, there is no Temple in this city (21.22). The Temple in
Jerusalem was always designed, it seems, as a pointer to, and
an advance symbol for, the presence of God himself. When
the reality is there, the signpost is no longer necessary. As in
Romans and 1 Corinthians, the living God will dwell with and
among his people, filling the city with his life and love, and pour-
ing out grace and healing in the river of life that flows from
the city out to the nations. There is a sign here of the future
project that awaits the redeemed, in God's eventual new world.
So far from sitting on clouds playing harps, as people often imagine, the redeemed people of God in the new world will be
the agents of his love going out in new ways, to accomplish new
creative tasks, to celebrate and extend the glory of his love.

9. Conclusion

There are of course other passages in the New Testament
which speak of new creation. Ideally one would want to factor
in the glorious picture of the city which is to come, at present
in heaven but destined for earth, which we find in Hebrews
11 and 12. One would certainly want to discuss the famous
passage in 2 Peter which, echoing Isaiah, speaks of waiting for
new heavens and a new earth in which justice will dwell. I have
discussed these, of course, in *The Resurrection of the Son of God*.
We should certainly place here Ephesians 1.15–23, one of the
grandest of all statements of the theme. But I come back, as I
have often done over the years, to the great poem in Colossians
1. It has often been squashed into a shallow-level picture of a
supposed 'cosmic Christ', legitimating a dehistoricized Jesus and

an easygoing transition away from a Jewish creation-theology and towards various soft versions of Teilhardian and similar thought. But it stands there as a rebuke to all such attempts, not least because, if it is Jesus who is the key to the cosmos, it is of course the crucified and risen Jesus we are talking about:

> He is the image of God, the invisible one,
>> the firstborn of all creation.
> For in him all things were created,
>> in the heavens and here on the earth.
> Things we can see and things we cannot,
>> – thrones and lordships and rulers and powers –
> All were created both through him and for him.
>
>> And he is ahead, prior to all else,
>>> and in him all things hold together;
>> And he himself is supreme, the head
>>> over the body, the church.
>
> He is the start of it all,
>> firstborn from realms of the dead;
>> so in all things he might be the chief.
> For in him all the Fullness was glad to dwell
>> and through him to reconcile all to himself,
>> making peace through the blood of his cross,
>> through him – yes, things on the earth,
>> and also the things in the heavens.[11]

It is of course only through imagery, through metaphor and symbol, that we can imagine the new world that God intends to make. That is right and proper. All our language about the future, as I have said, is like a set of signposts pointing into a bright mist. The signpost doesn't provide a photograph of what we will find when we arrive, but a true indication of the direction we should be travelling in. What I am proposing is that the New Testament image of the future hope of the whole cosmos, grounded in the resurrection of Jesus, gives as coherent a picture as we need or could have of the future that is promised to the whole world, a future in which, under the sovereign and wise rule of the creator God, decay and death will be done away, and a new creation born to which the present one will stand as mother to child. This picture, as some recent writers like John Polkinghorne have shown, gives a shape to the Christian hope which can address, and enter into dialogue with, cutting-edge physics in a way which the synthesis offered by Teilhard de Chardin and others simply cannot do. What creation needs is not abandonment on the one hand, nor evolution on the other, but redemption and renewal; and this is both promised and guaranteed by the resurrection of Jesus from the dead. This is what the whole world's waiting for.

This, in turn, clears the way for the other topics concerning the Christian future hope: God's putting all things to rights through the coming of Jesus, and the bodily resurrection itself.

As I reflect on God's future plans for the world, I am reminded of the great teacher and pastor Bishop Lesslie Newbigin. Someone once asked him whether, as he looked to the future, he was optimistic or pessimistic. His reply was simple and characteristic. 'I am', he said, 'neither an optimist nor a pessimist. Jesus Christ is risen from the dead!' This chapter, building on the previous one, is a way of saying Amen to that. The whole world is waiting, on tiptoe with expectation, for the moment when that resurrection life and power sweeps through it, filling it with the glory of God as the waters cover the sea.

Before we get to the topic of resurrection itself, however, we must turn to the other vital element of the New Testament picture of God's ultimate future. Central to the unveiling of God's new world will be the personal presence of Jesus himself.

7

Jesus, heaven and new creation

1. The ascension

Belief that Jesus of Nazareth has been raised from the dead is closely linked in the New Testament with the belief that he has been taken into heaven, where, in the words of the Psalm, he has been seated at the right hand of God.[1] Only Luke tells an explicit story about this event (though he, as if making up for his colleagues' omissions, tells it twice, once at the end of his gospel and once at the beginning of Acts). But we are safe in saying that it is presupposed more or less throughout early Christianity.

What is more, despite the efforts of many, it is impossible to collapse the ascension into the resurrection, or vice versa. You can't get away with the suggestion that saying 'Jesus is raised from the dead' and 'Jesus is ascended into heaven' are two ways of saying the same thing. Paul, our earliest writer, clearly distinguishes the two.[2] John, despite popular impressions to the contrary, sees them as two separate events; John 20.17 ('don't touch me, since I haven't yet ascended to the Father') is puzzling in other respects, but not in this one. Resurrection and ascension play quite different (though of course closely related) roles within the thought of the early church.

In fact, some kind of belief in Jesus' ascension has recently been shown to be not just a strange added extra to Christian belief, as has sometimes been thought, but a central and vital feature without which all sorts of other things start to go demonstrably wrong. In his magisterial work, *Ascension and*

Ecclesia, Professor Douglas Farrow of McGill University goes through the entire range of Christian thought on the subject, showing that where the ascension has been ignored or mis-understood one can trace a slide into muddled and even dangerous ideas and practices.[3] In our own day, the problem has been not unlike the problems about the second coming to which we shall presently turn: flat literalism on the one hand facing modernist scepticism on the other, with each feeding off the other. Some people insist that Jesus must have done a kind of vertical take-off (despite the fact that the same people know that he isn't now living somewhere in outer space, and despite the fact that a vertical take-off in one part of the world would be a downward movement seen from the other side of the globe, and so on). Many people insist – and I dare say that this is the theology many of my readers have been taught – that the language of Jesus' 'disappearance' is just a way of saying that after his death he became, as it were, spiritually present every-where, especially with his own followers. This is then often correlated with a non-literal reading of the resurrection, i.e., a denial of its bodily nature: Jesus simply 'went to heaven when he died', in a rather special sense that makes him now close to each of us wherever we are. According to this view, Jesus has, as it were, disappeared without remainder. His 'spiritual pres-ence' with us is his only identity. In that case, of course, to speak of his 'second coming' would then only be a metaphor for his presence, in the same sense, eventually permeating all things.

What happens when people think like this? To answer this we might ask a further question: why has the ascension been such a difficult and unpopular doctrine in the modern west-ern church? The answer is not just that rationalist scepticism mocks at it (a possibility which the church has sometimes invited with those stained-glass windows that show Jesus' feet sticking downwards out of a cloud). It is that the ascension demands that we think differently about how the whole cosmos is, so to speak, put together; and that we also think differently about the church and about salvation. Both literalism and scepticism have regularly operated with what is called a 'receptacle' view of space; theologians who have taken the ascension seriously have insisted that it demands what some have called a 'relational' view.[4] Basically, heaven and earth, in biblical cosmology, are not two different locations within the same continuum of space or matter. They are two different dimensions of God's good creation. And the point about heaven is twofold. First, heaven relates to earth tangentially, so that the one who is in heaven can be present simultaneously anywhere and everywhere on earth: the ascension therefore means that Jesus is available, accessible, without people having to travel to a particular spot on the earth to find him. Second, heaven is as it were the control room for earth; it is the CEO's office, the place from which instructions are given. 'All authority is given to me,' said Jesus at the end of Matthew's gospel, 'in heaven and on earth.'[5]

The idea of the human being Jesus now being in 'heaven', in his thoroughly embodied risen state, comes as a shock to many people, including many Christians. Sometimes this is because many people think that Jesus, having been divine, stopped being divine and became human, and then, having been human for a while, stopped being human and went back to being divine (at least, that's what many people think Christians are supposed to believe). More often it's because our culture is so used to the Platonic idea that 'heaven' is, by definition, a place of 'spiritual', 'non-material', reality, so that the idea of a solid body being not only present but thoroughly at home there seems like a category mistake. The ascension invites us to rethink all this; and, after all, why did we suppose we knew what 'heaven' was? Only because our culture has suggested things to us. Part of Christian belief is to find out what's true about Jesus and let that challenge our culture.

This applies in particular to the idea of Jesus being 'in charge' not only in heaven but also on earth, not only in some ultimate future but also in the present. Many will snort the obvious objection: it certainly doesn't look as though he's in charge, or, if he is, he's making a proper mess of it. But that misses the point. The early Christians knew the world was still a mess. But they announced, like messengers going off on behalf of a global company, that a new CEO had taken charge. They discovered through their own various callings how his new way of running things was to be worked out. It wasn't a matter (as some people anxiously suppose to this day) of Christians simply taking over and giving orders, in a kind of 'theocracy' where the church could simply tell everyone what to do. That has sometimes been tried, of course, and it's always led to disaster. But nor is it a matter, either, of the church backing off, letting the world go on its sweet way, and worshipping Jesus in a kind of private sphere.

Somehow there is a third option, which we shall explore in the third Part of the present book. We can glimpse it in the book of Acts: the *method* of the kingdom will match the *message* of the kingdom. The kingdom will come as the church, energized by the Spirit, goes out into the world vulnerable, suffering, praising, praying, misunderstood, misjudged, vindicated, celebrating: always – as Paul puts it in one of his letters – bearing about in the body the dying of Jesus, so that the life of Jesus may also be displayed.

What happens when you downplay or ignore the ascension? The answer is that *the church expands to fill the vacuum*. If Jesus is more or less identical with the church – if, that is, talk about Jesus can be reduced to talk about his presence within his people, rather than his standing over against them and addressing them from elsewhere as their Lord, then we have created a high road to the worst kind of triumphalism. This, indeed, is what twentieth-century English liberalism has always tended towards: by compromising with rationalism and trying to maintain that talk of the ascension is 'really' talk about Jesus being with us everywhere, the church has effectively presented *itself* (with its structures and hierarchy, its customs and quirks), instead of presenting Jesus as its Lord and itself as the world's servant, as Paul puts it.[6] And the other side of triumphalism is of course despair. If you put all your eggs into the church-equals-Jesus basket, what are you left with when, as Paul says in the same passage, we ourselves are found to be cracked earthenware vessels?

If the church identifies its structures, leadership, liturgy, buildings or anything else with its Lord – and that's what happens if you ignore the ascension, or turn it into another way of talking about the Spirit – what do you get? You get, on the one hand, what Shakespeare called 'the insolence of office'; on the other hand, the despair of late middle age, as people realize it doesn't work. (I see this all too frequently among those who bought heavily into the soggy rationalism of the 1950s and 1960s.) Only when we grasp firmly that the church is *not* Jesus and Jesus is *not* the church – when we grasp, in other words, the truth of the ascension, that the one who is indeed present with us by the Spirit is *also* the Lord who is strangely absent, strangely other, strangely different from us and over against us, the one who tells Mary Magdalene not to cling on to him – only then are we rescued from hollow triumphalism on the one hand and shallow despair on the other.

Conversely, only when we grasp and celebrate the fact that Jesus has gone on ahead of us into God's space, God's new world, and is both already ruling the rebellious present world as its rightful Lord and also interceding for us at the father's right hand – when we grasp and celebrate, in other words, what the ascension tells us about Jesus' continuing *human* work in the present – only then are we rescued from a wrong view of world history and equipped for the task of justice in the present (we'll come back to both of those later).[7] We are also, significantly, rescued from the attempts that have been made to create alternative mediators, and in particular an alternative mediatrix, in his place.[8] Get the ascension right, and your view of the church, of the sacraments, and of the mother of Jesus can get back into focus.[9]

You could sum all this up by saying that the doctrine of the Trinity, which has in fact been making quite a comeback in current theology, is essential if we are to tell the truth not only about God, and more particularly about Jesus, but also about ourselves. The Trinity is precisely a way of recognizing and celebrating the fact of the human being Jesus of Nazareth as distinct from, while still identified with, God the father on the one hand (he didn't just 'go back to being God again' after his earthly life) and the Spirit on the other hand (the Jesus who is near us and with us by the Spirit remains the Jesus who is other than us).[10] This places a full stop against all human arrogance, including Christian arrogance. And now we see at last why the Enlightenment world was determined to make the ascension appear ridiculous, using the weapons of rationalism and scepticism to do so: if the ascension is true, then the whole project of human self-aggrandisement represented by eighteenth-century European and American thought is rebuked and brought to heel. To embrace the ascension is to heave a sigh of relief, to give up the struggle to be God (and with it the inevitable despair at our constant failure), and to enjoy our status as *creatures*: image-bearing creatures, but creatures none the less.

The ascension thus speaks of the Jesus who remains truly human, and hence in an important sense absent from us while in another equally important sense present to us in a new way. At this point the Holy Spirit on the one hand, and the sacraments on the other, become enormously important, since they are precisely the means by which Jesus is present. Often in the church we have been so keen to stress the presence of Jesus by these means that we have failed to indicate his simultaneous absence, and have left people wondering whether this is, so to speak, 'all there is to it'. The answer is: no, it isn't. The lordship of Jesus; the fact that there is already a human being at the helm of the world; his present intercession for us; all this is over and above his presence with us. It is even more over and above our *sense of* that presence, which of course comes and goes with our own moods and circumstances.

Now it is of course one thing to say all this, to show how it fits together and sets us free from some of the nonsenses we would otherwise get into. It's quite another to be able to envisage or imagine it, to know what it is we're really talking about when we speak of Jesus being still human, still in fact an *embodied* human – actually, a *more solidly embodied* human than we are – but absent from this present world. We need, in fact, a new and better cosmology, a new and better way of thinking about the world, than the one which our culture, not least post-Enlightenment culture, has bequeathed us. The early Christians, and their fellow first-century Jews, were not, as many modern thinkers have supposed, locked into thinking of a three-decker universe with heaven up in the sky and hell down beneath their feet. When they spoke of 'up' and 'down' like that they, like the Greeks in their different ways, were using metaphors that were so obvious that they didn't need spelling out. As some recent writers have pointed out, when a pupil at school moves 'up a form', from (say) the fifth form to the sixth form, it is unlikely that this means relocating to a classroom on the floor above. And though the move 'up' from vice-chairman of the board to chairman of the board may indeed mean that at last you get an office in the penthouse suite, it would be quite wrong to think that 'moving up' in this context meant merely being a few feet further away from terra firma.

The mystery of the ascension is of course just that, a mystery. It demands that we think what is, to many today, almost un-thinkable: that we recognize that when the Bible speaks of 'heaven' and 'earth' it isn't talking about two localities related to each other within the same space-time continuum, nor yet about a 'non-physical' world on the one hand and a 'physical' one on the other, but about two different *kinds* of what we call 'space', two different kinds of what we call 'matter', and also, quite possibly (though this does not necessarily follow from the other two), two different kinds of what we call 'time'. We post-Enlightenment westerners are such wretched flatlanders. Although New Age thinkers, and indeed quite a lot of contemporary novelists, are quite capable of taking us into other parallel worlds, spaces and times, we retreat into our rationalistic closed-system universe as soon as we think about Jesus. C. S. Lewis of course did a great job, in the Narnia stories and elsewhere, of imagining how two worlds could relate and interlock. But the generation that has grown up knowing its way around Narnia has not usually been helped to see how to make the transition from a children's story to the real world of grown-up Christian devotion and theology.

Some church buildings have done their best to indicate the interrelation of heaven and earth. The Eastern Orthodox churches do it by envisaging 'heaven' as the inner sanctuary, the space around the altar, and 'earth' as the part of the building outside that space. The two are separated by the iconostasis upon which are portrayed the saints whose presence in 'heaven' is not far from the worshippers on 'earth'. Western cathedrals and abbeys have often done a similar thing through soaring Gothic architecture, giving us at floor level a sense of belonging within (but unable at the moment to inhabit more than a little of) great spaces of light and beauty into which, significantly, only our music can penetrate.

All such aids to the Christian imagination are to be welcomed as long, of course, as they are not mistaken for the real thing. What we are encouraged to grasp precisely through the ascension itself is that God's space and ours – heaven and earth, in other words – are, though very different, not far away from one another. Nor is talk about 'heaven' simply a metaphorical way of talking about our own spiritual lives. God's space and ours interlock and intersect in a whole variety of ways, even while they retain, for the moment at least, their separate and distinct identities and roles. One day, as we saw in the last chapter, they will be joined in a quite new way, open and visible to one another, married together for ever.

One day, in other words, the Jesus who is right now the central figure of God's space – the human Jesus, still wearing (as Wesley put it) 'those dear tokens of his passion' on his 'dazzling body' – will be present to us, and we to him, in a radically different way to what we currently know. The other half of the truth of the ascension is that Jesus will return, as the angels said in Acts 1.11.

At this point some of the regular prayers, in my tradition, let us down with a bump – which is actually the wrong metaphor, because what they do is to say, in effect, 'Jesus has been raised to heaven, and we pray that we may be raised there too.' There is indeed a sense in which this is true, as in Ephesians 2.6 and Colossians 3.1–4. But when people hear those prayers today (speaking of Jesus being exalted to heaven, and of ourselves going in heart and mind to be with him for ever; or speaking of the Holy Spirit as the one who will exalt us to the place where he has gone before), they are almost bound, within today's muddled worldview, to be reinforced in their view that the whole point of the Christian faith is to follow Jesus away from earth to heaven and stay there for ever. And the New Testament insists, on the contrary, that the one who has gone into heaven will come back. At no point in the gospels or Acts does anyone say anything remotely like, 'Jesus has gone into heaven, so let's be sure we can follow him.' They say, rather, 'Jesus is in heaven, ruling the whole world, and he will one day return to make that rule complete.'

But what is this 'second coming' all about? Isn't that, too, a strange, outlandish idea which we should abandon in our own day?

2. What about the 'second coming'?

'Christ has died,' we say in the Anglican eucharist, 'Christ is risen; *Christ will come again.*' And of course in the creed, too: 'He will come again in glory to judge the living and the dead.' If we sing it once during the season of Advent, we sing it a dozen times. 'Alleluia! Come, Lord, come!'

And if we are ordinary mainstream Christians in Britain today – and in many other places too, including parts of North America – we may well add under our breath, 'even though I haven't a clue what it means'. The so-called 'second coming' of Jesus is not a hot topic in the preaching of the mainstream churches, even in Advent. (There are of course some churches which speak of little else; I shall come to them presently.) The more recent lectionaries we use in my church have rather steered us away from it. What's more, the revival of a lively eucharistic life in the Church of England in the post-war years carried with it, in some circles at least, a theology which seemed to leave no room for a final 'coming'. 'Why do we say "Christ will come again"?' asked one puzzled worshipper in the 1970s when the threefold phrase was first used in Anglican liturgy. 'Surely we've been taught that he comes – that he is here with us – in the eucharist itself?'

What then can we say about the 'second coming' of Jesus?

We have reached the point in this book where we can address this question within the larger framework where it makes sense. We have looked in earlier chapters at the beliefs about life after death, and the future of the world, that are held in our own time and that were held in Jesus' day. We have seen that there are good historical arguments pointing to belief in Jesus' own bodily resurrection. In particular, I sketched in the last chapter the large-scale future hope of Christians, the hope for the renewal of the whole world. Now, before we turn to examine more particularly the hope, or the fate, of the individual within this scheme of thought, we come to one central

129

and vital aspect of the large-scale hope. When God renews the whole cosmos, the New Testament insists, Jesus himself will be personally present as the centre and focus of the new world that will result. What does the Christian faith teach at this point? What is its sharp edge for us today? How can we make it our own?

Answering these questions has become more difficult in the last century. There are two reasons for this, more or less equal and opposite.

On the one hand, the 'second coming' of Jesus Christ has become the favourite topic of a large swathe of North American Christianity, particularly but not exclusively in the fundamentalist and 'dispensationalist' segment. Growing out of some millenarian movements of the nineteenth century, particularly those associated with J. N. Darby and the Plymouth Brethren, a belief has arisen, and taken hold of millions of minds and hearts, that we are now living in the 'end times', in which all the great prophecies are to be fulfilled at last. Central to these prophecies, it is believed, is the promise that Jesus will return in person, snatching the true believers away from this wicked world to be with him, and then, after an interval of ungodliness, returning to reign over the world for ever. The attempt to correlate these prophecies with the geopolitical events of the 1960s and 1970s, which reached a height in Hal Lindsey's best-selling book *The Late Great Planet Earth*,[11] has somewhat palled, but its place has been taken by the fictional scenarios offered by a series of books by Tim LaHaye and Jerry Jenkins. The first volume of the series, called *Left Behind*, has given its name to a sequence of twelve books in all, most of which have done astonishingly well in the current American best-seller lists. In their fictitious scenario, the 'rapture' has happened; all true Christians have been snatched away from the earth; and those 'left behind' are now struggling to survive in a godless world. This is an exciting and entertaining scenario; I leave it to others to probe the social and political psychology that is going on when pseudo-theological fiction takes off like this. Nor is it purely an American phenomenon. The books sell quite well in the UK too, though who is buying them in my own country I do not know.[12]

The American obsession – I don't think that's too strong a word – with the second coming of Jesus, or rather with one particular and, as we shall see, highly distorted interpretation of it, continues unabated. I first met it in person when I was giving some lectures in Thunder Bay, Ontario, in the early 1980s. I was talking about Jesus in his historical context; and to my surprise almost all the questions afterwards were about ecology – about trees and water and crops, which is after all what there mostly is at Thunder Bay. It turned out (as I indicated in the previous chapter) that many conservative Christians in the area, and more importantly just to the south in the United States, had been urging that since we were living in the 'end times', with the world about to come to an end, there was no point worrying about trying to stop polluting the planet with acid rain and the like. Indeed, wasn't it 'unspiritual', and even a sign of a lack of faith, to think about such things? If God was intending to bring the whole world to a shuddering halt, what was the problem? If Armageddon was just around the corner, it didn't matter – and here, I suspect, is part of the real agenda – if General Motors went on pumping out poisonous gases into the Canadian atmosphere.

We face similar questions today. So-called end-time speculation, which is the daily bread of many in the American 'religious right', is not unconnected to the agenda of some of America's leading politicians. More of that anon. For many millions of believing Christians in today's world, the second coming is part of a scenario in which the present world is doomed to destruction while the chosen few are snatched up to heaven.

Partly in reaction against such an idea, but partly powered by the energy of good old Enlightenment liberalism, many in the mainstream churches of the West have for some time been doing their best to divest themselves of the doctrine that Jesus Christ 'will come again in glory to judge the living and the dead', at least in any recognizable form.

Both parts have been disliked: the coming on the one hand, the judging on the other. The idea that Jesus will 'come' to this world, invading it like a spaceman, smacks to many of an older 'supernatural' or 'interventionist' theology which they have spent a lifetime rejecting or, at best, reinterpreting. They don't imagine that Jesus is still, so to speak, around the place somewhere in that way. The language of his 'coming' must therefore be reinterpreted in terms of a general hope for world renewal. After all, they say, the early church expected Jesus to come very soon, and he didn't; we should obviously reinterpret their hope in a way which makes sense two thousand years later. In addition, the idea of judgment makes many people think of a vengeful, wrathful deity, determined to throw as many people as possible into hell. We have learnt to distrust people who love accusing and punishing others. In the same way, we have learnt to dislike and distrust theologies in which accusing and punishing takes centre stage. The Hebrew for 'the accuser' is after all *hasatan*, 'the satan'.

We are therefore faced, as we look at today's large-scale picture, with two polar opposites. On the one hand, some have made the second coming so central that they can see little else. On the other, some have so marginalized or weakened it that it ceases to mean anything at all.

Both positions need to be challenged. I shall shortly show that the focus on the so-called 'rapture' is based on a misunderstanding of two verses in Paul, and that when we get that out of the way there is a doctrine of Jesus' coming that remains central and vital if the whole Christian faith is not to unravel before our eyes. At the same time, the older Enlightenment liberalism, with its dislike of all 'judgment', has itself been under attack. We have become a very moralistic, very judgmental, generation. We have judged apartheid and found it wanting. We judge child-abusers and find them guilty. We judge geno- cide and find it outrageous. We have rediscovered what the Psalmists knew: that for God to 'judge' the world meant that he would, in the end, put it all to rights, straighten it out, pro- ducing not just a sigh of relief all round but shouting for joy from the trees and the fields, the seas and the floods.[13]

At the same time, we may not as a culture be fond of old- fashioned supernaturalism, but we certainly like spirituality in whatever form we can get it.[14] I suspect that if anyone other than Jesus (Krishna, say, or Buddha) were suddenly put forward as being due for a 'second coming', there would be millions in our post-secular society who would embrace such a thing uncritically, leaving Enlightenment rationalism huffing and puffing in the rear. We are a puzzled and confused generation, embracing any and every kind of non-rationalism that may offer us a spiritual shot in the arm while lapsing back into rational- ism (in particular, the old modernist critiques) whenever we want to keep traditional or orthodox Christianity at bay.

And yet it is Christian orthodoxy, properly understood, that can help us find the way through this morass and muddle and out the other side. But before we get any further I need to say a word about a word – a much misunderstood word, a word which may get in the way unless we demystify it. I refer to the blessed term 'eschatology'.[15]

The word 'eschatology' has often been used, in relation to early Christianity, to mean the expectation of the return of Jesus within a generation – and the redefinitions that took place when this did not happen. This expectation, it used to be thought, was based on, and gave new focus to, the expectation of first- century Jews that the world was about to come to an end.

When I wrote *The New Testament and the People of God* in 1992 I argued that, though the early Christians did indeed expect Jesus' return, they were not bothered by its not happening with- in a generation, and indeed that the Jewish expectation which they had inherited was not about the end of the world, but about a dramatic change within the present world order. An Oxford colleague who read the book said to me, 'Now that you've abandoned eschatology . . .' – meaning, apparently, 'Now that you've abandoned the idea that first-century Jews and Christians expected the world to end at once'. I insisted then, and I insist now, that I have done no such thing. The word 'eschatology', which literally means 'the study of the last things', doesn't just refer to death, judgment, heaven and hell, as used to be thought (and as many dictionaries still define the word). It refers to the strongly held belief of most first-century Jews, and virtually all early Christians, that history was going somewhere under the guidance of God; and that where it was going was towards God's new world of justice, healing and hope. The transition from the present world to the new one would be a matter not of the destruction of the present space-time universe, but of its radical healing. As we saw in the last chapter, the New Testament writers, particularly Paul, looked forward to this time, and saw Jesus' resurrection as the beginning, the first fruits, of it. So when I (and many others) use the word 'eschatology', we don't simply mean 'the second coming', still less a particular theory about it, but rather the entire sense of God's future for the world, and the belief that that future has already begun to come forward to meet us in the present. This is what we find in Jesus himself, and in the teaching of the early church. They modified, but did not abandon, the Jewish eschatological beliefs that they had already shared.

So how can we understand the 'second coming'? How, for that matter, do the biblical writers themselves understand it? This will take a further chapter to set out.

8

When he appears

1. Introduction

Two chapters ago I sketched the big picture of cosmic redemption that the New Testament invites us to make our own. God will redeem the whole universe; Jesus' resurrection is the beginning of that new life, the fresh grass growing through the concrete of corruption and decay in the old world. That final redemption will be the moment when heaven and earth are joined together at last, in a burst of God's creative energy for which Easter is the prototype and source. When we put together that big picture with what we've said in the previous chapter about the ascension of Jesus, what do we get? Why, of course, the personal *presence* of Jesus, as opposed to his current *absence*.

The presence we know at the moment – the presence of Jesus with his people in word and sacrament, by the Spirit, through prayer, in the faces of the poor – is of course related to that future presence, but the distinction between them is important and striking. Jesus' appearing will be, for those of us who have known and loved him here, like meeting face to face someone whom we have only ever known by letter, telephone, or perhaps email. Communication theorists insist that for full human communication you need not only words on a page but a tone of voice. That's why a telephone call can say more than a letter, not in quantity but in quality. But for full communication between human beings you need not only a tone of voice but also body language, facial language, and the thousand small ways in which, without realizing it, we relate to one another. At the moment, by the Spirit, the word, the sacraments and prayer, and in those in need whom we are called to serve for his sake, the absent Jesus is present to us; but one day he will be there with us, face to face. Mrs Alexander got it partly right in a classic nineteenth-century compromise:

> And our eyes at last shall see him,
> Through his own redeeming love,
> For that child so dear and gentle
> Is our Lord in heaven above.

Unless we feel the pull and yearning of those lines, we may not yet have learnt to know him as we may know him in the present, or to feel the tension between our present knowing and that which is promised in the future. But the hymn is quite wrong to suggest that for this knowledge *we* need to go and find *him*:

> And he leads his children on
> To the place where he is gone.

This is indeed true, as we shall see, of what happens to his people after death, in the interim state. But it isn't the main truth that the New Testament teaches, the main emphasis which the early Christians insisted on over and over again. The main truth is that *he* will come back to *us*.[1] That is the thing of which we must now speak, in two main movements. He will come again; and he will come again as judge.

2. Coming, appearing, revealing, royal presence

We still speak, in our culture, about the sun 'rising' and 'setting', even though we know that in fact it is we, or at least our planet, who are moving in relation to the sun rather than the other way round. In the same way, the early Christians often spoke of Jesus 'coming', or 'returning'; indeed, at least in John's gospel, Jesus himself speaks in that way. But the larger picture they use suggests that if we are to understand them properly that language, common and even credal though it is, may not be the most helpful way today of getting at the truth it affirms.

In fact, the New Testament uses quite a variety of language and imagery to express the truth that Jesus and his people will one day be personally present to each other, as full and re-newed human beings. It is perhaps an accident of history that the phrase 'the second coming', which is very rare in the New Testament, has come to dominate discussion. When that phrase is identified, as it has often been in North America in particu-lar, with a particular view of that 'coming' as a literal down-ward descent, meeting half-way with the redeemed who are making a simultaneous upward journey, all sorts of problems arise which are avoided if we take the New Testament's mul-tiple witness as a whole.

The first thing to get clear is that, despite widespread opin-ion to the contrary, during his earthly ministry Jesus said nothing about his return. I have argued this position at length and in detail in my various books about Jesus and don't have space to substantiate it here. Let me just say two things, quite baldly.[2]

First, when Jesus speaks of 'the son of man coming on the clouds', he is not talking about the second coming, but, in line with the Daniel 7 text he is quoting, about his vindication after suffering. The 'coming' is an upward, not a downward, movement. In context, the key texts mean that, though Jesus is going to his death, he will be vindicated by events that will take place afterwards.[3] What those events are remains cryptic from the point of view of the passages in question, which is one good reason for thinking them authentic; but they certainly include Jesus' resurrection on the one hand and the destruction of the Temple, the system that has opposed him and his mission, on the other. And the language, significantly, is precisely the language that the early church used as the least inadequate way of talking about the strange thing that happened after Jesus' resurrection: his 'ascension', his glorification, his 'coming', not to earth, but to heaven, to the father.

Second, the stories Jesus tells about a king, or master, who goes away for a while and leaves his subjects or servants to trade with his money in his absence, were not originally meant to refer to Jesus going away and leaving the church with tasks to get on with until his eventual second coming, even though they were read in that way from fairly early on.[4] They belong in the Jewish world of the first century, where everyone would at once 'hear' the story to be about God himself, having left Israel and the Temple at the time of the Exile, coming back again at last, as the post-exilic prophets had said he would,[5] back to Israel, back to Zion, back to the Temple. In their original setting, the point of these stories is that Israel's God, yhwh, is indeed coming at last to Jerusalem, to the Temple – in and as the human person Jesus of Nazareth. The stories are not, in that sense, about the *second* coming of Jesus, but about the first one. They are explaining, albeit cryptically, Jesus' own belief, that what he was doing in coming to Jerusalem to enact both judgment and salvation was what yhwh had said in scripture that he would do in person.

These two historical moves, about the 'son of man' sayings and about the parables of the returning master or king, have left me open to the attack, particularly from American readers, that I have thereby given up believing or teaching the second coming. This is absurd, as the present chapter will make clear. The fact that Jesus didn't teach it doesn't mean it isn't true. (Similarly, the fact that I have written books about Jesus without mentioning it doesn't mean I don't believe in it; when a football commentator goes through a whole game without mentioning cricket, that doesn't mean he doesn't believe it exists, or that he doesn't rate it highly as a sport.) Jesus was having a hard enough time explaining to his disciples that he had to die; they never really grasped that at all, and they certainly didn't take his language about his own resurrection as anything more than the general hope of all Jewish martyrs. How could they possibly have understood him saying something about further events in what would have been, for them, a still more unthinkable future?

Of course, when Jesus came to Zion as Israel's rightful Lord in the first century, that event did indeed point forward to his eventual return as the rightful Lord of the whole world. This means that, if we are careful what we are doing, we can read the parables I've mentioned in this new way if we so desire. The reason we need to be careful, though, is because they don't quite fit. Nowhere in the New Testament does any writer say that at Jesus' final coming there will be some of his servants, some actual believing Christians, who will be judged in the way that the wicked servant was judged for hiding his master's money in a napkin.

Nor will it do to say, as some have said who have grasped part of the point but not worked it through, that the events of AD 70 were themselves the 'second coming' of Jesus, so that ever since then we have been living in God's new age, and there is no further 'coming' to await. This may seem to many readers, as indeed it seems to me, a bizarre position to hold, but there are some who not only hold it but eagerly propagate it, and use some of my arguments to support it. This results from a confusion: if the texts which speak of 'the son of man coming on the clouds' refer to AD 70, as I have argued that (in part) they do, this doesn't mean that AD 70 was the 'second coming' – because the 'son of man' texts aren't 'second coming' texts at all, despite their frequent misreading that way. They are about Jesus' vindication. And Jesus' vindication – in his resurrection, ascension and judgment on Jerusalem – requires a still further event for everything to be complete. Let me say it quite emphatically for the sake of those who have been confused on the point (and to the amusement, no doubt, of those who haven't been): the 'second coming' has not yet occurred.

So: if the gospel accounts of Jesus' teaching do not refer to the second coming, where does the idea come from? Quite simply, from the rest of the New Testament. As soon as Jesus had been vindicated, raised and exalted, the church firmly believed and taught that he would return. 'This same Jesus who has gone from you into heaven', said the angel to the disciples, 'will return in the same way that you saw him go into heaven.'[6] And, though Acts doesn't often refer again to this belief, clearly the whole book takes place under this rubric. This is what the disciples are doing to make Jesus' lordship known in all the world against the day when he will come once more to renew all things.[7]

But of course the primary witness is Paul. Paul's letters are full of the future coming or appearing of Jesus.[8] His worldview, his theology, his missionary practice, his devotion are all inconceivable without it. Yet what he has to say about this great event has often been misunderstood, not least by the proponents of 'rapture' theology. It's almost time to address this directly, but first a word about another major and often misunderstood technical term.

Scholars and simple folk alike can get led astray by the use of a single word to refer to something when that word in its original setting means both more and less than the use to which it is subsequently put. In this case the word in question is the Greek word *parousia*. This is usually translated 'coming'; but literally it means 'presence' – that is, 'presence' as opposed to 'absence'.

The word *parousia* occurs in two of the key passages in Paul (1 Thessalonians 4.15 and 1 Corinthians 15.23), and it is found frequently elsewhere in Paul and the New Testament. It seems clear that the early Christians knew the word well, and knew what was meant by it. People often assume that the early church used *parousia* simply to mean 'the second coming of Jesus', and that by this event they all envisaged, in a quite literal fashion, the scenario of 1 Thessalonians 4.16–17 (Jesus coming down on a cloud and people flying upwards to meet him). Neither of these assumptions is in fact correct.

On the one hand, the word *parousia* had two lively meanings in non-Christian discourse at the time. Both of these seem to have influenced it in its Christian meaning.

The first meaning was the mysterious presence of a god or divinity, particularly when the power of this god was revealed in healing. People would suddenly be aware of a supernatural and powerful 'presence', and the obvious word for this was *parousia*. Josephus sometimes uses this word when he is talking about YHWH coming to the rescue of Israel.[9] God's powerful, saving presence is revealed in action, for instance when Israel under King Hezekiah was miraculously defended against the Assyrians.

The second meaning emerges when a person of high rank makes a visit to a subject state, particularly when a king or emperor visits a colony or province. The word for such a visit is 'royal presence': in Greek, *parousia*. In neither setting, we note, obviously but importantly, is there the slightest suggestion of anybody flying around on a cloud. Nor is there any hint of the imminent collapse or destruction of the space-time universe.

Now supposing Paul, and for that matter the rest of the early church, wanted to say two things. On the one hand, supposing they wanted to say that the Jesus they worshipped was near in spirit but absent in body, but that one day he would be present in body, and that then the whole world, themselves included, would know the sudden transforming power of that presence. A natural word to use for this would be *parousia*.

On the other hand, supposing they wanted to say that the Jesus who had been raised from the dead and exalted to God's right hand was the rightful Lord of the world, the true Emperor before whom all other emperors would shake in their shoes and bow their knees in fear and wonder. And supposing they wanted to say that, just as Caesar might one day visit a colony like Philippi or Thessalonica or Corinth (the normally absent but ruling emperor appearing and ruling in person), so the absent but ruling Lord of the world would one day appear and rule in person within this world, with all the consequences that would result. Again, the natural word to use for this would be *parousia*. (This was particularly significant in that Paul and the others were keen to say that Jesus was the true Lord and that Caesar was a sham.)

Now these things are not just suppositions. This is exactly how it was. Paul and the others used the word *parousia* because they wanted to evoke these worlds. But they evoke them within a different context. For neither the first nor the last time, the Jewish storyline and the Greco-Roman allusions and confrontations meet like two tectonic plates, throwing up the craggy mountain range we call New Testament theology. The Jewish storyline in question was, of course, the story of the Day of the Lord, the Day of YHWH, the Day when YHWH would defeat all Israel's enemies and rescue his people once and for all. Paul and the other writers regularly refer to 'the Day of the Lord', and now of course they mean it in a Christian sense: 'the Lord' here is Jesus himself.[10] In this sense, and in this sense only, there is a solid Jewish background for the Christian doctrine of the 'second coming' of Jesus.[11] Of course, there could be nothing stronger, because pre-Christian Judaism, including the disciples during Jesus' lifetime, never envisaged the death of the Messiah. That is why they never thought of his resurrection, let alone an interim period between such events and the final consummation, during which he would be installed as the world's true Lord while still waiting for that sovereign rule to take full effect.

What happened, it seems, was this. The early Christians had lived within, and breathed and prayed, that old Jewish storyline. In the resurrection and ascension of Jesus, shocking and unexpected though they were, they grasped the fact that in this way Israel's God had indeed done what he'd always intended, though it hadn't looked like they thought it would. Through this they came to see that Jesus, as Israel's Messiah, was already the world's true Lord, and that his secret presence by his Spirit in the present time was only a hint of what was still to come, when he would finally be revealed as the one whose power would trump all other powers both earthly and heavenly. The Jesus-story thus created a radical intensification and transformation from within the Jewish story; and the language that results in describing the Jesus-event that is yet to come is the language that says, in relation to the future: Jesus is Lord and Caesar isn't.

Parousia is itself, in fact, one of those terms in which Paul is able to say that Jesus is the reality of which Caesar is the parody. His theology of the second coming is part of his political theology of Jesus as Lord.[12] In other words, we have the language of *parousia*, of royal presence, sitting in a typically Pauline juxtaposition with the language of Jewish apocalyptic. This would not, I think, have presented many problems for Paul's first hearers. It has certainly created problems for subsequent readers, not least in the last century or so.

This is so especially when we read 1 Thessalonians 4.16–17:

> The Lord himself will come down from heaven with a shouted order, with the voice of an archangel and the sound of God's trumpet. The Messiah's dead will rise first; then we who are alive, who are left, will be snatched up with them among the clouds, to meet the Lord in the air. And in this way we shall always be with the Lord.

The point to notice above all about these tricky verses is that they are *not* to be taken as a literal description of what Paul thinks will happen. They are simply a different way of saying what he is saying in 1 Corinthians 15.23–27 and 51–54, and in Philippians 3.20–21.

We had better get those other passages straight in our minds to start with. In 1 Corinthians 15.23–27 Paul speaks of the *parousia* of the Messiah as the time of the resurrection of

the dead, the time when his present though secret rule will become manifest in the conquest of the last enemies, especially
death. Then in verses 51–54 he speaks of what will happen
to those who, at Jesus' coming, are not yet dead. They will be
changed, transformed. This is clearly the same event as he is
speaking of in 1 Thessalonians 4; we have the trumpet in
both, and the resurrection of the dead in both; but whereas
in 1 Thessalonians he speaks of those presently alive being
'snatched up in the air', in 1 Corinthians he speaks of them
being 'transformed'. So too in Philippians 3.21, where the context is quite explicitly ranging Jesus over against Caesar, Paul
speaks of the *transformation* of the present lowly body to be
like Jesus' glorious body, as a result of his all-conquering power.

So why does Paul speak in this peculiar way in 1 Thessalonians, about the Lord descending and the living saints being
snatched up in the air? I suggest that he is finding richly metaphorical ways of alluding to three other stories which he is
deliberately bringing together. (Paul was good at richly mixed
metaphors: in the next chapter, 1 Thessalonians 5, he says that
the thief will come in the night, so the woman will go into labour,
so you mustn't get drunk but must stay awake and put on your
armour. As the television programmes say, don't try that one
at home.)

We must remind ourselves yet once more that all Christian
language about the future is a set of signposts pointing into
a mist. Signposts don't normally provide you with advance
photographs of what you'll find at the end of the road, but that
doesn't mean they aren't pointing in the right direction. They
are telling you the truth, the particular sort of truth that can
be told about the future.

The three stories which Paul is here bringing together start
with the story of Moses coming down the mountain. The
trumpet sounds, a loud voice is heard, and after a long wait
Moses appears and descends from the mountain to see what's
been going on in his absence.

Then there is the story of Daniel 7, in which the per-secuted people of God are vindicated over their pagan enemy by being raised up on the clouds to sit with God in glory. This 'raising up on the clouds', which Jesus applies to himself in the gospels, is now applied by Paul to the Christians who are presently suffering persecution.[13]

Putting these two stories together, in a typically outrageous mix of metaphors, enables Paul to bring in the third story, to which we have already alluded. When the emperor visited a colony or province, the citizens of the country would go to meet him at some distance from the city. It would be disrespectful to have him arrive at the gates as though they his subjects couldn't be bothered to greet him properly. When they met him, they wouldn't then stay out in the open country; they would escort him royally into the city itself. When Paul speaks of 'meeting' the Lord 'in the air', the point is precisely not – as in the popular rapture theology – that the saved believers would then stay up in the air somewhere, away from earth. The point is that, having gone out to meet their returning Lord, they will escort him royally into his domain, that is, back to the place they have come from. Even when we realize that this is highly charged metaphor, not literal description, the mean-ing is the same as in the parallel in Philippians 3.20. Being citizens of heaven, as the Philippians would know, doesn't mean that one is expecting to go back to the mother city, but rather that one is expecting the emperor to come *from* the mother city to give the colony its full dignity, to rescue it if need be, to subdue local enemies and put everything to rights.

These two verses in 1 Thessalonians 4, then, have been grievously abused by those who have constructed out of them a big picture of a supposed 'rapture'. This has had its effect not only on popular fundamentalism, but on a fair amount of New Testament scholarship, which has assumed that Paul really meant what the fundamentalists think he meant. Only when we put together the several different things that he says on the same topic does the truth emerge. This is a typical piece of highly charged and multiply allusive rhetoric. The reality to which it refers is this: Jesus will be personally present, the dead will be raised, and the living Christians will be transformed. That, as we shall now see, is pretty much what the rest of the New Testament says as well.

Note, though, something else of great significance about the whole Christian theology of resurrection, ascension, second coming and hope. This theology was born out of confrontation with the political authorities, out of the conviction that Jesus was already the true Lord of the world who would one day be manifested as such. The 'rapture' theology avoids this confrontation, because it suggests that Christians will miraculously be removed from this wicked world. Perhaps that is why such theology is often gnostic in its tendency towards a private dualistic spirituality, and towards a political laissez-faire quietism. And perhaps that is partly why such theology, with its dreams of Armageddon, has quietly supported the political status quo in a way that Paul would never have done.

Before turning away from Paul, notice a significant pair of passages. First, at the end of 1 Corinthians, Paul suddenly writes a phrase in Aramaic: *Marana tha.*[14] It means 'Our Lord, come!', and goes back (like the word *Abba*, 'father') to the very early Aramaic-speaking church. There is no reason why the Greek-speaking church would have invented a prayer in Aramaic; we must be in touch at this point with extremely early and pre-Pauline tradition. The early church was from the beginning praying to Jesus that he would return.

Second, a very different passage in Colossians 3. Here we have in a nutshell Paul's theology of resurrection and ascension, as applied to present Christian living and future Christian hope:

> If you've been raised with the Messiah, seek the things that are above, because that's where the Messiah is, sitting at God's right hand. Think about the things above, not about the things below; for you died, and your life is hidden with the Messiah in

God. When the Messiah appears [*hotan ho Christos phanerōthē*], the one who is your life, then you too will appear with him in glory.[15]

This is clearly in the same ballpark as the other texts we've been looking at. But notice the key thing: that instead of 'coming', or the blessed word *parousia*, Paul can here use the word 'appear'. It's the same thing from a different angle, and this helps us to demystify the idea that the 'coming' of Jesus means that he will descend like a spaceman from the sky. Jesus is at present in heaven. But, as we saw earlier, heaven, being God's space, is not somewhere within the space of our world, but is rather a different though closely related space. The promise is not that Jesus will simply reappear within the present world order, but that, when heaven and earth are joined together in the new way God has promised, then he will appear to us – and we will appear to him, and to one another, in our own true identity.

This is, in fact, remarkably close to a key passage in the first letter of John (1 John 2.28; 3.2):

Now, children, abide in him; so that, when he appears [*ean phanerōthē*], we may have confidence and not shrink from him in shame at his presence [*parousia*] . . . Beloved, we are now God's children; and it has not yet appeared [*oupō ephanerōthē*] what we shall be; but we know that when he appears [*ean phanerōthē*], we shall be like him, because we shall see him just as he is.

Here we have more or less exactly the same picture as in Colossians, though this time with 'appearing' and *parousia* happily side by side. Of course, when he 'appears' he will be 'present'. But the point of stressing 'appearing' here is that, though in one sense it will seem to us that he is 'coming', he will in fact be 'appearing' right where he presently is – not a long way away within our own space-time world, but in his own world, God's world, the world we call 'heaven'. This world is different from ours ('earth'), but intersects with it in countless ways, not least in the inner lives of Christians themselves. One day the two worlds will be integrated completely, and be fully visible to one another, producing that transformation of which both Paul and John speak.

Of course, Paul and John are not the only writers to mention all of this. The Revelation of St John the Divine also speaks of the coming of Jesus; and here we find the word 'come' itself. The Spirit and the Bride say 'Come', and the closing prayer of the book, as with 1 Corinthians, is that the Lord Jesus will come, and come soon. The same theme is scattered elsewhere in the book.[16] There is no space here to look at these in detail, or indeed at the relevant passages in the other, smaller, New Testament books.[17] Famously, 2 Peter 3 is the one place in the New Testament where the issue of delay is addressed head on; and it's worth noting that those who reckon this a problem are precisely, in context, those who are arguing for a rather different, non-historical, form of Christianity.[18]

What we have here, with minor variations, is a remarkably unanimous view spread throughout the early Christianity known to us. There will come a time, which might indeed come at any time, when, in the great renewal of the world which Easter itself foreshadowed, Jesus himself will be personally present, and will be the agent and model of the transformation that will happen both to the whole world and also to believers. This expectation and hope, expressed so clearly in the New Testament, continues undiminished in the second and subsequent centuries. Mainstream Christians throughout the early period were not worried by the fact that the event had not happened within a generation. The idea that the problem of 'delay' set out in 2 Peter 3 was widespread in second-generation Christianity is a modern scholars' myth rather than a historical reality.[19] Nor was the idea of Jesus' 'appearing' or 'coming' simply part of a tradition that was passed on uncritically without later generations really tuning in to what it was saying. As with the ascension, so with Jesus' appearing: it was seen as a vital part of a full presentation of the Jesus who was, and is, and is to come. Without it the church's proclamation makes no sense. Take it away, and all sorts of things start to unravel. The early Christians saw this as clearly as anyone since, and we would do well to learn from them.

But it is now high time to look at the second aspect of the appearing or coming of Jesus. When he comes, according to the same biblically grounded tradition, he will have a specific role to play: that of judge.

9

Jesus the coming judge

1. Introduction

From the very beginning of Christianity – it's already there in some of the earliest traditions – we discover the belief that the Jesus who will appear at the end will take the role of judge. This is not an isolated belief. Indeed, within its Jewish context, it is more readily explicable than the *parousia* itself. However, it's important that we explore its meaning within early Christianity, and its significance for today and tomorrow.

The picture of Jesus as the coming judge is the central feature of another absolutely vital and non-negotiable Christian belief: that there will indeed *be* a judgment in which the creator God will set the world right once and for all. The word 'judgment' has carried negative overtones for a good many people in our liberal and post-liberal world. We need to remind ourselves that throughout the Bible, not least in the Psalms, God's coming judgment is a good thing, something to be celebrated, longed for, yearned over. It causes people to shout for joy, and indeed the trees of the field to clap their hands.[1] In a world of systematic injustice, bullying, violence, arrogance and oppression, the thought that there might be a coming day when the wicked are firmly put in their place and the poor and weak are given their due is the best news there can be. Faced with a world in rebellion, a world full of exploitation and wickedness, a good God *must* be a God of judgment. The liberal optimism of the nineteenth century had a long run for its money, outlasting some of the more obvious counter-arguments provided by the huge systemic evil of the twentieth century. But more recent theology has returned to the theme of judgment, recognizing that the biblical analysis of evil corresponds more closely to reality.[2]

The Old Testament hope for the creator God to bring judgment and justice to the world, to set the world right, became focused in the later biblical period on Israel's longing to see God overturn the oppressive regimes of the pagan world. It would be like a great, cosmic law-court scene. Israel (or at least the righteous within Israel) would play the part of the helpless defendant. The Gentiles (or at least the particularly wicked ones) would play the part of the arrogant bullies who would at last meet their match, and get the justice (the 'judgment') they deserved.

The most famous scenario which expresses all this is Daniel 7. There, the Gentile nations are depicted as huge, powerful monsters, while Israel, or the righteous within Israel, are depicted as an apparently defenceless human being, 'one like a son of man'. The scene is a great law-court setting, whose climax comes when the judge, the Ancient of Days, takes his seat and finds in favour of the son of man against the monsters, of Israel against the pagan empires. The son of man is then given authority and dominion over all the nations, in a deliberate echo of Adam being given authority over the animals in Genesis 1 and 2.

What happens when this is transposed to the New Testament? Answer: we find Jesus himself taking on the role of the 'son of man', suffering then vindicated. Then, as in Daniel, he receives from the Supreme Judge the task of bringing this judgment to bear on the world. This accords with numerous biblical and post-biblical passages in which Israel's Messiah, the one who represents Israel in person, is given the task of judgment. In Isaiah 11, the Messiah's judgment creates a world where the wolf and the lamb lie down side by side. In Psalm 2, the Gentiles tremble when the Messiah is enthroned. Again and again the Messiah is stated to be God's agent to bring the whole world, not just Israel, back into the state of justice and truth for which God longs as much as we do. So the early Christians, who had concluded from Easter that Jesus was indeed the Messiah, naturally identified him as the one through whom God would put the world to rights. They didn't simply deduce this from their belief in his future coming or appearing. Actually, it may have been the other way round: their belief in Jesus' messiahship may have been a decisive factor in the emergence of the belief in his final coming as judge.

Certainly by the time of Paul this belief is well established. The summary of what Paul said on the Areopagus in Athens concludes with the statement that God has fixed a day on which he will judge the world by a man whom he has appointed, giving assurance of the fact by raising him from the dead.[3] Paul can refer almost casually (in Romans 2.16) to the fact that, according to the gospel he preaches, God will judge the secrets of all hearts through Jesus the Messiah. Although people often suppose that, because Paul taught justification by faith, not works, there can be no room for a future judgment 'according to works', this only goes to show how much some have radically misunderstood him. The future judgment according to deeds, a judgment exercised by Jesus at his 'judgment seat', is clearly taught in, for instance, Romans 14.9–10, 2 Corinthians 5.10 and elsewhere. Equally important, these are not isolated places where Paul is quoting a tradition that doesn't fully fit with his developed theology. They are fully and tightly integrated into his thinking and preaching. For him, as much as for anyone else in the early church, the final judgment, exercised by Jesus the Messiah, was a vital element, without which all sorts of other things simply wouldn't stand up.

In particular (though there isn't space to develop this here) this picture of future judgment according to works is actually the *basis* of Paul's theology of justification by faith.[4] The point of justification by faith isn't that God suddenly ceases to care about good behaviour or morality. Justification by faith cannot be collapsed, as so many in the last two centuries have effectively tried to do, either into a generalized liberal view of a laissez-faire morality or into the romantic view that what we do outwardly doesn't matter at all since the only thing that matters is what we're like inwardly. (Those who over-anxiously defend a doctrine from which all mention of 'works' has been rigorously excluded should consider with whom they are colluding at this point!) No: justification by faith is what happens in the *present time*, anticipating the verdict of the *future day* when God judges the world. It is God's advance declaration that, when someone believes the gospel, that person is already a member of his family no matter who their parents were, that their sins are forgiven because of Jesus' death, and that on the future day, as Paul says, 'there is now no condemnation' (Romans 8.1). Clearly there are further questions to be asked about how the verdict issued in the present can so confidently be supposed to anticipate correctly the verdict issued in the future on the basis of the entire life led. Paul addresses those questions in several ways at several points, particularly in his expositions of the work of the Holy Spirit. But for Paul (and this is the only point I am making in the present context) there was no clash between present justification by faith and future judgment according to works. The two need, and depend upon, one another. To go any further would demand a fairly thorough exposition of Romans and Galatians, for which there is obviously no space here.[5]

Once again, the Pauline picture is filled out by other references in the New Testament. This is no flash in the pan or Pauline idiosyncrasy; it is common early Christian belief.[6] It is the central point in that long paragraph in John 5 which caused so many headaches to those earlier scholars who tried to make John's gospel teach simply a present eternal life, rather than also the future one:

The father doesn't judge anyone; he has handed over all judgment to the son, so that everyone should honour the son just as they honour the father. Anyone who doesn't honour the son doesn't honour the father who sent him. I'm telling you the solemn truth: anyone who hears my word, and believes in the one who sent me, has eternal life. Such a person won't come into judgment; they will have passed out of death into life. I'm telling you the solemn truth: the time is coming – in fact, it's here already! – when the dead will hear the voice of God's son, and those who hear it will live. You see, just as the father has life in himself, in the same way he has given the son the privilege of having life in himself. He has even given him authority to pass judgment, because he is the son of man. Don't be surprised at this. The time is coming, you see, when everyone in the tombs will hear his voice. They will come out – those who have done good, to the resurrection of life, and those who have done evil, to the resurrection of judgment. I can't do anything on my own authority. I judge on the basis of what I hear. And my judgment is just, because I'm not trying to carry out my own wishes, but the wishes of the one who sent me.[7]

The main point to notice, once more, is that all the future judgment is highlighted basically as good news, not bad. Why so? It is good news, first, because the one through whom God's justice will finally sweep the world is not a hard-hearted, arrogant or vengeful tyrant, but the Man of Sorrows, who was acquainted with grief; the Jesus who loved sinners and died for them; the Messiah who took the world's judgment upon himself on the cross. Of course, this also means that he is quite uniquely placed to judge the systems and rulers that have carved up the world between them, and the New Testament points this out here and there.[8] In particular, as we have already seen and as some medieval theologians and artists highlighted, Jesus comes as judge much as Moses descended the mountain into the camp where idolatry and revelry was in full swing. The Sistine Chapel itself reminds us of the day when careless and casual living, as well as downright wickedness, will be brought to book.[9]

Within the New Testament, and within subsequent Christian theology, this judgment is *anticipated* under certain circumstances. I have already spoken of justification by faith. The same is true, in 1 Corinthians, for the eucharist: eating and drinking the body and blood of Jesus means confronting here and now the one who is the judge as well as the saviour of all.[10] And the same is true, of course, of the work of the Spirit, as we see once more in John 16. When the Spirit comes, declares Jesus, he will convict the world of sin, of righteousness and judgment.[11] The final judgment, in other words, will be anticipated in the present world through the Spirit-led work and witness of Jesus' followers.

2. Second coming and judgment

The so-called second coming of Jesus, then, when properly understood in the New Testament and subsequent Christian teaching, is no afterthought to the basic Christian message. It hasn't been as it were bolted on to the outside of a gospel message which could stand complete without it. We cannot relegate it to the margins of our thinking, our living and our praying; if we do, we shall pull everything else out of shape. I now want, briefly, to draw out a few final points of relevance for us today.

First, the appearing or coming of Jesus offers the complete answer to the literalist fundamentalists on the one hand and to the proponents of that 'cosmic Christ' idea I outlined in Chapter 5. Jesus remains other than the church, other than the world, even while being present to both by the Spirit. He confronts the world in the present, and will do so personally and visibly in the future. He is the one to whom every knee shall bow (Philippians 2.10–11), as well as the one who took the form of a servant and was obedient to the death of the cross (Philippians 2.6–8). Indeed, as Paul stresses, he is the first *because* he did the second. In his appearing we find neither a dualist rejection of the present world, nor simply his arrival like a spaceman into the present world, but the *transformation* of the present world, and ourselves within it, so that it will at last be put to rights, and we with it. Death and decay will themselves be overcome, and God will be all in all.

This means, second, that a proper shape and balance are given to the Christian worldview. Like the Jewish worldview, but radically opposed to the Stoic, the Platonic, the Hindu and the Buddhist worldviews, Christians tell a story with a beginning, a middle and an end. Not to have closure at the end of the story – to be left with a potentially endless cycle, round and round with either the same things happening again and again, or simply perhaps the long outworking of karma – would be the very antithesis of the story told by the apostles, and by the long line of their Jewish predecessors. And, precisely because Jesus is not collapsed into the church, or indeed the world, we can renounce on the one hand the triumphalism that conveniently makes his sovereign lordship an excuse for its own, and on the other hand the despair that comes when we see such hopes dashed, as they always will be, in the follies and failings of even the best and greatest Christian organizations, structures, leaders and followers. Because we live between ascension and appearing, joined to Jesus Christ by the Spirit but still awaiting his final coming and presence, we can be *both* properly humble *and* properly confident. 'We proclaim not ourselves, but Jesus Christ as Lord, and ourselves as your servants through Jesus.'[12]

Third, following directly from this, the task of the church between ascension and *parousia* is therefore set free both from the self-driven energy that imagines it has to build God's kingdom all by itself, and the despair that supposes it can't do anything until Jesus comes again. We do not 'build the kingdom' all by ourselves, but we do build *for* the kingdom. All that we do in faith, hope and love in the present, in obedience to our ascended Lord and in the power of his Spirit, will be enhanced and transformed at his appearing.[13] This too brings a note of judgment, of course, as Paul makes clear in 1 Corinthians 3.10–17. The 'day' will disclose what sort of work each builder has done.

In particular, the present rule of the ascended Jesus Christ and the assurance of his final appearing in judgment should give us – which goodness knows we need today – some clarity and realism in our political discourse. Far too often Christians slide into a vaguely spiritualized version of one or other major political system or party. What would happen if we were to take seriously our stated belief that Jesus Christ is already the Lord of the world, and that at his name, one day, every knee would bow?

You might suppose that this would inject merely a note of pietism, and make us then avoid the real issues – or, indeed, to attempt a theocratic take-over bid. But to think in either of those ways would only show how deeply we have been conditioned by the Enlightenment split between religion and politics. What happens if we reintegrate them? As with specifically Christian work, so with political work done in Jesus' name: confessing Jesus as the ascended and coming Lord frees up the political task from the necessity to pretend that this or that programme or leader has the key to Utopia (if only we would elect him or her). Equally, it frees up our corporate life from the despair that comes when we realize that, once again, our political systems let us down. The ascension and appearing of Jesus constitute a radical challenge to the entire thought-structure of the Enlightenment (and of course several other movements). And, since our present western politics is very much the creation of the Enlightenment, we should think seriously about the ways in which, as thinking Christians, we can and should bring that challenge to bear. I know this is giving a huge hostage to fortune, raising questions to which I certainly don't know the answer, but I do know that unless I point all this out one might easily get the impression that these ancient doctrines are of theoretical or abstract interest only. They aren't. People who believe that Jesus is already Lord, and that he will appear again as judge of the world are called and equipped (to put it mildly) to think and act quite differently in the world from those who don't. I shall pursue these questions a bit further in the final Part of the book.

In particular, of course, the hope of Jesus' coming as judge, to put right all that is wrong in the world and to give new life to the dead, is the context for one of our central themes, to which we can at last turn. If all this is so, what can we say about the future that awaits every one of us, every baptized believer in Jesus Christ? What precisely do we mean, for ourselves, when we speak of the future resurrection?

10

The redemption of our bodies

1. Introduction

As we saw in the first two chapters, there is no agreement in the church today about what happens to people when they die. Not surprisingly, therefore, there is also confusion in the wider, non-Christian world not only about the fate of the dead but about *what Christians are supposed to believe* on the subject.

This is all the more curious in that the New Testament itself, which most churches officially regard as their primary doctrinal source, is crystal clear on the matter. In a classic passage, Paul speaks of 'the redemption of our bodies' (Romans 8.23). There is no room for doubt as to what he means: God's people are promised a new type of bodily existence, the fulfilment and redemption of our present bodily life. The rest of the early Christian writings, where they address the subject, are completely in tune with this.

This expression of hope, hope for the resurrection of the body, has however been so out of tune with several of the prevailing moods of Christian thought down the years that it has become muzzled, distorted and then not even known. In this chapter I shall lay out the basic picture of final bodily resurrection offered by the New Testament and the early fathers of the church, and explain how I think it can be re-emphasized today. This can be done the more briefly in that I am merely drawing together what I have set out in much more detail elsewhere.[1]

My proposition is that the traditional picture of people 'going to heaven' on the one hand or 'going to hell' on the other, as a one-stage post-mortem journey (with or without the option of some kind of 'purgatory' or 'continuing journey' as an intermediate stage), represents a serious distortion and diminution of the Christian hope. Bodily resurrection is not just one odd bit of that hope. It is the element which gives shape and meaning to the rest of the story we tell about God's ultimate purposes. If we squeeze it to the margins, as many have done by implication, or indeed if we leave it out altogether, as some have done quite explicitly, we don't just lose an extra component of the machine, like choosing to buy a car which happens not to have electrically operated mirrors. We lose the central engine which drives it and gives every other component its reason for working. Instead of talking vaguely about 'heaven', and then trying to fit the language of resurrection into that, we should talk with biblical precision about the resurrection, and reorganize our language about heaven around *that*. What is more, as I shall show in the final Part of this book, when we do this we discover an excellent foundation, not, as some suppose, for an escapist or quietist piety (that belongs more with the traditional and misleading language about 'heaven'), but for lively and creative Christian work within the present world.

2. Resurrection: life *after* 'life after death'

We saw in the second chapter that, whereas Greco-Roman paganism on the one hand and second-Temple Judaism on the other held a wide variety of beliefs about life beyond death, the early Christians were remarkably unanimous on the topic. There is space here only for a brief survey of the massive evidence.

We begin once more with Paul. I stressed in the previous chapter that when Paul speaks in Philippians 3 of being 'citizens of heaven', he doesn't mean that we shall retire there when we have finished our work here. He says in the next line that Jesus will come *from* heaven in order to transform the present humble body into a glorious body like his own; and that he will do this by the power through which he makes all things subject to himself. This little statement contains in a nutshell more or less all Paul's thought on the subject. The risen Jesus is both the *model* for the Christian's future body and the *means* by which it comes about.

Similarly in Colossians 3.1–4: when the Messiah appears, the one who is your life, then you too will appear with him in glory. Paul does not say 'one day you will go to be with him'. No; you already possess life in him. This new life which the Christian possesses secretly, invisible to the world, will burst forth into full bodily reality and visibility.

The clearest and strongest passage, often ignored, is Romans 8.9–11. If the Spirit of God, the Spirit of Jesus the Messiah, dwells in you, says Paul, then the one who raised the Messiah from the dead will give life to your mortal bodies as well, through his Spirit who dwells in you. God will give life, not to a disembodied spirit, not to what many people have thought of as a 'spiritual body' in the sense of a non-physical one, but 'to your mortal bodies also'.

Paul is not the only New Testament writer to hold this view. The first letter of John declares that when Jesus appears, we shall be like him, for we shall see him as he is.[2] The resurrection body of Jesus, which at the moment is almost unimaginable to us in its glory and power, will be the model for our own. And of course within John's gospel, despite the puzzlement of those who want to read the book in a very different way, we have some of the clearest statements of future bodily resurrection. Jesus reaffirms the widespread Jewish expectation of resurrection, and announces that the hour for this has already arrived. In the passage we glanced at in the previous chapter, it is quite explicit:

the hour is coming indeed, it is already here, when the dead
will hear the voice of the son of God, and those who hear will
live; when all in the graves will come out, those who have done
good, to the resurrection of life, and those who have done evil,
to the resurrection of judgment.[3]

This clearly depends on Daniel 12, and other passages such as
Isaiah 26 and Ezekiel 37. It exhibits a surface tension with the
position of Paul, who mostly seems to regard resurrection as
God's future gift by the Spirit for those who are in Christ, not
for everyone (though, as we shall see presently, 2 Corinthians
5.10 may indicate otherwise). Some of the early church fathers
enthusiastically follow John at this point, emphasizing that resurrection is necessary for the wicked as well so that they may
be judged in the body. To this we shall return.

Here we need to revisit a point we made earlier. What does
Jesus mean when he declares that there are 'many dwelling-
places' in his father's house?[4] This has regularly been taken,
not least when used in the context of bereavement, to mean
that the dead (or at least dead Christians) will simply go to
'heaven' permanently, rather than being raised again subsequently to new bodily life. But the word for 'dwelling-places'
here, *monai*, is regularly used in ancient Greek not for a final
resting place but for a temporary halt on a journey that will
take you somewhere else in the long run.

This fits closely with Jesus' words to the dying brigand in Luke:
'Today you will be with me in paradise.'[5] Despite a long tradition of misreading, 'paradise' is here, as in some other Jewish
writing, not a final destination, but the blissful garden, the park-
land of rest and tranquillity, where the dead are refreshed as
they await the dawn of the new day.[6] The main point of the
sentence lies in the apparent contrast between the brigand's
request and Jesus' reply: 'Remember me,' he says, '*when you
come in your kingdom*', implying (whether ironically or not
does not concern us here) that this will be at some far distant
future. Jesus' answer brings this future hope into the present,

implying of course that with his death the kingdom is indeed coming, even though it doesn't look like what anyone had imagined: '*Today* you will be with me in paradise.' There will still, of course, be a future completion involving ultimate resurrection; Luke's overall theological understanding leaves no doubt on that score. Jesus, after all, didn't rise again 'today', i.e., on Good Friday. Luke must have understood him to be referring to a state of being-in-paradise which would be true, for him and for the man dying beside him, at once, that very day – in other words, *prior to the resurrection*. With Jesus the future hope has come forwards into the present. For those who die in faith, before that final reawakening, the central promise is of being 'with Jesus' at once. 'My desire is to depart', wrote Paul, 'and be with Christ, which is far better.'[7]

'Resurrection' itself then appears as what the word always meant, whether (like the ancient pagans) people disbelieved it, or whether (like many ancient Jews) they affirmed it. It wasn't a way of talking about 'life after death'. It was a way of talking about a new bodily life *after* whatever state of existence one might enter immediately upon death. It was, in other words, life *after* 'life after death'.

What then about such passages as 1 Peter 1, which speak of a salvation that is 'kept in heaven for you', so that in your present believing you are receiving 'the salvation of your souls'? Here, I suggest, the automatic assumption of western Christianity leads us badly astray. Most Christians today, reading a passage like this, assume that it means that heaven is where you go to receive this 'salvation' – or even that 'salvation' *consists in* 'going to heaven when you die'. This then provides a dangerously distorted framework within which some of the key gospel sayings are interpreted, such as those in Matthew where Jesus talks of 'entering the kingdom of heaven', or 'having a reward in heaven', or of 'storing up riches in heaven'. Quite simply, the way we now understand that language in the western world at least is totally different from what Jesus and his hearers would have meant and understood.

For a start, 'heaven' is actually a reverent way of speaking about God, so that 'riches in heaven' simply means 'riches in God's presence' (as we see when, elsewhere, Jesus talks about someone being, or not being, 'rich towards God').[8] But then, by derivation from this primary meaning, 'heaven' is the place where *God's purposes for the future are stored up*. It isn't where they are meant to stay, so that one would need to go to heaven to enjoy them; it is where they are kept safe against the day when they will become a reality on earth. If I say to a friend 'I've kept some beer in the fridge for you', that doesn't mean that he has to get into the fridge in order to drink the beer. God's future inheritance, the incorruptible new world and the new bodies that are to inhabit that world, are already kept safe, waiting for us, not so that we can go to heaven and put them on there, but so that they can be brought to birth in this world, or rather in the new heavens and new earth, the renewed world of which I spoke earlier.

We should note as well, in relation to the passage in 1 Peter and some others, that the language of the 'soul' is rare in this sense in the early Christian writings. The word *psychē* was very common in the ancient world, and carried a variety of meanings. Despite its frequency both in later Christianity and (for instance) in Buddhism, the New Testament doesn't use it to describe, so to speak, 'the bit of you that will ultimately be saved'. The word *psychē* seems here to refer, like the Hebrew *nephesh*, not to a disembodied inner part of the human being, but to what we might call the 'person' or even the 'personality'. And the point in 1 Peter 1 is that this 'person', the 'real you', is *already* being saved, and will one day receive that salvation in full bodily form. That is why Peter quite rightly plants the hope for salvation firmly in the resurrection of Jesus. God has, he says, 'given us new birth to a living hope by the resurrection of Jesus the Messiah from the dead'.[9]

3. Resurrection in Corinth

All discussions of the future resurrection must sooner or later do business with Paul, and particularly with his two letters to Corinth. These are tricky and controversial, and I've spent a long time elsewhere going through them in detail. Let me simply sum up the main argument, working back from 2 Corinthians to 1 Corinthians.[10]

The passage about resurrection in 2 Corinthians 4 and 5 comes within Paul's long and passionate description of his own apostleship. He speaks of his ministry in terms of 'having treasure in jars of clay, to show that what matters is God's power and not his own'. To give substance to this, he spells out the future hope within which the present life of ambiguity and suffering makes sense. If all we had were the final verses of chapter 4, it might have been possible to say, and some still try to argue this, that Paul was referring to a future hope in which the body would be left behind and a pure spirit would remain: 'the outer nature', he says, 'is wasting away, but the inner nature is being renewed day by day.' Is this not three-quarters of the way down the road to Plato, eager to be done with the perishable mortal body and to be left with the glorious, immortal and disembodied soul?

Certainly not. In chapter 5 Paul speaks of the new 'tent' or 'tabernacle' which is waiting for us. There is a new house, a new dwelling, a new body, waiting within God's sphere (again, 'heaven'), ready for us to put it on over the present one, so that what is mortal may be swallowed up with life. As always, so here, Paul insists that God will accomplish this by the Spirit.

This is the point at which we modern westerners are called to make a huge leap of the imagination. We have been buying our mental furniture for so long in Plato's factory that we have come to take for granted a basic ontological contrast between 'spirit' in the sense of something immaterial and 'matter' in the sense of something material, solid, 'physical'. We think we know that solid objects are one sort of thing, and ideas, or values, or spirits, or ghosts, are a different sort of thing (often not noticing that they are themselves all rather different sorts of things). We know that bodies decay and die; that houses, temples, cities and civilizations fall to dust; and so we assume that to be bodily, to be physical, is to be impermanent, changeable, transitory, and that the only way to be permanent, unchanging and immortal is to become non-physical.

Paul's point here is that this is not so. Actually, it wasn't so even in the dominant cosmology of his day, which was Stoic rather than Platonic. Still less was it so within the Jewish creation theology which formed the seedbed out of which, because of the resurrection of Jesus himself, Paul grew his theology of new creation.[11] Paul is making his Corinthian readers think in new patterns, and he has the same effect on us.

What Paul is asking us to imagine is that there will be a new mode of physicality which stands in relation to our present body as our present body does to a ghost. It will be as much more real, more firmed up, more *bodily*, than our present body as our present body is more substantial, more touchable, than a disembodied spirit. We sometimes speak of someone who's been very ill as being 'a shadow of their former self'. If Paul is right, a Christian in the present life is a mere shadow of his or her *future* self, the self they will be when the body which God has waiting in his heavenly storeroom is brought out, already made to measure, and put on over the present one – or over the self that will still exist after bodily death. This is where one of the great Easter hymns gets it exactly right:

> O how glorious and resplendent
> Fragile body, shalt thou be,
> When endued with so much beauty,
> Full of health, and strong, and free!
> Full of vigour, full of pleasure,
> That shall last eternally.[12]

Paul is anxious not to pretend he has already attained this state. Indeed, he is anxious to stress that the present work of an apostle involves him precisely in sharing the weakness and suffering of the present state of the world. But his point is that we must all appear before the judgment seat of the Messiah (2 Corinthians 5.10); and for that we shall need bodies. Here Paul, like John, is on track with Daniel 12 and other similar Jewish texts. Indeed, it may be at this point that Paul hints after all at a re-surrection of the wicked (in order to be judged in the body) as well as of the righteous.

This brings us to the heart of the New Testament view of the resurrection, 1 Corinthians 15.

The hope of resurrection underlies the whole of 1 Corinthians, not just chapter 15. But here Paul addresses it head on as of central importance. Some in Corinth have denied the future resurrection, almost certainly on the normal pagan grounds that everyone knew dead people didn't rise again. In reply, Paul speaks, as we saw in the previous chapter, of Jesus as the first fruits, and of the great harvest still to come when all Jesus' people are raised as he has been.

The whole chapter echoes and alludes to Genesis 1—3. It is a theology of new creation, not of the abandonment of creation. The heart of the chapter is an exposition of the two different types of bodies, the present one and the future one. This is where all sorts of problems have arisen.

Several popular translations, notably the Revised Standard Version and its offshoots, have translated Paul's key phrases as 'a physical body' and 'a spiritual body'.[13] Simply in terms of the Greek words Paul uses, this cannot be correct. The technical arguments are overwhelming and conclusive. The contrast is between the present body, corruptible, decaying and doomed to die, and the future body, incorruptible, undecaying, never to die again. The key adjectives, which are quoted endlessly in discussions of this topic, do not refer to a 'physical' body and a 'non-physical' one, which is how people in our culture are bound to hear the words 'physical' and 'spiritual'.

The first word, *psychikos*, does not in any case mean anything like 'physical' in our sense. For Greek-speakers of Paul's day, the *psychē*, from which the word derives, means the soul, not the body.

But the deeper, underlying point is that adjectives of this type, Greek adjectives ending in *-ikos*, do not describe *the material out of which things are made*, but *the power or energy which animates them*. It is the difference between asking on the one hand 'is this a wooden ship or an iron ship?' (the material from which it is made) and asking on the other 'is this a steam ship or a sailing ship?' (the energy which empowers it). Paul is talking about the present body, which is animated by the normal human *psychē* (the life-force we all possess here and now, which gets us through the present life but is ultimately powerless against illness, injury, decay and death), and the future body which is animated by God's *pneuma*, God's breath of new life, the energizing power of God's new creation.

This is why, in a further phrase which became controversial as early as the mid-second century, Paul declares that 'flesh and blood cannot inherit God's kingdom'.[14] He doesn't mean that physicality will be abolished. 'Flesh and blood' is a technical term for that which is corruptible, transient, heading for death. The contrast, again, is not between what we call physical and what we call non-physical, but between *corruptible physicality* on the one hand and *non-corruptible physicality* on the other.

This underlies the remarkable concluding verse of 1 Corinthians 15, to which we shall return. For Paul, the bodily resurrection does not leave us saying 'so that's all right; we shall go, at the last, to join Jesus in a non-bodily, Platonic heaven', but 'so, then, since the person you are and the world God has made will be gloriously reaffirmed in God's eventual future, you must be steadfast, immovable, always abounding in the Lord's work, because you know that in the Lord your labour is not in vain.' Belief in the bodily resurrection includes the belief that what is done in the present in the body, by the power of the Spirit, will be reaffirmed in the eventual future, in ways at which we can presently only guess.

4. Resurrection: later debates

There were of course all kinds of debates and further discussions about the bodily resurrection in the second century and beyond.[15] What is remarkable is that, apart from the small corpus of gnostic and semi-gnostic writings, the early fathers at least as far as Origen insisted on this doctrine, though the pressures on them to abandon it must have been very great. Ignatius of Antioch, Justin Martyr, Athenagoras, Irenaeus, Tertullian – all of them stress bodily resurrection.

What is more, they all link this doctrine very closely to two others which enable them to stand out against all kinds of other teachings, not least docetism and gnosticism: first, the doctrine of creation, and second the doctrine of God's justice and final judgment. As in Judaism, resurrection is the point where creation and judgment meet. Where one is abandoned, for whatever reason, the others soon follow.

With Tertullian in particular, we start to find questions about what precisely bodily resurrection will involve. (Some of these questions are also raised in the rabbinic sources which were wrestling with similar problems around the same time.) Suppose a cannibal eats a Christian; and suppose the cannibal is then himself converted. The Christian's body has become part of the cannibal's body; who will have which bits at the resurrection?

Tertullian gives a brusque answer. It's God's business, he says; he's the creator, so he can and will sort it out. Origen, faced with similar questions, replies more subtly. Our bodies, he points out, are in any case in a state of flux. It isn't just that hair and fingernails grow, and are cut off; our entire physical substance is slowly changing. What we today call atoms and molecules pass through us, leaving us with continuity of form but transience of matter. (C. S. Lewis, summarizing this argument, offers an illustration: I am in that respect, he says, like a curve in a waterfall.[16]) This argument is repeated by Thomas Aquinas a millennium after Origen and nearly a millennium before Lewis. It's a good argument: as we now know, we change our entire physical kit, every atom and molecule, over a period of, at most, every seven years or so. I am physically a totally different person now from the person I was ten years ago. And yet I am still me. Thus it really doesn't matter whether we get the identical molecules back or not, though some continuity is perfectly possible. The ones we use for a while have been used by other organisms before us, and will be used by others when we are done with them. Dust we are, and to dust we shall return. But God can do new things with dust.

Many of the leading theologians in the Patristic and medieval periods were quite clear about the two-stage post-mortem future. Gregory the Great (540–604), for instance, taught that the soul of the dead Christian enjoys the beatific vision while still awaiting the resurrection of the body. Anselm (1033–1109) stressed that our resurrection bodies will transcend our present bodies in a new kind of being. The Victorine theologians, following Hugh of St-Victor (d. 1142), taught that the resurrection body will be identical with our earthly body but transfigured:

> it will be immune from death and sorrow; it will be at the height of its powers, free from disease and deformity, and around thirty years old, the age at which Christ began his ministry. It will surpass anything we can imagine, even from the accounts of Christ's appearances on earth after his own resurrection.[17]

Mainstream medieval theologians like Thomas and Bernard insisted on the bodily resurrection. They, like the New Testament and the fathers, held a strong view of God's good creation. They knew that it must be reaffirmed, not abandoned. But a good deal of western medieval piety then took a very different turn, in which the twin destinations of heaven and hell, and the possible intermediate destination of purgatory, became far more important, and in which the language of 'resurrection', in so far as it was retained at all, seemed simply to be a rather special way of talking about 'heaven', which was the primary category. This has had all kinds of unfortunate results, to which we shall come in a moment. But first we must draw out and underline the key elements of the early Christian view of the resurrection, and consider how we can reappropriate it for today.

5. Rethinking resurrection today: who, where, what, why, when and how

Who will be raised from the dead? All people, according to John and perhaps Paul; but for Paul at least there is a special sense of resurrection which clearly applies to those who are in Christ and indwelt by the Spirit. This raises other questions which we shall have to address in the next chapter.

Where will the resurrection take place? On the new earth, joined as it will then be to the new heaven. That has been the burden of my song in the shape and argument of this whole Part of the book. In this new world there will be no problem of overcrowding (as some, at the risk of bathos, have ventured to suggest). Apart from the question of whether every human will be raised or only some, we need to remind ourselves that roughly half the humans who have ever lived are alive at the moment. World population has grown at an enormous rate in the last century; we easily forget that for much of history huge tracts of land have been hardly inhabited at all. Even the civilized and somewhat crowded cities of biblical times were mostly, by today's standards, like small market towns. In any case, if we take seriously the promise of new heavens and new earth, none of this is a problem. God is the creator, and his new world will be exactly what we need and want, with the love and beauty of this present world taken up and transformed.

More fully, then, what precisely will the resurrection body be? Here I pay homage again to one of the few modern writers who has tried to help us with the task of *imagining* what the risen body might be like: C. S. Lewis. In a variety of places, but particularly in his remarkable book *The Great Divorce*, he manages to get us to envisage bodies that are more solid, more real, more substantial than our present ones.[18] That is the task that 2 Corinthians in particular invites us to. These will be bodies of which the phrase 'the weight of glory', taken from that letter (4.17), will be seen, felt and known to be appropriate.

Further questions were asked in the ancient world at this point, and often re-emerge in contemporary discussion. Which of our present characteristics, and indeed present blemishes, will be retained in the transformed physicality? When I taught a course on resurrection at Harvard in 1999, one of my students complained, in her term paper, that since she had never liked the shape of her nose she hoped she wouldn't have to put up with it in a future life as well. There is no way we can answer such questions. All we can surmise from the picture of Jesus' resurrection is that, just as his wounds were still visible, not now as sources of pain and death but as signs of his victory, so the Christian's risen body will bear such marks of his or her loyalty to God's particular calling as are appropriate, not least where that has involved suffering.

In particular, this new body will be immortal. That is, it will have passed *beyond* death, not just in the *temporal* sense (that it happens to have gone through a particular moment and event), but in the *ontological* sense of no longer being subject to sickness, injury, decay and death itself. None of these destructive forces will have any power over the new body. That, indeed, may be one of the ways of understanding the *strange-*

ness of the risen body of Jesus. The disciples were looking at the first, and so far the only, piece of incorruptible physicality.

At this point we must notice that, once again, our language gets us into trouble. The word 'immortality' has often been used to mean '*disembodied* immortality', and it has sometimes then been used in a sharp contrast with 'resurrection'. As a result, we easily forget Paul's point about the resurrection body. It will be a body; but it will not be subject to mortality. An 'immortal body' is something most people find so strange that they don't even pause to wonder if that's what Paul and the other early Christians were talking about. But it is.

There is a world of difference between this belief and a belief in an 'immortal soul'. Platonists believe that all humans have an immortal element within them, normally referred to as 'soul'. (Having praised C. S. Lewis, I should say that he seems to fall into this trap.) In the New Testament, however, 'immortality' is something which only God possesses by nature, and which he then shares, as a gift of grace rather than an innate possession, with his people.[19]

Why will we be given new bodies? According to the early Christians, the purpose of this new body will be to rule wisely over God's new world. Forget those images about lounging around playing harps. There will be work to do and we shall relish doing it. All the skills and talents which we have put to God's service in this present life – and perhaps, too, the interests and likings we gave up because they conflicted with our vocation – will be enhanced and ennobled and given back to us to be exercised to his glory. This is perhaps the most mysterious, and least explored, aspect of the resurrection life. But there are several promises in the New Testament about God's people 'reigning', and these cannot just be empty words.[20] If, as we have already seen, the biblical view of God's future is of the renewal of the entire cosmos, there will be plenty to be done, entire new projects to undertake. In terms of the vision of original creation in Genesis 1 and 2, the garden will need to be tended once more, and the animals renamed. These are only images, of course, but like all other future-oriented language they serve as true signposts to a larger reality – a reality to which most Christians give little or no thought.

The new body will be a gift of God's grace and love. However, there are several passages in the New Testament, not least in the words of Jesus himself, which speak of God's future blessings in terms of *reward* (a further kind of answer, in other words, to the question 'why'). Many Christians find this uncomfortable. Not only have we been taught that we are justified by faith, not works. Somehow, the very idea of being a Christian for what we will get out of it is distasteful.

But the image of reward in the New Testament doesn't work like that. It isn't a matter of calculation, of doing a difficult job in order to be paid a wage. It is much more like working at a friendship, or a marriage, in order to enjoy the other person's company more fully. It is more like practising golf in order that we can go out on the course and hit the ball in the right direction. It is more like learning German or Greek so that we can read some of the great poets and philosophers who wrote in those languages. The 'reward' is *organically connected to the activity*, not some kind of arbitrary pat on the back, otherwise unrelated to the work that has been done. And it is always far in abundance beyond any sense of direct or equivalent payment. The reward of being able to read and enjoy Homer for the rest of your life is way beyond any kind of one-for-one 'payment' for the slog of learning Greek. As we have already seen and shall pick up again later, all this relates directly to what Paul says in 1 Corinthians 15.58: the resurrection means that what you do in the present, in working hard for the gospel, is not wasted. It is not in vain. It will be completed, will have its fulfilment, in God's future.

When will the resurrection happen? Some have supposed that we go, immediately upon death, into the resurrection state.[21] I find that very difficult. Paul says that, if Christ is the first fruits, those who belong to him will be raised 'at his coming' – which clearly hasn't happened yet. The book of Revelation speaks, as do many Jewish writings of the period, of the dead waiting patiently, and sometimes not so patiently, for the time when they will finally be raised to new life.[22] This intermediate state, in fact, is more or less a constant feature of resurrection belief both Jewish and Christian.

In particular, if it is true (as I argued earlier) that the new creation will be in important senses continuous with the present one, we cannot think that it has already arrived, any more than it would have made sense for Jesus' resurrection body to be already alive and active before his crucifixion. The new is the *transformation*, not merely the replacement, of the old. And since the old is quite obviously not yet transformed, the resurrection, its central feature, cannot yet have happened. Time matters; it was part of the original good creation. Though it may well itself be transformed in ways we cannot at present even begin to imagine, we should not allow ourselves to be seduced by the language of 'eternity' (as in the phrase 'eternal life', which in the New Testament regularly refers, not to a non-temporal future existence but to 'the life of the coming age') into imagining, as one old song puts it, that 'time shall be no more'.[23] No: 'the old field of space, time, matter and the senses is to be weeded, dug, and sown for a new crop. We may be tired of that old field: God is not.'[24]

How will it happen? As John Polkinghorne and others have urged, what we are talking about is a great act of new creation. Polkinghorne, in fact, offers a contemporary metaphor which I find appealing (but which, I have discovered, some people find appalling). He, of course, puts it in a much more nuanced way, but I don't think it's too much of a caricature to express it like this: God will download our software onto his hardware, until the time when he gives us new hardware to run the software again.[25] Paul says that God will give us new bodies; there may well be some bodily continuity, as with Jesus himself, but

God is well capable of recreating people even if (as with the martyrs of Lyons) their ashes are scattered into a fast-flowing river.

Whenever the question of 'how' is raised in the early Christian writings, the answer comes back: by the Spirit. The Spirit who brooded over the waters of chaos, the Spirit who indwelt Jesus so richly that it became known as the Spirit *of* Jesus: this Spirit, already present within Jesus' followers as the first fruits, the down payment, the guarantee of what is to come, is not only the beginning of the future life, even in the present time, but also the energizing power through which the final transformation will take place. The early creed spoke of 'the Holy Spirit, the Lord *and giver of life*'. That is exactly true to the New Testament.

All this raises in an acute form the question: so where are the dead right now? How should we think of them?

11

Purgatory, paradise, hell

1. Introduction

Before the sixteenth century, most western Christians thought of the church as divided into three parts. First there was the church triumphant, consisting of the saints, the holy souls, who had already arrived at the beatific vision of God. Officially they were still awaiting the final resurrection; but increasingly that wasn't emphasized, and in many medieval portrayals it has dropped out altogether. Think of Dante, and the medieval mystery plays. There was such a place as heaven; some souls had already made it there, and they were therefore to be thought of as 'saints'; they were in the presence of God; what more could they want?

Within this picture, some saints had got there by the direct route, immediately upon death, while others had arrived in 'heaven' after a period elsewhere, to which we shall come presently. But, once there, such saints could act as friends at court for those already on the way. And these triumphant saints had their own celebration: All Saints' Day.

At the other end was the church militant. ('Militant' means 'fighting', in the sense of 'fighting the good fight of faith', as in 1 Timothy.[1]) This is, of course, the company of God's people in the present life, about whom we are not presently concerned.

In between was the church 'expectant', that is, 'waiting'; and the place where they were waiting was purgatory. This is a complex topic and needs further examination.

2. Purgatory

Purgatory is basically a Roman Catholic doctrine. It is not held as such in the Eastern Orthodox Church, and it was decisively rejected, on biblical and theological grounds and not merely because of antipathy to particular abuses, at the Reformation. The main statements of purgatory come from Aquinas in the thirteenth century and Dante in the early fourteenth, but the notion became woven deeply into the entire psyche of the whole period.[2] Huge energy was expended in the late medieval period in developing the picture of purgatory and rearranging present Christian life around it. Most Christians, it was taught, remain sinful in some measure right up to death; they therefore need both punishment and purging, though they can be helped through this time by the prayers, and especially the masses, of the church militant. It was as an outcrop from this that the sale of indulgences was invented in the early sixteenth century, to the horror not only of Martin Luther but of several other Roman Catholic theologians of the day.

The poetic and dramatic power of the idea of purgatory is evident both from Dante seven hundred years ago and, closer to our time, from works like Cardinal Newman's famous *Dream of Gerontius*, set to music even more famously by Elgar. This vision, and the teaching which goes with it, still forms the staple diet of a large part of the Roman Church, and of some others that look to it for a lead. But in the last generation two major and central Roman teachers have expounded very different views.

Karl Rahner, who died in 1984, attempted to combine Roman and Eastern teaching on the place of the soul between death and resurrection. Instead of concentrating on what he saw as the over-individualized concern with the fate of a particular soul, he supposed that after death souls became more closely united with the cosmos as a whole, through which process, while still awaiting the resurrection, the soul is more aware of the effects of its own sin on the world in general. This, he thought, is purgatory enough.[3]

More remarkable still is the view of Cardinal Ratzinger, now Pope Benedict XVI. Building on 1 Corinthians 3, he argued that the Lord himself is the fire of judgment which transforms us as he conforms us to his glorious, resurrected body. This happens, not during a long-drawn-out process, but in the moment of final judgment itself. By thus linking purgatory to Jesus Christ himself as the eschatological fire, Ratzinger detaches the doctrine of purgatory from the concept of an intermediate state, and breaks the link that, in the Middle Ages, gave rise to the idea of indulgences and so provided a soft target for Protestant polemic. Whatever we think of that, it is clear that two of the most central, important and conservative Roman theologians of the last generation have offered a quite radical climb-down from Aquinas, Dante, Newman and all that went in between.[4]

At the same time, however – and this is where many Anglicans come in – there has been a tendency in much twentieth-century theology to soft-pedal the 'sure and certain hope' spoken of so enthusiastically by the Reformers. It seems (we are often told) very arrogant. If we know our own hearts, and those of the people to whom we minister, we know that we are not ready for final bliss. In addition, the tendency towards universalism so evident in the last hundred years of Protestant thinking has produced a new situation, where not only professed Christians, but the mass of professed non-Christians, are going to have to be got ready for salvation in the time after death. Like a badly sprung double bed, this has propelled the people who used to be positioned at either side, in either heaven or hell, into an uneasy huddle in the middle. Non-Christians, in this view, will continue after death to pursue whatever 'journey' they have been on up till then, until they eventually come round to accepting God's salvation. Christians, likewise, will continue the 'journey' they have been on, proceeding by unhurried steps through uncharted spiritual country until they, too, arrive at the goal. Sometimes, as in the American Prayer Book, this process is spoken of as 'growth' – though why that metaphor is preferred to others is not clear. We thus have a sort of purgatory-for-all. It isn't very unpleasant, and it's certainly not punitive – since the liberalism that gives rise to these ideas doesn't make much fuss of sin, and certainly doesn't want to think it needed or needs to be punished.[5]

Purgatory, in either its classic or its modern form, provides the rationale for All Souls' Day (2 November), a tenth-century Benedictine innovation. This commemoration assumes a sharp distinction between the 'saints', who are already in heaven, and the 'souls', who aren't, and who are therefore still less than completely happy, and need our help (as we say today) to 'move on'. The double commemoration of All Saints and All Souls stands on the foundation of this radical distinction. It is this that I now want to challenge.

There are four points to be made.

First, as I said earlier, the resurrection is still in the future. This is the official view of all mainstream orthodox theologians, Catholic and Protestant, East and West, except for those who think that after death we pass into an eternity in which all moments are present. We should recall in particular that the use of the word 'heaven' to denote the *ultimate* goal of the redeemed, though of course hugely popularized by medieval and subsequent piety, is severely misleading and does not begin to do justice to the Christian hope. I am repeatedly frustrated by how hard it is to get this point through the thick wall of traditional thought and language that most Christians put up. The ultimate destination is (once more) *not* 'going to heaven when you die', but being bodily raised into the transformed, glorious likeness of Jesus Christ. (The point of all this is not, of course, merely our own happy future, important though that is, but the glory of God as we come fully to reflect his image.) Thus, if we want to speak of 'going to heaven when we die', we should be clear that this represents the first, and far less important, stage of a two-stage process. Resurrection isn't 'life after death'; it is life *after* 'life after death'.

Second, there is no reason in the New Testament to suppose that there are any category distinctions between different Christians in heaven as they await the resurrection. In the early Christian writings, all Christians are 'saints', including the muddled and sinful Corinthians. When Paul speaks of his desire 'to depart and be with Christ, for that is far better', he isn't suggesting that he is going to be 'with Christ' while less proficient Christians will have an interim waiting period.[6] He will not, in that sense, be with the 'saints' *while the 'souls' are somewhere else.* This is recognized in Eastern Orthodoxy, which celebrates the saints in all sorts of ways, but doesn't imagine that they have already obtained final bliss. They won't until we all do. That's why the Orthodox pray *for* the saints as well as with them.

The only passage in the New Testament which makes any kind of distinction at this point is 1 Corinthians 3, which speaks of Christian workers who build with gold, silver and precious stones, and others who build with wood, hay and stubble. But Paul doesn't say that the one group will go straight to 'heaven' while the others go to purgatory. Both will be saved; the same destination awaits both; but the first group will arrive gloriously, the second by the skin of their teeth. This is a solemn passage, to be taken very seriously by Christian workers and teachers, but, as the Pope now appears to acknowledge, it doesn't indicate that there is a difference of status, or of celestial geography, or of temporal progression, between one category of Christians after death and another.

In fact, there are so many things said in the New Testament about the greatest becoming least and the least becoming greatest that we shouldn't be surprised at this lack of distinction between the post-mortem state of different Christians. I appreciate that it may be hard for some to come to terms with this, but in the light of the basic and central Christian gospel, the message and achievement of Jesus, and the preaching of Paul and the others, there is no reason whatever to say, for instance, that Peter or Paul, Aidan or Cuthbert, or even, dare I say, the mother of Jesus herself, are more 'advanced', closer to God, have achieved more spiritual 'growth', or whatever, than those Christians who have been martyred in our own day, or indeed those who have died quietly in their beds. If we are to be true to our foundation charter, we must say that all Christians, living and departed, are to be thought of as 'saints'; and that all Christians who have died are to be thought of, and treated, as such.

Third, therefore, I do not believe in purgatory as a place, a time or a state. It was in any case a late western innovation, without biblical support, and its supposed theological foundations are now questioned, as we saw, by leading Roman Catholic theologians themselves. As the Reformers insisted, bodily death itself is the destruction of the sinful person. Someone once accused me of suggesting that God was a magician if he could wonderfully make a still-sinful person into a no-longer-sinful person, just like that. But that's not the point. Death itself gets rid of all that is still sinful; this isn't magic, but good theology. There is nothing then left to purge. Some older teachers suggested that purgatory would still be necessary because one would still need to bear some punishment for one's sins, but any such suggestion is of course abhorrent to anyone with even a faint understanding of Paul, who teaches that 'there is no condemnation for those who are in Christ'.[7]

The last great paragraph of Romans 8, so often and so appropriately read at funerals, leaves no room for purgatory in any form:

> Who shall lay any charge against us . . . who shall condemn us . . . who shall separate us from the love of Christ? Neither death nor life nor anything in all creation shall be able to separate us from the love of God in Christ Jesus our Lord.[8]

And if you still want to say that Paul really meant 'though of course you'll probably have to go through purgatory first', I think with great respect that you ought to see, not a theologian, but a therapist.

In fact, Paul makes it clear here and elsewhere that it's the *present* life that is meant to function as a purgatory. The sufferings of the present time, not of some post-mortem state, are the valley through which we have to pass in order to reach the glorious future. I think I know why purgatory became so popular, why Dante's middle volume is the one people most easily relate to. *The myth of purgatory is an allegory, a projection, from the present on to the future.* This is why purgatory appeals to the imagination. It is our story, here and now. If we are Christians, if we believe in the risen Jesus as Lord, if we are baptized members of his body, then we are passing right now through the sufferings which form the gateway to life. Of course, this means that for millions of our theological and spiritual ancestors death will have brought a pleasant surprise. They had been gearing themselves up for a long struggle ahead, only to find it was already over.

The revival of a quasi-purgatory in our own day, therefore, is beside the point. It is a strange return to mythology, just when we should be having our feet on the ground. It is ironic that in some circles the aim seems to be to sidle up to Rome in a friendly way, at the very moment when two of the leading conservative theologians in Rome, Rahner and Ratzinger, have been transforming the doctrine into something else. It's time for a deep breath, some clear thinking, and a sigh of relief.

3. Paradise

I therefore arrive, fourthly, at this view: that all the Christian departed are in substantially the same state, that of restful happiness. Though this is sometimes described as 'sleep', we shouldn't take this to mean that it is a state of unconsciousness.

Had Paul thought that, I very much doubt that he would have described life immediately after death as 'being with Christ, which is far better'. Rather, 'sleep' here means that the *body* is 'asleep' in the sense of 'dead', while the real person – however we want to describe him or her – continues.

This state is not, clearly, the final destiny for which the Christian dead are bound, which is as we have seen the bodily resurrection. But it is a state in which the dead are held firmly within the conscious love of God and the conscious presence of Jesus Christ, while they await that day. There is no reason why this state should not be called 'heaven', though we must note once more how interesting it is that the New Testament routinely doesn't call it that, and uses the word 'heaven' in other ways.

An important point follows from all this. Since both the departed saints and we ourselves are in Christ, we share with them in the 'Communion of Saints'. They are still our brothers and sisters in Christ. When we celebrate the eucharist they are there with us, along with the angels and archangels. Why then should we not pray for and with them? The reason the Reformers and their successors did their best to outlaw 'praying for the dead' was because that had been so bound up with the notion of purgatory, and the need to get people out of it as soon as possible. Once we rule out purgatory, I see no reason why we should not pray for and with the dead, and every reason why we should – not that they will get out of purgatory, but that they will be refreshed, and filled with God's joy and peace. Love passes into prayer; we still love them; why not hold them, in that love, before God?

I do not, however, find in the New Testament, or in the earliest Christian fathers, any suggestion that those at present in 'heaven' or (if you prefer) 'paradise' are actively engaged in praying *for* those of us in the present life. Nor do I find any suggestion that Christians who are still alive should pray to the 'saints' to intercede to the father on their behalf. I know that I touch here on a sensitive nerve within the devotional habits of many Christians, but I think this point of view deserves to be heard. It is true that, if the Christian dead are conscious, and if they are 'with Christ' in a sense which, as Paul implies, is closer than we ourselves are at the moment, there is every reason to suppose that they are at least, like the souls under the altar in Revelation, urging the father to complete the work of justice and salvation in the world. If that is so, there is no reason in principle why they should not urge the father similarly on our behalf. Or if, from another point of view, they are indeed 'with Christ', and if part of the work of the ascended Christ is indeed to be ruling the world as the agent of his father, we might indeed suppose that the dead are somehow involved in that, not merely as spectators of that ongoing work. But – and this is very important for those who, like me, believe that it's vital to ground one's beliefs in scripture itself – I see no evidence in the early Christian writings to suggest that the Christian dead are in fact engaged in work of that sort, still less any suggestion that presently alive Christians should, so to speak, encourage them to do it by invoking them specifically.

In particular, we should be very suspicious of the medieval idea that the 'saints' can function as 'friends at court', so that, while we might be shy of approaching the King ourselves, we know someone who is, as it were, 'one of us', to whom we can talk freely and who will maybe put in a good word for us. The practice seems to me to call into question, and even to deny by implication, the immediacy of access to God through Jesus Christ and in the Spirit which is promised again and again in the New Testament. In the New Testament it is clear: because of Christ and the Spirit, every single Christian is welcome at any time to come before the father himself. If you have a royal welcome awaiting you in the throne room, for whatever may be on your heart and mind, whether great or small, why would you bother hanging around the outer lobby trying to persuade someone there, however distinguished, to go in and ask for you?

To question this, even by implication, is to challenge one of the central blessings and privileges of the gospel.

Explicit invocation of saints may be, in fact – I do not say it always is, but it may be – a step towards that semi-paganism of which the Reformers were rightly afraid. The world of late Roman antiquity found it difficult to rid its collective imagination of the many-layered panoply of gods and lords, of demigods and heroes, that had been collecting in the culture for well over a thousand years. The second-century church began, quite understandably, to venerate the martyrs as special witnesses to the victory of Christ over death. Once Christianity had become established, and persecution ceased, it was not a large transition to nominate for veneration others who, though not martyred, had nevertheless been notable Christians in whatever way. But the whole process of developing not only hierarchies among such people but also elaborate systems for designating them (canonization and the like) seems to me a huge exercise in missing the point.

So then: instead of the three divisions of the medieval church – triumphant, expectant and militant – I believe that there are only two. The church in heaven/paradise is both triumphant and expectant. I do not expect all my readers to agree with this conclusion, but I would urge them at least to search the scriptures and see whether these things be so. And in particular I urge those whose churches, like my own, have revived the practice of All Souls' commemorations, not least those who find them pastorally helpful, to think seriously about the theology they are, at least implicitly, embracing and teaching. The appropriate times for remembering the Christian dead, and for doing so in a way which expresses genuine Christian hope, are Easter on the one hand and All Saints on the other. To add other commemorations detracts from the meaning of those great festivals. Here, as in some other points of theology and liturgy, more is less.

These are of course matters of detail, applying to some churches but not all. But all churches are rightly concerned, at least from time to time, with addressing the questions of what happens immediately after death, as well as the ultimate future. Without some reflection on these matters, which have been so central and contentious within the tradition, our discussions will be impoverished and run the risk of repeating old mistakes. The important thing is that we grasp the central hope of the ultimate resurrection, set within the new creation itself, and that we reorder all our thinking and speaking about every other 'after-death' question in that light.

4. Beyond hope, beyond pity

Whenever I have spoken about these issues over the last decade or so, someone always asks, 'what about hell?' This question really demands a book to itself, and I am torn between my lack of desire to write such a book and my recognition that one must at least say something.

Part of the difficulty of the topic, as with the others we have been studying, is that the word 'hell' itself conjures up an image gained more from medieval imagery than from the earliest Christian writings. Just as many who were brought up to think of God as a bearded old gentleman sitting on a cloud decided that, when they stopped believing in such a being, they had therefore 'stopped believing in God', so many who were taught to think of hell as a literal underground location full of worms and fire, or for that matter as a kind of torture chamber at the centre of God's castle of heavenly delights, decided that, when they stopped believing in that, so they stopped believing in hell. The first group decided that, because they couldn't believe in childish images of God, they must be atheists. The second decided that, because they couldn't believe in childish images of hell, they must be universalists.

There are of course better reasons for becoming an atheist, and better reasons for becoming a universalist. Many who occupy one of those positions have gone by a much more sophisticated route than the ones I have described. But, at least at a popular level, it is not the serious early Christian doctrine of final judgment that has been rejected, but one or other gross caricature.

The most common New Testament word sometimes translated as 'hell' is *Gehenna*. Gehenna was a place, not just an idea: it was the rubbish heap outside the south-west corner of the old city of Jerusalem. There is to this day a valley at that point which bears the name *Ge Hinnom*. When I was in Jerusalem a few years ago, I was taken to a classy restaurant on the western slope of this famous valley, and we witnessed a spectacular firework display, organized no doubt without deliberate irony, on the site to which Jesus was referring when he spoke about the smouldering fires of Gehenna. But, as with his language about 'heaven', so with his talk of Gehenna: once Christian readers had been sufficiently distanced from the original meaning of the words, alternative images would come to mind, generated not by Jesus or the New Testament, but by the stock of images, some of them extremely lurid, supplied by ancient and medieval folklore and imagination.

The point is that when Jesus was warning his hearers about Gehenna he was not, as a general rule, telling them that unless they repented in this life they would burn in the next one. As with God's kingdom, so with its opposite: it is *on earth* that things matter, not somewhere else. His message to his contemporaries was stark, and (as we would say today) 'political'. Unless they turned back from their hopeless and rebellious dreams of establishing God's kingdom in their own terms, not least through armed revolt against Rome, then the Roman juggernaut would do what large, greedy and ruthless empires have always done to smaller countries (not least in the Middle East) whose resources they covet or whose strategic location they are anxious to guard. Rome would turn Jerusalem into a hideous, stinking extension of its own smouldering rubbish heap. When Jesus said 'unless you repent, you will all likewise perish', that is the primary meaning he had in mind.[9]

It is therefore only by extension, and with difficulty, that we can extrapolate from the many gospel sayings which articulate this urgent, immediate warning to the deeper question of a warning about what may happen after death itself. The two parables which appear to address this question directly are, we should remember, *parables*, not actual descriptions of the after-life. They use stock ancient Jewish imagery, such as 'Abraham's bosom', not to teach about what happens after death but to insist on justice and mercy within the present life.[10] This is not to say that Jesus would have dissented from their implied picture of post-mortem realities. It is, rather, to point out that to take the scene of Abraham, the Rich Man and Lazarus 'literally' is about as sensible as trying to find out the name of the Prodigal Son. Jesus simply didn't say very much about the future life; he was, after all, primarily concerned to announce that God's kingdom was coming 'on earth as in heaven'. He gave (as we have seen) no fresh teaching on the question of the resurrection, apart from dark hints that it was going to happen, and happen soon, to one person ahead of everyone else; for the rest, he was content to reinforce the normal Jewish picture. In the same way, he was not concerned to give any fresh instruction on post-mortem judgment, apart from the strange hints that it was going to be dramatically and horribly anticipated in one particular way, in space-time history, within a generation.

We cannot therefore look to Jesus' teaching for any fresh detail on whether there really are some who finally reject God, and who as it were have that rejection ratified. All the signs, of course, are that he went along with the normal first-century Jewish perception: there would indeed be such people, with the only surprise being the one experienced, by sheep and goats alike, both at their fate and at the evidence on which it was based.[11] And the early Christian writers go along with this. Hell, and/or final judgment, is not a major topic in the letters (though when it comes, it is very important, as for instance in Romans 2.1–16); it is not mentioned at all in Acts; and the vivid pictures towards the end of the book of Revelation, while being extremely important, have always proved among the hardest parts of scripture to interpret with any certainty. All this should warn us against the cheerful double dogmatism which has bedevilled discussion of these topics – the dogmatism, that is, both of the person who knows exactly who is and who isn't 'going to hell', and that of the universalist who is absolutely certain that there is no such place, or that if there is it will, at the last, be empty.

That latter kind of universalism was the normal working assumption of many theologians and clergy in the liberal heyday of the 1960s and 1970s, and has remained a fixed point, almost in some cases *the* fixed point, for many whose thinking was shaped in that period. I well remember, in one of my first tutorials at Oxford, being told by my tutor that he and many others believed that 'though hell may exist, it will at the last be untenanted' – in other words, that hell would turn out to be purgatory after all, an unpleasant preparation for eventual bliss. The merest mention of final judgment has been squeezed out of Christian consciousness in several denominations, including my own, by the cavalier omission of verses from public biblical reading. Whenever you see, in an official lectionary, the command to omit two or three verses, you can normally be sure that they contain words of judgment. Unless, of course, they are about sex.

But the worm has turned, theologically speaking, in the last twenty years. The failure of liberal optimism in western society has been matched by the obvious failure of the equivalent liberal optimism in theology, driven as it was by the spirit of the age. It is a shame to have to rerun the story of nearly a hundred years ago, with Karl Barth furiously rejecting the liberal theology that had created the climate for the First World War; but it does sometimes feel as though that is what has happened. Faced with the Balkans, Rwanda, the Middle East, Darfur and all kinds of other horrors which enlightened western thought can neither explain nor alleviate, opinion in many quarters has, rightly in my view, come to see that there must be such a thing as judgment. Judgment – the sovereign declaration that *this* is good and to be upheld and vindicated, and *that* is evil and to be condemned – is the only alternative to chaos. There are some things, quite a lot of them in fact, which one must not 'tolerate', lest one merely collude with wickedness. We all know this perfectly well, yet we conveniently forget it whenever squeamishness or the demands of social convention make it easier to go with the flow of current opinion. The problem is that much theology, having for so long lived on the convenience food of an easygoing tolerance-of-everything, an 'inclusivity' with as few boundaries as McWorld, has become depressingly flabby, unable to climb even the lower slopes of social and cultural judgment, let alone the steep upper reaches of that judgment of which the early Christians spoke and wrote.

But judgment is necessary – unless we were to conclude, absurdly, that nothing much is wrong, or, blasphemously, that God doesn't mind very much. In the justly famous phrase of Miroslav Volf, there must be 'exclusion' before there can be 'embrace': evil must be identified, named and dealt with before there can be reconciliation. That is the basis on which Desmond Tutu has built his mind-blowing work on the South African 'Commission for Truth and Reconciliation'.[12] And – this is of course the crunch – where those who have acted wickedly refuse to see the point, there can be no reconciliation, no embrace.

God is utterly committed to set the world right in the end. This doctrine, like that of resurrection itself, is held firmly in place by the belief in God as creator on the one side and the belief in his goodness on the other. And that setting-right must necessarily involve the elimination of all that distorts God's good and lovely creation, and in particular of all that defaces his image-bearing human creatures. Not to put too fine a point upon it, there will be no barbed wire in the kingdom of God. And those whose whole being has become dependent upon barbed wire will have no place there either.

For 'barbed wire', of course, read whichever catalogue of awfulnesses you prefer: genocide, nuclear bombs, child prostitution, the arrogance of empire, the commodification of souls, the idolization of race. The New Testament has several such categories, functioning as red flashing lights to warn against going down a road that leads straight to a fenceless cliff. And in the analysis offered by early Christians from Paul onwards, such patterns of behaviour have three things to be said about them.

First, they all stem from the primal fault, which is idolatry, worshipping that which is not God as if it were. Second, they all show the telltale marks of the consequent fault, which is subhuman behaviour, that is, the failure fully to reflect the image of God, that 'missing-the-mark' as regards full, free and genuine humanness for which the New Testament's regular word is *hamartia*, 'sin'. ('Sin', we note, is not the breaking of arbitrary rules; rather, the rules are the thumbnail sketches of different types of dehumanizing behaviour.) Third, it is perfectly possible, and it really does seem to happen in practice, that this idolatry and dehumanization become so endemic in the life and chosen behaviour of an individual, and indeed of groups, that, unless there is a specific turning away from such a way of life, those who persist are conniving at their own ultimate dehumanization.

This is at the heart of the way in which I believe we can today restate the doctrine of final judgment. I find it quite impossible, reading the New Testament on the one hand and the newspaper on the other, to suppose that there will be no ultimate condemnation, no final loss, no human beings to whom, as C. S. Lewis put it, God will eventually say '*Thy* will be done'. I wish it were otherwise, but one cannot for ever whistle 'There's a wideness in God's mercy' in the darkness of Hiroshima, of Auschwitz, of the murder of children and the careless greed that enslaves millions with debts not their own. Humankind cannot, alas, bear very much reality, and the massive denial of reality by the cheap and cheerful universalism of western liberalism has a lot to answer for.

But if there is indeed final condemnation for those who, by their idolatry, dehumanize themselves and drag others down with them, the account I have suggested of how this works in practice provides a somewhat different picture from those normally imagined.

The traditional view is that those who spurn God's salvation, who refuse to turn from idolatry and wickedness, are held for ever in conscious torment. Sometimes this is sharpened up by over-enthusiastic preachers and teachers, who claim to know precisely which sorts of behaviour are bound to lead to hell and which, though reprehensible, are still forgivable. But the traditional picture is clear: such human beings will continue to be, in some sense, human beings, and they will be punished in an endless time.

This account is then opposed by the universalists. Sometimes they suggest (rather after the manner of Shakespeare in *Measure for Measure*) that God will be merciful even to the utterly abhorrent, to mass-murderers and child-rapists. Sometimes they modify this: God will continue, after death, to offer all people the chance of repentance, until they finally give in to the offer of his love.

A middle way is offered by the so-called 'conditionalists'. They propose 'conditional immortality': those who persistently refuse God's love and his way of life in the present world will simply cease to exist. Immortality, such theories point out, is not (despite the popularity of Platonism!) an innate human characteristic; it is something which, as Paul says, only God possesses as of right, and hence is a gift which God can choose to bestow or withhold.[13] According to this theory, then, God will simply not confer immortality on those who, in this life, have continued impenitently to worship idols and thereby to destroy their own humanness. This view is therefore sometimes known as 'annihilationism'; such people will cease to exist. That word, however, is perhaps too strong, suggesting that such people are actively destroyed, rather than merely failing to receive a gift that had been held out to them and which they consistently rejected.

Over against these three options, I propose a view which combines what seem to me the strong points of the first and third. The greatest objection to the traditional view in recent times – and the last two hundred years have seen a massive swing towards universalism in the western churches, at least the so-called 'mainstream' ones – has come from the deep revulsion many have felt at the idea of the torture-chamber in the middle of the castle of delights, the concentration camp in the middle of the beautiful countryside, the idea that, among the joys of the blessed, we should include the contemplation of the torments of the wicked. However much we tell ourselves that God must condemn evil if he is a good God, and that those who love God must endorse that condemnation, as soon as these pictures present themselves to our minds we turn away in disgust. The 'conditionalist' avoids this at the apparent cost of belittling those scriptural passages which appear to speak unambiguously of a *continuing* state for those who have rejected the worship of the true God and the way of humanness which follows from it.

Using that analysis, though, presents us with the following possibility, which I believe does justice both to the key texts and to the realities of human life of which, after a century of horror mostly dreamed up by human beings, we are now all too well aware. When human beings give their heartfelt allegiance and worship to that which is not God, they progressively cease to reflect the image of God. One of the primary laws of human life is that you become like what you worship; what's more, you *reflect* what you worship, not only back to the object itself but outwards to the world around. Those who worship money increasingly define themselves in terms of it, and increasingly treat other people as creditors, debtors, partners or customers rather than as human beings. Those who worship sex define themselves in terms of it (their preferences, their practices, their past histories), and increasingly treat other people as actual or potential sexual objects. Those who worship power define themselves in terms of it, and treat other people as either collaborators, competitors or pawns. These and many other forms of idolatry combine in a thousand ways, all of them damaging to the image-bearing quality of the people concerned and of those whose lives they touch. My suggestion is that it is possible for human beings so to continue down this road, so to refuse all whisperings of good news, all glimmers of the true light, all promptings to turn and go the other way, all signposts to the love of God, that after death they become at last, by their own effective choice, *beings that once were human but now are not*, creatures that have ceased to bear the divine image at all. With the death of that body in which they inhabited God's good world, in which the flickering flame of goodness had not been completely snuffed out, they pass simultaneously not only beyond hope but also beyond pity. There is no concentration camp in the beautiful countryside, no torture chamber in the palace of delight. Those creatures that still exist in an ex-human state, no longer reflecting their maker in any meaningful sense, can no longer excite, in themselves or others, the natural sympathy some feel even for the hardened criminal.

I am well aware that I have now wandered into territory that no one can claim to have mapped. Jesus, Christians believe, has been to hell and back, but to say that is to stand gaping into the darkness, not to write a travel brochure for future visitors. The last thing I want is for anyone to suppose that I (or anyone else) know very much about all this. Nor do I want anyone to suppose I enjoy speculating in this manner. But I find myself driven, by the New Testament and the sober realities of this world, to this kind of a resolution to one of the darkest theological mysteries. I should be glad to be proved wrong, but not at the cost of the foundational claims that this world is the good creation of the one true God, and that he will at the end bring about that judgment at which the whole creation will rejoice.

5. Conclusion: human goals and new creation

But I cannot end this chapter on that note – for the very good reason that the New Testament, again and again, refuses to end on it either. Paul in Romans is quite clear that there will indeed be final condemnation for 'those who are factious and disobey the truth, but obey wickedness'; but, as the letter goes on, his great emphasis falls on the fact that God has shut up all people in the prison-house of disobedience in order that he may have mercy upon all.[14] True, it is clear from that passage and others like it that he does not mean 'all people individually', but rather 'people of all sorts'. But when Paul says 'all' he regularly reaches out beyond what his hearers might have expected, to show that God's powerful love embraces the unexpected as well as the obvious. Since Paul knew that his own hard and bitter heart had been changed by God's grace, he also knew that there was nobody, this side of the grave, who could not in principle be similarly reached and changed.

Likewise, the majestic but mysterious ending of the Revelation of St John leaves us with fascinating and perhaps frustrating hints of future purposes, further work of which the eventual new creation is just the beginning. The description of the new Jerusalem in chapters 21 and 22 is quite clear that some categories of people are 'outside': the dogs, the fornicators ... those who speak and make lies. But then, just when we have in our minds a picture of two nice, tidy categories, the insiders and the outsiders, we find that the river of the water of life flows *out of* the city; that growing on either bank is the tree of life, not a single tree but a great many; and that 'the leaves of the tree are for the healing of the nations'. There is a great mystery here, and all our speaking about God's eventual future must make room for it. This is not at all to cast doubt on the reality of final judgment for those who have resolutely worshipped and served the idols that dehumanize us and deface God's world. It is to say that God is always the God of surprises.

But the most important thing to say at the end of this discussion, and of this section of the book, is that 'heaven and hell' are not, so to speak, what the whole game is about. This is one of the central 'surprises' in the Christian hope. The whole point of my argument so far is that the question of 'what happens to me after death' is *not* the major, central, framing question that centuries of theological tradition have supposed. The New Testament, true to its Old Testament roots, regularly insists that the major, central, framing question is that of God's purpose of rescue and re-creation for the whole world, the entire cosmos. The destiny of individual human beings must be understood within that context – not simply in the sense that we are only part of a much larger picture, but in the sense that part of the whole point of being 'saved' in the present is so that we can play a vital role (Paul speaks of this role in the shocking terms of being 'fellow workers with God') within that larger picture and purpose. And that in turn makes us realize that the question of our own 'destiny', in terms of the alternatives of joy or woe, is probably the wrong way of looking at the whole question. The question ought to be, '*How will God's new creation come?*' and then, '*How will we humans contribute to that renewal of creation, and to the fresh projects which the creator God will launch in his new world?*' The choice before humans would then be framed differently: are you going to worship the creator God, and discover thereby what it means to become fully and gloriously human, reflecting his powerful, healing, transformative love into the world? Or are you going to worship the world as it is, boosting your corruptible human-ness by gaining power or pleasure from forces within the world, but merely contributing thereby to your own dehumanization and the further corruption of the world itself?

This reflection leads to a further, and sobering, thought. If what I have suggested is anywhere near the mark, then to insist on 'heaven and hell' as the ultimate question – to insist, in other words, that what happens eventually to individual humans is the most important thing in the world – may be to make a similar mistake to the one made by the Jewish people in the first century, the mistake which both Jesus and Paul addressed. Israel believed (so Paul tells us, and he should know) that the purposes of the creator God all came down to the question: how is God going to rescue Israel? What the gospel of Jesus revealed, however, was that the purposes of God were reach-ing out to the question: how is God going to rescue the world *through Israel*, and thereby rescue Israel itself as part of the pro-cess but not as the point of it all? Maybe what we are faced with in our own day is a similar challenge: to focus, not on the ques-tion of which human beings God is going to take to heaven, and how he is going to do it, but on the question of how God is going to redeem and renew his creation *through human beings*, and how he is going to rescue those humans themselves, as part of the process but not as the point of it all. If we could reread Romans and Revelation – and the rest of the New Testa-ment, of course – in the light of this reframing of the question, I think we would find much food for thought. And if – to re-visit for a moment the discussions we had in Chapter 2 – we could rework the church's liturgies so that they expressed the surprising hope held out in the New Testament, we would find ourselves sustained and strengthened by that larger vision.

We would find, in particular, that the question of the church's mission was suddenly catapulted into centre stage, and reshaped in the process. But for that we must move to the final Part of the book.

Part 3

HOPE IN PRACTICE: RESURRECTION AND THE MISSION OF THE CHURCH

12

Rethinking salvation: heaven, earth and the kingdom of God

1. Introduction

We have now reached the point where we must ask: 'so what'? Is all this talk about God's ultimate future, about 'life after life after death', simply a matter of tidying up our beliefs about what will happen in the very end, or does it have any practical consequences here and now? Is it simply a matter of getting our teaching and preaching right, and of ordering our funerals and other liturgies so that they reflect biblical teaching about death and what lies beyond instead of non-biblical and even anti-biblical ideas which have crept into the church here and there?

Let me approach this question obliquely. Among the objections that are regularly raised to believing in the bodily resurrection of Jesus, I have recently come across a remarkable one which shows, it seems to me, a total misunderstanding of what Christianity is all about. One of the leading American writers on early Christianity, Dominic Crossan, has asked on a number of occasions: even if Jesus did rise from the dead, so what? Very nice for him, but what's it got to do with anything else? Why should he be so specially favoured? If God can pull off a stunt like that, why can't he intervene and do a lot more useful things like stopping genocide or earthquakes?[1] And this objection chimes in with things that have been said, for instance, by my distinguished predecessor Bishop David Jenkins, constituting what you might call the moral objection (as opposed to the historical or scientific one) to believing in Jesus' bodily resurrection.

I don't want to comment here on the objection itself – though we may note that when historians start to make arguments about 'what in fact happened' on the grounds of 'what ought (or ought not) to have happened' they put themselves on very thin ice indeed. What I want to do, rather, is to show what the New Testament says by way of answer to the question, 'what's the resurrection of Jesus got to do with anything else?', and to point to some conclusions from this for the life of the church and of Christians today.[2]

Part of the energy for this undertaking comes from two further observations, this time about the way we keep Easter in the contemporary church. (The church I know best is the Church of England, but conversations with friends in other churches indicates that similar phenomena can be found in plenty of other churches too.)

A good many Easter hymns start by assuming that the point of Easter is that it proves the existence of 'life after death' and encourages us to hope for it. This is then regularly, but ironically, combined with a view of that life after death in which the specific element of *resurrection* has been quietly removed. 'May we go where he is gone,' we sing at the end of one well-known hymn, 'Rest and reign with him in heaven!' But that is precisely *not* the point which the New Testament draws from Jesus' resurrection. Yes, there is a promised 'rest' after the labours of this life, and the word 'heaven' may be an appropriate, though vague, way of denoting where this 'rest' takes place. But this time of rest is the prelude to something very different which will emphatically involve earth as well. Earth – the renewed earth – is where the 'reign' will take place, which is why the New Testament regularly speaks, not of our going to be where Jesus is, but of his coming to where we are, as we have seen in the previous Part of the book.

But even when we become more precise and focused about what the New Testament says about our own future hope – the final resurrection itself, and whatever intermediate state may precede it, which we have discussed in Chapters 10 and 11 – this is still, maybe to our surprise, not the main emphasis of what the New Testament sees as the direct result of the resurrection of Jesus of Nazareth. Yes, that resurrection does indeed give us a sure and certain hope. If that's not the case, we are of all people, as Paul says, most to be pitied.[3] But when the New Testament strikes the great Easter bell, the main resonances it sets up are not simply about ourselves and about whatever future world God is ultimately going to make, when heaven and earth are joined together and renewed at last from top to bottom. Precisely because the resurrection has happened as an event *within our own world*, its implications and effects are to be felt within our own world, here and now.

This is one of the points at which it simply won't do to say (as, according to various opinion polls, a lot of clergy and even some bishops are inclined to say) that believing in the bodily resurrection of Jesus is a take-it-or-leave-it option. There is a watershed here. It may look like only a few steps this way or that to move from one side to the other, but if you accept the bodily resurrection of Jesus all the streams flow in one direction, and if you don't they all flow in the other direction. And, to put it kindly but bluntly, if you go in the other direction, away from the bodily resurrection, you may be left with something that looks a bit like Christianity, but it won't be what the New Testament writers were talking about. Please note, this is not at all a matter of putting a tick beside some dogmas and leaving a blank beside others, with the resurrection simply being a rather more difficult box to tick than some others. It is a matter of a belief which is a symptom of an entire worldview, an accurate index to a way of looking at everything else.

The point of this final section of the book is that a proper grasp of the (surprising) *future* hope which is held out to us in Jesus Christ leads directly and, to many people, equally surprisingly, to a vision of the *present* hope which is the basis of all Christian mission. To hope for a better future in this world – for the poor, the sick, the lonely and depressed, for the slaves, the refugees, the hungry and homeless, for the abused, the paranoid, the downtrodden and despairing, and in fact for the whole wide, wonderful and wounded world – is not something *else*, something extra, something tacked on to 'the gospel' as an afterthought. And to work for that intermediate hope, the surprising hope that comes forward from God's ultimate future into God's urgent present, is not a *distraction from* the task of 'mission' and 'evangelism' in the present. It is a central, essential, vital and life-giving part of it. Mostly, Jesus himself got a hearing from his contemporaries because of what he was *doing*. They saw him 'saving' people from sickness and death, and they heard him talking about a 'salvation', the message for which they had longed, which would go beyond the immediate into the ultimate future. But the two were not unrelated, the present one a mere 'visual aid' of the future one, or a trick to gain people's attention. The whole point of what Jesus was up to was that he was doing, close up, in the present, what he was promising long-term, in the future. And what he was promising for that future, and doing in that present, was not about saving souls for a disembodied eternity, but rescuing people from the corruption and decay of the way the world presently is so that they could enjoy, already in the present, that renewal of creation which is God's ultimate purpose – and so that they could thus become colleagues and partners in that larger project itself.

When we turn to Paul, the verse which has always struck me in this connection is 1 Corinthians 15.58. Paul, we remind ourselves, has just written the longest and densest chapter in any of his letters, discussing the future resurrection of the body in great and complex detail. How might we expect him to finish such a chapter? By saying, 'therefore, since you have such a great hope, sit back and relax, because you know God's got a great future in store for you'? No. Instead, he says, 'Therefore, my beloved ones, be steadfast, immovable, always abounding in the work of the Lord, because you know that in the Lord your labour is not in vain.'

What does he mean? How does believing in the future resurrection lead to getting on with the work in the present? Quite straightforwardly. The point of the resurrection, as Paul has been arguing throughout the letter, is that *the present bodily life is not valueless just because it will die*. God will raise it to new life. What you do with your body in the present matters, because God has a great future in store for it. And if this applies to ethics, as in 1 Corinthians 6, it certainly also applies to the various vocations to which God's people are called. What you *do* in the present – by painting, preaching, singing, sewing, praying, teaching, building hospitals, digging wells, campaigning for justice, writing poems, caring for the needy, loving your neighbour as yourself – all these things *will last into God's future*. They are not simply ways of making the present life a little less beastly, a little more bearable, until the day when we leave it behind altogether (as the hymn so mistakenly puts it, 'until that day when all the blest to endless rest are called away'). They are part of what we may call *building for God's kingdom*.

I shall come back to the meaning of 'God's kingdom' presently. But let us note, at the outset of this final section of the book, that the promise of new creation – the promise we have been studying throughout this book – is not and cannot be simply about straightening out ideas about 'life after death'. It is about the mission of the church. There has been a lot of talk, where I work, about what we have called 'Mission-Shaped Church', following a report with that title, urging today's church not to regard 'mission' as an extra, something to fit in if there's any time left over from other concerns, but as the central, and shaping, dynamic of its life.[4] But if this is to mean what it ought to mean we must also reshape our ideas of mission itself. It's no good falling back into the tired old split-level world where some people believe in 'evangelism' in terms of 'saving souls for a timeless eternity' and other people believe in 'mission' in terms of 'working for justice, peace and hope in the present world'. That great divide has nothing to do with Jesus and the New Testament, and everything to do with the silent enslavement of many Christians (both 'conservative' and 'radical') to the Platonic ideology of the Enlightenment. Once we get the resurrection straight, we can and must get mission straight. If we want a 'mission-shaped church', what we need is a hope-shaped mission. And if that is surprising, we ought to be getting used to it by now.

We begin with one of the largest topics of all, which most Christians take for granted but which is in urgent need of a radical rethink: salvation.

2. The meaning of 'salvation'

The truly exciting, surprising and perhaps frightening thing about where we have now got to in this book is that we have been forced to rethink the very meaning of 'salvation' itself.

Mention 'salvation', and almost all western Christians assume that you mean 'going to heaven when you die'. But a moment's thought, in the light of all we have said so far, will reveal that this simply cannot be right. 'Salvation' means, of course, 'rescue'. But what are we ultimately to be rescued from? The obvious answer is 'death'. But if, when we die, all that happens is that our bodies decompose while our souls (or whatever other word we want to use for our continuing existence) go on elsewhere, this doesn't mean we've been *rescued from* death. It simply means that we've died.

And if God's good creation – of the world, of life as we know it, of our glorious and remarkable bodies, brains and blood-streams – really *is* good, and if God wants to reaffirm that good-ness in a wonderful act of new creation at the last, then to see the death of the body and the escape of the soul as 'salvation' is not simply slightly off course, in need of a few subtle alter-ations and modification. It is totally and utterly wrong. It is colluding with death. It is conniving at death's destruction of God's good, image-bearing human creatures, while consoling ourselves with the (essentially non-Christian and non-Jewish) thought that the 'really important' bit of ourselves is 'saved' from this wicked, nasty body and this sad, dark world of space, time and matter! As we have seen, the whole of the Bible, from Genesis to Revelation, speaks out against such nonsense. *It is, however, what most western Christians, including most 'Bible Christians' of whatever sort, actually believe.* This is a seri-ous state of affairs, reinforced not only in popular teaching but in liturgies, public prayers, hymns and homilies of every kind.

All this was borne in on me recently when I read a popular-level book by the well-known Christian writer Adrian Plass. Plass wouldn't claim to be a profound theologian, though actually his great contribution, through humour, irony and the occasional deeply poignant story, is often to make us think afresh about things we take for granted. So when someone gave me his new book, *Bacon Sandwiches and Salvation*, I looked for-ward to more of the same. And I wasn't disappointed: the book is funny, shrewd, deliberately silly and deliberately serious.[5]

When it came to the most serious bit, on salvation itself, I was looking forward to some fresh thinking. Plass himself raises the questions that puzzle many people today:

> But what is it all about? What does it mean to be saved? Saved from what? Saved *for* what? Should the whole business of sal-vation have a significant impact on my present as well as on my future? Speaking of the future, what can we expect from an

eternity spent in heaven? How can we possibly make sense of heaven when our feet remain so solidly on Earth? Where is the interface, the meeting point between the flesh and the Spirit? And when all the strange religious terms and voices and patterns and mantras and man-made conventions have faded away, what will be left?[6]

Well, quite. That is indeed the puzzle we found in the early chapters of the present book. I turned over the page, eager to see what Plass would come up with as a fresh statement of 'salvation'. But I was disappointed:

[God's] plan was for us to live in perfect harmony with him . . . Then something went horribly, dreadfully wrong . . . This truly ghastly thing that happened somehow separated human beings from God, who nevertheless continued to love them/us with a passion that is impossible to comprehend. Desperate to heal the rift, he devised a rescue plan . . . Because Jesus was executed on the cross it is now possible for any or all of us, through repentance, baptism and obedience, *to recover the magnificent relationship with God* that was destroyed in days gone by . . . If you and I accept the death and resurrection of Jesus as a living, divine, working mechanism in our own lives *we shall one day go home to God and find peace* . . . The Holy Spirit, sent by Jesus himself after his death, offers support and strength for those who call on him.[7]

Now I know it is hardly fair to take on Adrian Plass in a book like the present one. He is not claiming to be writing a work of theology, and, as I have said, his book has many wonderful insights (as well as many corny jokes). I cite him simply as a classic example – all the more powerful because at this point he is so clearly articulating what so many take for granted – of the 'normal' western Christian view: that 'salvation' is about 'my relationship with God' in the present and about 'going home to God and finding peace' in the future. The fact that, though asking so many probing questions and clearly being dissatisfied with the stock answers he has received, he has not thought to question these answers themselves shows how deeply rooted they are in an entire tradition. Those of us who have known this tradition all our lives – not just an 'evangelical' tradition, by the way, but at this point the entire tradition of the western church – will recognize his summary as being 'what most Christians believe' and, indeed, what most non-Christians assume Christians believe. And, to make the point once more as forcibly as I can, this belief is simply not what the New Testament teaches.

The day after writing this paragraph I had another, and sharply personal, example of the same problem. An anguished email appeared from the man who is translating my book *Judas and the Gospel of Jesus* into one of the Balkan languages. He had just got to the point where I was warning that some western Christians have embraced something worryingly similar to second-century gnosticism when they think of the present world as evil and the only solution being to escape it and to go to heaven instead. This produced a tirade of accusations from the translator, for whom that seemed to be precisely what he thought the gospel was all about. Hadn't I read the Bible? Didn't I believe in heaven? Or in Jesus? Was I trying to invent a new religion?

Thus far, I am simply rubbing in the point I have been making throughout the book. But in this closing section we have to look, head on, at the problem which directly results from this widespread misperception of the Christian view of 'salvation'. As long as we see 'salvation' in terms of 'going to heaven when we die', the main work of the church is bound to be seen in terms of saving souls for that future. But when we see 'salvation', as the New Testament sees it, in terms of God's promised new heavens and new earth, and of our promised resurrection to share in that new, and gloriously embodied, reality – what I have called 'life after life after death' – then the main work of the church here and now demands to be rethought in consequence.

At this point the well-known slogan of Christian Aid, 'We believe in life before death', comes into its own. Life *before* death is what is threatened, called into question, by the idea that salvation is merely 'life *after* death'. If we're heading for a time-less, bodiless eternity, then what's the fuss about putting things right in the present world? But if what matters is the newly em-bodied life *after* 'life after death', then the presently embodied 'life *before* death' can at last be seen, not as an interesting but ultimately irrelevant present preoccupation, not simply as a 'vale of tears and soul-making' through which we have to pass to a blessed and disembodied final state, but as the essential, vital time, place and matter into which God's future purposes have already broken in the resurrection of Jesus and in which those future purposes are now to be further anticipated through the mission of the church. 'Life after death', it seems, can be a serious distraction not only from the ultimate 'life *after* "life after death"', but also from 'life *before* death'. To ignore this is in fact to collude not only with death, but with all sorts of other powers that gain their force from their own alliance with that ultimate enemy.

'Salvation', then, is not 'going to heaven', but 'being raised to life in God's new heaven and new earth'. But as soon as we put it like this we realize that the New Testament is full of hints, indications and downright assertions that this 'salvation' isn't just something we have to wait for in the long-distance future. We can enjoy it here and now (always partially, of course, since we all still have to die), genuinely anticipating in the present what is to come in the future. 'We were saved', says Paul in Romans 8.24, 'in hope'. The verb 'we were saved' indicates a past action, something that has already taken place, referring obviously to the complex of faith and baptism of which Paul has been speaking in the letter so far. But this remains 'in hope', because we still look forward to the ultimate future salvation of which he speaks in (for instance) Romans 5.9, 10.

This explains at a stroke the otherwise puzzling fact that the New Testament often refers to 'salvation' and 'being saved' in terms of bodily events within the present world. 'Come and save my daughter', begs Jairus; as Jesus is on his way to do so, the woman with the issue of blood thinks to herself, 'If I can only touch his clothes I will be saved'; 'Daughter,' says Jesus to her after her healing, 'your faith has saved you.'[8] Matthew, telling the same story, abbreviates it drastically, but at this point he adds an extra note: 'and the woman was saved from that moment on'.[9] It is fascinating to see how passages like this – and there are many of them – are often juxtaposed with others which speak of 'salvation' in larger terms, which seem to go beyond present physical healing or rescue. This juxtaposition makes some Christians nervous (surely, they think, 'salvation' ought to be a *spiritual* matter!) but it doesn't seem to have troubled the early church at all.[10] For the first Christians, the ultimate 'salvation' was all about God's new world; and the point of what Jesus and the apostles were doing when they were healing people, or being rescued from shipwreck, or whatever, was that this was a proper anticipation of that ultimate 'salvation', that healing transformation of space, time and matter. The future rescue which God had planned and promised was starting to come true in the present. We are saved, not as souls, but as wholes.

(All sorts of things follow from this. We might notice, for instance, that theories of 'atonement', of the meaning of the cross, are not simply a set of alternative answers to the same question. They give the answers they give because of the questions they ask. If the question is 'how can I get to heaven despite the sin because of which I deserve to be punished?', the answer may well be 'because Jesus has been punished in your place'. But if the question is 'how can God's plan to rescue and renew the entire world go ahead, despite the corruption and decay which has come about because of human rebellion?', the answer may well be 'because on the cross Jesus defeated the powers of evil which have enslaved rebel humans and so ensured continuing corruption'. Please note, *these and other possible questions and answers are not mutually exclusive.* My point is that reframing the question will mean rethinking the various answers we might give, and the relationship between them. This is a large topic for another occasion.[11])

But as soon as we grasp this – and I appreciate it takes quite a bit of latching on to for people who have spent their whole lives thinking the other way – we see that if salvation is that sort of thing, it can't be confined to human beings. When a human being is 'saved', in the past as a single coming-to-faith event, in the present through acts of healing and rescue, including answers to the prayer 'lead us not into temptation, but deliver us from evil', and in the future when they are finally raised from the dead, this is always so that they can be genuine human beings in a fuller sense than they otherwise would have been. And genuine human beings, from Genesis 1 onwards, are given the mandate of looking after creation, of bringing order to God's world, of establishing and maintaining communities. To suppose that we are saved, as it were, for our own private benefit, for the restoration of our own relationship with God (vital though that is!) and for our eventual home-coming and peace in 'heaven' (misleading though that is!) is like a boy being given a cricket bat as a present and insisting that, since it belongs to him, he must always and only play with it in private. But of course you can only do what you're meant to do with a cricket bat when you're playing with other people. And salvation only does what it's meant to do when those who have been saved, are being saved and will one day fully be saved realize that they are saved, not as souls but as wholes, and not for themselves alone but for what God now longs to do through them.

The point is this. When God 'saves' people in this life, by working through his Spirit to bring them to faith, and by leading them to follow Jesus in discipleship, prayer, holiness, hope and love, such people are designed – it isn't too strong a word – to be a sign and foretaste of what God wants to do for the entire cosmos. What's more, such people are not just to be a sign and foretaste of that ultimate 'salvation'; they are to be *part of the means by which* God makes this happen in both the present and the future. That is what Paul insists on when he says that the whole creation is waiting with eager longing – not just for its own redemption, its liberation from corruption and decay, but *for God's children to be revealed*: in other words, for the un-veiling of those redeemed humans through whose stewardship creation will at last be brought back into that wise order for which it was made.[12] And since Paul makes it quite clear that those who believe in Jesus Christ, who are incorporated into him through baptism, are already God's children, are already themselves 'saved', this stewardship cannot be something to be postponed for the ultimate future. It must begin here and now.

In other words – to sum up where we've got so far – the work of 'salvation', in its full sense, is (1) about whole human beings, not merely 'souls'; (2) about the present, not simply the future; and (3) about what God does *through* us, not merely what God does *in and for* us. If we can get this straight, we will rediscover the historic basis for the full-orbed mission of the church. To pursue this further we need to look at the larger picture with-in which all this makes sense: the kingdom of God.

3. The kingdom of God

We have seen at several points in this book that the normal Christian understanding of 'kingdom', especially of 'kingdom of heaven', is simply mistaken. 'God's kingdom' and 'kingdom of heaven' mean the same thing: the sovereign rule of God (i.e., the rule of 'heaven', that is, of the one who lives in heaven), which according to Jesus was and is breaking in to the present world, to 'earth'. That is what Jesus taught us to pray for. We have no right to omit that clause from the Lord's Prayer, or to suppose that it doesn't really mean what it says.

This, as we have seen, is what the resurrection and ascension of Jesus, and the gift of the Spirit, are all about. They are not designed to take us away from this earth, but to make us agents of the transformation of this earth, anticipating the day when, as we are promised, 'the earth shall be full of the knowledge of the Lord, as the waters cover the sea'. When the risen Jesus appears to his followers at the end of Matthew's gospel, he declares that all authority in heaven *and on earth* has been given to him. When John the Seer hears the thundering voices in heaven, they are singing, 'the kingdom of the world has become the kingdom of our Lord and of his Messiah, and he shall reign for ever and ever'.[13] And the point of the gospels – of Matthew, Mark, Luke and John, together with Acts – is that *this has already begun.*

The question of *how* it has begun – in what sense it is 'inaugurated', 'anticipated' or whatever – has been the stuff of debate for a long time. But part of the problem with that debate is that those taking part in it have not usually clarified the question of *what precisely it is* that is begun, launched or initiated. At one level it is clearly the hope of Israel, as expressed in classic 'kingdom passages' such as Isaiah 52.7–12. There, 'God becoming king at last' means the end of exile, the defeat of evil, and the return of Israel's God to Zion. We can see all of that becoming the major theme, not only of Jesus' life and public career, but of his own interpretation of his death.[14]

But underneath that again, when we stand back, is the meaning of 'God's kingdom' to which the hope of Israel was designed to contribute – or, to put it another way, the meaning because of which God called Israel in the first place. Faced with his beautiful and powerful creation in rebellion, God longed to set it right, to rescue it from continuing corruption and impending chaos and to bring it back into order and fruitfulness. God longed, in other words, to re-establish his wise sovereignty over the whole creation, which would mean a great act of healing and rescue. He did not want to rescue humans *from* creation, any more than he wanted to rescue Israel *from* the Gentiles. He wanted to rescue Israel *in order that Israel might be a light to the Gentiles*, and he wanted thereby to rescue humans *in order that humans might be his rescuing stewards over creation*. That is the inner dynamic of the kingdom of God.

That, in other words, is how the God who made humans to be his stewards over creation, and who called Israel to be the light of the world, is to become king, in accordance with his original intention in creation on the one hand and his original intention in the covenant on the other. To snatch saved souls away to a disembodied 'heaven' would destroy the whole point. God is to become king of the whole world at last. And he will do this, not by declaring that the inner dynamic of creation (that it be ruled by humans) was a mistake, nor by declaring that the inner dynamic of his covenant (that Israel would be the means of saving the nations) was a failure, but by fulfilling them both. That is more or less what Paul's letter to the Romans is all about.[15]

This is the purpose that has been realized in Jesus Christ. One of the greatest problems of the western church, ever since the Reformation at least, is that it hasn't really known what the gospels were there for. Imagining that the point of Christianity was to enable people to 'go to heaven', most western Christians have supposed that the mechanism by which this happened was the one they found in the writings of Paul (I stress, the one *they found*; I have argued elsewhere that this involved misunderstanding Paul as well), and that the four gospels were simply there to give back-up information about Jesus, his teaching, his moral example and his atoning death. This long tradition has screened out the possibility that when Jesus spoke of 'God's kingdom' he wasn't talking about a 'heaven' for which he was preparing his followers, but about something that was happening in and on this earth, through his work, then through his death and resurrection, and then through the Spirit-led work to which they would be called.

Part of the difficulty people still have in coming to terms with the gospels, read in this way, is that 'kingdom of God' has been a flag of convenience under which all sorts of ships have sailed. Some have used the phrase as a cover for pursuing business of their own – programmes of moral, social or political improvement or upheaval, agendas of the left and the right, of the well-meaning but muddled and of the less well-meaning but all too clear. Many who have gone this route have treated the gospels as though they were simply stories about Jesus going around helping people as best he could, with the unfortunate sequel of his untimely death. And many other Christians, seeing this shallow and confused exegesis and application, have reacted angrily against what is called 'kingdom theology' as though it were simply an outdated and shallow corporate version of faddish self-help moralism. (This is a serious problem in some parts of America, where 'kingdom' has become a slogan of this kind, and has then been used to rule out or marginalize many aspects of orthodox Christian faith – precipitating among some would-be orthodox Christians a reaction against any social or political dimension to the gospel, and against 'kingdom' language altogether. By such means do we project our own confusions on to the text.)

But the fact that some people, and some movements, have misappropriated the 'kingdom theology' of the gospels doesn't mean there isn't a reality of which such ideas are a caricature. What we find in the gospels is much, much more profound. Here we meet again a familiar problem, the problem of how Jesus' initial ministry joins up with his self-giving to death. I have argued at length elsewhere that Jesus never imagined that the 'kingdom' which he was launching through his healings, feastings and teachings would be fulfilled without his death. Or, to put it the other way round, I and others have stressed that Jesus' death was not (and he did not think it was) about something other than the kingdom-work to which he had devoted his short public career. The problem of evil which looms up as the backdrop to the gospels is not going to be dealt with even by Jesus' healings, feastings and teachings. It certainly won't be dealt with by his then providing his followers with a fast-track route to a distant and disembodied heaven. It can only be dealt with – the kingdom can only come on earth as in heaven – through Jesus' own death and resurrection. That is a whole other story, though of course a central and vital one.[16]

But when we reintegrate what should never have been separated – the kingdom-inaugurating public work of Jesus on the one hand and his redemptive death and resurrection on the other – we find that the gospels tell a different story. It isn't just a story of some splendid and exciting social work with an unhappy conclusion. Nor is it just a story of an atoning death with an extended introduction. It is something much bigger than the sum of those two diminished perspectives. It is the story of God's kingdom being launched on earth as in heaven, generating a new state of affairs in which the power of evil has been decisively defeated, the new creation has been decisively launched, and Jesus' followers have been commissioned and equipped to put that victory, and that inaugurated new world, into practice. 'Atonement', 'redemption' and 'salvation' are what happens on the way, because for people to engage in this work demands that they themselves be rescued from the powers that enslave the world, in order that they can in turn be rescuers. To put it another way, if you want to help inaugurate God's kingdom, you must follow in the way of the cross; and if you want to benefit from Jesus' saving death, you must become part of his kingdom-project. There is only one Jesus, only one gospel story, albeit told in four kaleidoscopic patterns.[17]

Heaven's rule, God's rule, is thus to be put into practice in the world, resulting in salvation in both the present and the future, a salvation which is both *for* humans and, *through* saved humans, for the wider world. This is the solid basis for the mission of the church. But to explore this further will need another chapter.

13

Building for the kingdom

1. Introduction

Many people, faced with the challenge to work for God's kingdom in the present, will at once object. 'Doesn't that sound', they will ask, 'as though you're trying to build God's kingdom by your own efforts?' Well, if it does sound like that, I'm sorry. It wasn't meant like that. Perhaps some further clarification is needed.

Let's be quite clear on two points. First, God builds God's kingdom. But God has ordered his world in such a way that his own work within that world would take place not least through one of his creatures in particular, namely the human beings who reflect his image. That, I believe, is central to what the notion of 'being made in God's image' is all about. God intends his wise, creative, loving presence and power to be *reflected*, 'imaged' if you like, into his world *through* his human creatures. He has enlisted us to act as his stewards in the project of creation. And, following the disaster of rebellion and corruption, he has built into the gospel message the fact that, through the work of Jesus and the power of the Spirit, he equips humans to help in the work of getting the project back on track. So the objection about us trying to build God's kingdom by our own efforts, though it seems humble and pious, can be a way of hiding from responsibility, of keeping one's head well down when the boss is looking for volunteers. Not that one can go on eluding God's call for ever . . . but still.

The second point is to distinguish between the final kingdom and the present anticipations of it. The final coming together of heaven and earth is, of course, God's supreme act of new creation, for which the only real prototype – other than the first creation itself – was the resurrection of Jesus. God alone will sum up all things in Christ, things in heaven and things on earth. He alone will make the 'new heavens and new earth'. It would be the height of folly to think that we could assist in that great work.

But what we can and must do in the present, if we are obedient to the gospel, if we are following Jesus, and if we are indwelt, energized and directed by the Spirit, is to build *for* the kingdom. This brings us back to 1 Corinthians 15.58 once more: what you do in the Lord *is not in vain*. You are not oiling the wheels of a machine that's about to fall over a cliff. You are not restoring a great painting that's shortly going to be thrown on the fire. You are not planting roses in a garden that's about to be dug up for a building site. You are – strange though it may seem, almost as hard to believe as the resurrection itself – accomplishing something which will become, in due course, part of God's new world. Every act of love, gratitude and kindness; every work of art or music inspired by the love of God and delight in the beauty of his creation; every minute spent teaching a severely handicapped child to read or to walk; every act of care and nurture, of comfort and support, for one's fellow human beings, and for that matter one's fellow non-human creatures; and of course every prayer, all Spirit-led teaching, every deed which spreads the gospel, builds up the church, embraces and embodies holiness rather than corruption, and makes the name of Jesus honoured in the world – all of this will find its way, through the resurrecting power of God, into the new creation which God will one day make. That is the logic of the mission of God. God's recreation of his wonderful world, which has begun with the resurrection of Jesus and continues mysteriously as God's people live in the risen Christ and in the power of his Spirit, means that what we do in Christ and by the Spirit in the present is not wasted.

It will last all the way into God's new world. In fact, it will be enhanced there.

I have no idea what precisely this will mean in practice. I am putting up a signpost, not offering a photograph of what we will find when we get to where the signpost is pointing. I don't know what musical instruments we shall have to play Bach in God's new world, though I'm sure Bach's music will be there. I don't know how my planting a tree today will relate to the wonderful trees that there will be in God's recreated world, though I do remember Martin Luther's words about the proper reaction to knowing the kingdom was coming the next day being to go out and plant a tree. I do not know how the painting an artist paints today in prayer and wisdom will find a place in God's new world. I don't know how our work for justice for the poor, for remission of global debts, will reappear in that new world. But I know that God's new world of justice and joy, of hope for the whole earth, was launched when Jesus came out of the tomb on Easter morning; and I know that he calls his followers to live in him and by the power of his spirit, and so to be new-creation people here and now, bringing signs and symbols of the kingdom to birth on earth as in heaven. The resurrection of Jesus and the gift of the Spirit mean that we are called to bring real and effective signs of God's renewed creation to birth even in the midst of the present age. Not to bring works and signs of renewal to birth within God's creation is ultimately to collude, as gnosticism always does, with the forces of sin and death themselves. But don't focus on the negative. Think of the positive: of the calling, in the present, to share in the surprising hope of God's whole new creation.

The image I have often used, in trying to explain this strange but important idea, is that of the stonemason working on part of a great cathedral. The architect has already got the whole plan in mind, and has passed on instructions to the team of masons as to which stones need carving in what way. The foreman distributes these tasks among the team. One will shape stones for a particular tower or turret; another will carve the delicate pattern that breaks up the otherwise forbidding straight lines; another will work on gargoyles or coats of arms; another will be making statues of saints, martyrs, kings or queens. They will be vaguely aware that the others are getting on with their tasks; and they will know, of course, that many other entire departments are busy about quite different tasks as well. When they've finished with their stones and their statues they will hand them over, without necessarily knowing very much about where, in the eventual building, their work will find its home. They may not have seen the complete architect's drawing of the whole building with 'their bit' identified in its proper place. Nor may they live to see the completed building, with their work at last where it belongs. But they will trust the architect that the work they have done in following instructions will not be wasted. They are not, themselves, building the cathedral; but they are building *for* the cathedral, and when the cathedral is complete their work will be enhanced, ennobled, will mean much more than it could have meant as they were chiselling it and shaping it down in the stonemasons' yard.

That image, of course, is itself incomplete, since the cathedral is eventually built by the combination of all the artisans and craftspeople working together, whereas God's eventual kingdom will, as I have said, be a fresh gift of transformation and renewal from the Architect himself. But it is enough to indicate the way in which there is continuity, as well as discontinuity, between the present life and the work we do in it, and the ultimate future life in which God has gathered all things together and transformed them, 'making all things new' in Christ. What we do in the Lord is 'not in vain'; and that is the mandate we need for every act of justice and mercy, every programme of ecology, every effort to reflect God's wise stewardly image into his creation. In the new creation the ancient human mandate to look after the garden is dramatically reaffirmed, as John hints in his resurrection story, where Mary supposes

Jesus is the gardener. The resurrection of Jesus is the reaffirmation of the goodness of creation, and the gift of the Spirit is
there to make us the fully human beings we were supposed to
be, precisely so that we can fulfil that mandate at last.

The work we do in the present, then, gains its full significance from the eventual design in which it is meant to
belong. Applied to the mission of the church, this means that
we must work in the present for the advance signs of that eventual state of affairs when God is 'all in all', when his kingdom
has come and his will is done 'on earth as in heaven'. This
will of course be radically different from the kind of work we
would engage in if our sole task was to save souls for a disembodied heaven, or simply to help people enjoy a fulfilling
'relationship with God' as though that were the end of the
matter. It will also be significantly different from the kind of
work we might undertake if our sole task was to forget any God-
dimension at all and to try simply to make life better within
the continuation of the world as it is.

This throws us headlong into some contentious, but important and necessary, areas. Today's church (including 'emerging
church', 'liquid church', 'fresh expressions of church', 'mission-
shaped church' and many others) is grappling with the question of what its mission and life might look like in the days
to come. But the present mood of frustration with existing
patterns of church life, coupled with postmodern free-for-all
experimentation on the one hand and residual Protestant fears
about the created order on the other, have conspired together
to produce cheerful and sometimes not-so-cheerful chaos.
This is the context within which a proper vision of biblical
eschatology can and should generate a fresh, and no doubt
controversial, vision of the church's mission.

To put it bluntly, creation is to be redeemed; that is, space
is to be redeemed, time is to be redeemed, and matter is to
be redeemed. God said 'very good' over his space-time-and-
matter creation, and, though the redeeming of this world from

its present corruption and decay will mean transformations we cannot imagine, the one thing we can be sure of is that this re-deeming of creation will not mean that God will say, of space, time and/or matter, 'oh well, nice try, good while it lasted but obviously gone bad, so let's drop it and go for a non-spatio-temporal, non-material world instead.' But if God really does intend to *redeem* his created world of space, time and matter, rather than rejecting it, we are faced with the question: what might it look like to celebrate that redemption, that healing and transformation, in the present, and thereby appropriately to anticipate God's final intention?

A note before we launch in, to anticipate the obvious objec-tion. As long as the present world lasts, there will be an ever-present danger of idolatry, of worshipping the creature instead of the creator. Since space, time and matter are the raw mater-ials out of which idols have been formed, some devout people have supposed that they must reject space, time and matter themselves, so that any object used in worship, any action per-formed, any 'holy place', become instantly suspect.

Fair enough: there is such a thing as idolatry, and we must guard against it. Indeed, we must put it to death without pity. *But idolatry is always the perversion of something good.* Greed – worshipping the appetites and what they feed on – is the perversion of the God-given instinct for the proper enjoy-ment of the good creation. The proper response to idolatry is therefore not dualism, the rejection of space, time or matter as themselves evil or dangerous, but the renewed worship of the Creator God, which sets the context for the proper enjoyment and use of the created order without the danger of worship-ping it. Our living within, and enjoyment and use of, space, time and matter must constantly be measured against the story of Jesus, both in his sharing of space, time and matter as the Incarnate Son, in his death which passes judgment on all idolatry and sin, and in his resurrection in which space, time and matter are renewed in his body, anticipating the final renewal of all things. The danger of idolatry, and the proper response to it, stand as a rubric over what is now to come. The church is called to a mission of implementing Jesus' resurrection, and thereby anticipating the final new creation. What might that look like?

2. Justice

The first major category I want to explore is justice. I use this word as a shorthand for the intention of God, expressed from Genesis to Revelation, to set the whole world right – a plan gloriously fulfilled in Jesus Christ, supremely in his resurrection (following his victory over the powers of evil and death on the cross) and now to be implemented in the world. We cannot get off the hook of present responsibility, as many Christians try to do, not least within some parts of fundamentalism, by declaring that the world is currently in such a mess and there's nothing that can be done about it until the Lord returns. That is classic dualism. Many people embrace it enthusiastically. It leaves the church with nothing to do in the present except care for the wounded as best we can while we wait for a different kind of salvation altogether.

To say that there's more to it than that, though, is not to return to the old 'social gospel'. It is, rather, to live consciously between the resurrection of Jesus in the past and the making of God's new world in the future. This is why the theology of liberal modernism, at its best, was always fighting its social agendas with one hand tied behind its back. Of course some Christians have spoken of the resurrection as a way of reinforcing a dualism which leaves them with no social concern. But that always was a gross distortion. Precisely because Jesus Christ rose from the dead, God's new world has already broken in to the present, and Christian work for justice in the present, for instance in the ongoing campaigns for debt remission and ecological responsibility, take the shape they do. If Jesus left his body behind in the tomb, and if we are going to do the same, as many theologians of the last generation thought, then we are robbed both of the ground and the energy for our work to bring real, bodily, concrete signs of hope to the present world.

Think back to the Sadducees. They were the powerful elite in Jesus' world. They were held in place by Rome, and they enjoyed wealth, status and prestige within Judaean society. Their denial of the resurrection, and of any future life, was argued, it seems, on the basis of their belief that the doctrine was a new-fangled thing, invented by late prophets like Daniel; you couldn't find it, they claimed, in the Five Books of Moses. The Pharisees argued against this, as did Jesus himself, with his quotation from Exodus, where God declares that he is the God of Abraham, Isaac and Jacob. Now when Jesus quotes that verse he isn't simply pulling a rabbit out of an exegetical hat, finding a passage in the Books of Moses which speaks of the patriarchs as still alive, and therefore by implication still awaiting their final resurrection. The point of God saying to Moses that he is the God of Abraham, Isaac and Jacob is to underline what he's going to say in the next few verses: that he has heard the cry of his people in slavery, and is coming down to rescue them and to bring them to their promised land.[1]

Within the first-century world of Jesus, the Pharisees and the Sadducees, the doctrine of resurrection was a *revolutionary* doctrine. It spoke of God's determination to bring about the new Exodus, the real return from exile, the great liberation from oppression and slavery, the liberation for which Israel longed. And the real reason the Sadducees opposed it – behind the smokescreen of theological argument on the one hand and silly stories about women with seven husbands on the other – was that they knew that the resurrection doctrine was a threat to their own position. They knew it meant that God was turning the world upside down. And people who believe that God will turn the world upside down – people like Mary with her Magnificat, pulling down the mighty from their thrones and exalting the humble and meek – are not going to be backward in getting on with some world-changing activities in the present. It isn't that, like suicide bombers, people who believe in the resurrection are more cheerful about dying for the cause because they are happy to leave this present world and escape into a glorious future. It is, rather, that people who believe in the resurrection, in God making a whole new world in which everything will be set right at last, are unstoppably motivated to work for that new world in the present.

If that was true even of the Pharisees, even before anyone *had* in fact been raised from the dead, how much more ought it to be true of us, who celebrate and proclaim Jesus not only as risen from the dead but as the one who has thereby been installed as Lord of the whole world? The world has *already* been turned upside down; that's what Easter is all about. It isn't a matter of waiting until God eventually does something different at the end of time. God has brought his future, his putting-the-world-to-rights future, into the present in Jesus of Nazareth, and he wants that future to be implicated more and more in the present. That's what we pray for every time we say the Lord's Prayer: Thy kingdom come, thy will be done, on earth as it is in heaven. And that's why that prayer goes on to pray for bread and forgiveness; which is, I suggest, where the issue of justice comes closest to our global village today.

Once again there are two extremes towards which Christian people tend to slide. To begin with, there are those who declare that if Jesus is the true revolutionary then the single main Christian task is to build the kingdom here on earth through social, political and cultural revolution. Alas, this social gospel (as it used to be called) has singularly failed to deliver the goods in the century or so since it has been advocated in this modern form. An enormous amount of good has been done: social conditions have been improved vastly, though how much has been due to Christian work and how much to other influences it's hard to say. But we are still a fragmented, frightened and battered world. Even in the affluent West there are many places where Dickensian conditions, or worse, still obtain, all the more appalling for being mostly out of sight and mind as far as the glossy media are concerned.

At the other end of the scale there are those who declare that nothing can be done until the Lord returns and everything is put to rights. The forces of evil are too entrenched, and nothing save a great apocalyptic moment of divine power can address them or change the deep structures of the way things are. This kind of dualism breeds very effectively within societies where, though injustice can be seen and named, it is politically inconvenient to do anything about it. We will get on, such a view says, with the real business of the gospel, which is that of saving souls for the future world. We will even do mopping-up operations, sticking-plaster activities, to look after the people at the bottom of the pile. But we won't do anything about the structures that put them there and keep them there. This kind of dualism banishes the continuing healing activity of the Father from the world he made, of the Son from the world of which he is already the Lord, and of the Spirit from the world within which he (she?) groans in travail.

Neither of these views begins to do justice – in any sense – to Paul's injunction to be steadfast and immovable in doing the work of the Lord, because in the Lord our labour is not in vain. The universal early Christian belief was that Jesus had already been demonstrated publicly to be Israel's Messiah and the world's true Lord through his resurrection. That, as we've seen, is part of the whole point of the Christian story. And if we believe it, and pray, as he taught us, for God's kingdom to come on earth as in heaven, there is no way we can rest content with major injustice in the world. We must recognize, as the second view does, that the final putting to rights of everything does indeed wait for the last day. We must therefore avoid the arrogance or triumphalism of the first view, imagining that we can build the kingdom by our own efforts without the need

for a further great divine act of new creation. But we must agree
with the first view that doing justice in the world is part of the
Christian task, and we must therefore reject the defeatism of
the second view that says there's no point in even trying.

As far as I can see, the major task that faces us in our generation, corresponding to the issue of slavery two centuries ago,
is that of the massive economic imbalance of the world, whose
major symptom is the ridiculous and unpayable Third World
debt. I have spoken about this many times over the last few years,
and I have a sense that some of us, like old Wilberforce on the
subject of slavery, are called to bore the pants off people by
going on and on about it until eventually the point is taken and
the world is changed. There are many good books on the subject, from different points of view, and I don't want to go into
the arguments now. I simply want to record my conviction that
this is the Number One moral issue of our day. Sex matters
enormously but global justice matters far, far more. The present system of global debt is the real immoral scandal, the dirty
little secret – or rather the dirty enormous secret – of glitzy,
glossy western capitalism. Whatever it takes, we must change
this situation or stand condemned by subsequent history alongside those who supported slavery two centuries ago and those
who supported the Nazis seventy years ago. It is that serious. I
can't develop the arguments here; I just want to make four brief
comments, in the light of the subject matter we have explored
in this book, about the nature of the debates that you run into
when you raise the subject. (I know this only too well: every
time I write on these issues some commentators, usually in
America, write to tell me that I should stick to Jesus and Paul
and not meddle in economics and politics. Fortunately there
are plenty of others, in America and elsewhere, who encourage me to keep going.)

First, notice how the rhetoric regularly employed against the
remission of global debts echoes the arguments used against
the abolition of slavery. Read the writings of the eighteenth-

century Quaker John Woolman (1720–72). Read again the story of Wilberforce (1759–1833).[2] The patronizing, temporizing and sometimes bullying they had to put up with; the tone of voice that says 'we know how the world works; don't bother us with moral arguments'; the powerful interests that lobbied the great and the good against them; all this is routine today as the western global empire fights back against the cry for justice. But every time we put it off one more day, several hundred children die. And that's just the start.

We must learn, therefore, to recognize the complex arguments against debt remission for what they are. People tell you it's a tricky and many-sided subject. Yes, it is; so was slavery. So are all major moral problems. The fact remains that what is now going on amounts to theft by the strong from the weak, by the rich from the poor. I am choosing my words carefully; read the literature and see. If a policeman catches a thief red-handed, he doesn't need complicated arguments about the thief's motives, the complexities of his and his victim's intertwined economic situations, or any other prevarication; the important thing is to stop the thieving and stop it right away. In the light of this, we should learn to recognize the complex stories told by those with vested interests as corresponding closely to the complex stories told by the Sadducees to show how impossible it was to believe in the resurrection. Jesus' answer was blunt and to the point: you're wrong, because you don't know the Bible and you don't know God's power (Mark 12.24). Our response must be that because we believe in the resurrection of Jesus as an event within history we believe that the living God has already begun the process of new creation, and what may seem impossible in human terms is possible to God.

Thus when people object, as they do, to me and others pointing out that the rich are getting richer and the poor are getting poorer, by commenting that wealth is not finite, that 'statist' and 'globalist' solutions and handouts will merely strip the poor of their human dignity and vocation to work, and that all this will encourage the poor towards a sinful envy of the rich, a slothful escapism and a counterproductive reliance on Caesar rather than God – when I hear this kind of thing, I want to take such commentators to refugee camps, to villages where children die every day, to towns where most adults have already died of AIDS, and to show them people who haven't got the energy to be envious, who aren't slothful because they are using all the energy they've got to queue for water and to care for each other, who know perfectly well that they don't need handouts so much as justice. I know, and such people will often know in their bones, that wealth isn't a zero-sum game, but reading the collected works of F. A. Hayek in a comfortable chair in North America simply doesn't address the moral questions of the twenty-first century.[3]

Second, return to what I said a few moments ago: the way in which the liberal theology of the last century has, in denying the bodily resurrection, joined forces with the Sadducees in keeping God at arm's length and thus holding at bay any chance of theologically grounded work for God's new world, for the kingdom to come on earth as in heaven. There are multiple ironies here too, as the social-gospel liberalism was also embracing the modernist denials of God's action in history, when that action was just what they needed as their basis. The heirs of that liberal theology are today keen to marginalize the Bible, declaring that it supports slavery and other wicked things, because they don't like what it says on other topics such as sexual ethics. But if you push the Bible off the table you are merely colluding with pagan empire, denying yourself the sourcebook for your kingdom-critique of oppression. The Sadducees didn't know the Bible or God's power; that's why they denied the resurrection and supported Rome.[4]

Third, however, look at the mirror-image point: that much conservative theology, not least in America where it counts heavily at the moment, has also served to reinforce the dominance of the West. The Cold War years enabled America to build up its persona as God's answer to Communism. Many conservative churches there still live by the belief that what's good for America is good for God – with the result, for instance, that if America needs to produce more acid rain in order to keep up car production, then God must be happy with it, and anyone who talks about pollution, or is disappointed that the President didn't sign the Kyoto protocol, is somehow anti-Christian, or is simply producing a 'baptized neo-socialism', as one reviewer accused me of. The rampant belief in the Rapture lends strong support to this, as we saw earlier: Armageddon is coming, so who cares what state the planet is in? The irony is that those American churches that protest most vocally against the teaching of Darwinism in their schools are often, in their public policies, supporting a kind of economic Darwinism, the survival of the fittest in world markets and military power.

In particular, fourth, the strong belief in Jesus' bodily resurrection among conservative Christians in many parts of the world, especially in America, has taken that belief out of its biblical context and put it instead in a different one, where it serves agendas diametrically opposed to the biblical ones. For many conservative Christians today, belief in Jesus' bodily resurrection is all about God's supernatural action in the world, legitimating an upstairs/downstairs view of reality – a dualism, in other words – in which the 'supernatural' is the real world and the 'natural', the this-worldly, is secondary and largely irrelevant. The resurrection is thus affirmed as the orthodox belief over against liberal modernism; but what you are left with is *conservative* modernism, leaving the modernism intact (the split between heaven and earth) and indeed reinforcing it. From this viewpoint, of course, what matters is the supernatural, world-denying salvation offered by the gospel. Any attempt to work for God's justice *on earth* as in heaven is condemned as the sort of thing those wicked anti-supernatural liberals try to do. That is precisely not what the resurrection is about, and in defending the orthodox position on Easter I have become aware, the last few years, that many liberals are really attacking not Easter itself but the escapist and socially conservative politics of those they perceive to be defending it. This convoluted distortion of the gospel is not, alas, confined to North American fundamentalism.

Thus from both sides within would-be Christian culture – those who deny the resurrection, and thereby cut off the branch from which true Christian work for justice must grow, and those who affirm it but use it to reinforce their anti-thisworldly theology – we find apparently powerful reasons for doing nothing about the plight of the world, and for letting things take their own course, which means of course letting the strong go on winning. Implicit social Darwinism again. We should know where that got us a hundred years ago, as preachers in Britain and Germany solemnly declared that a few good wars might be God's way of enabling the human race to become fitter and stronger. As we learn the lessons of God's future let us not forget the tragic lessons of our own past.

The paradigm I have set out in this book tells heavily against both sides. This is the point where a genuine biblical theology can come out of the forest and startle both those who thought that the Bible was irrelevant or dangerous for political ethics and those who thought that taking the Bible seriously meant being conservative politically as well as theologically. The truth is very different – as we should have guessed from Jesus' own preaching of the kingdom, not to mention his death as a would-be rebel king. His resurrection, and the promise of God's new world that comes with it, creates a programme for change and offers to empower it. Those who believe the gospel have no choice but to follow.

And if people tell you that after all there isn't very much they can do, remember what the answer is. What would you say to someone who said, rightly, that God would make them completely holy in the resurrection, and that they would never reach this state of complete holiness until then – and who then went on to say, wrongly, that therefore there was no point in even trying to live a holy life until that time? You would press for some form of inaugurated eschatology. You would insist that the new life of the Spirit, in obedience to the lordship of Jesus Christ, should produce radical transformation of behaviour in the present life, *anticipating* the life to come even though we know we shall never be complete and whole until then. That is the lesson of Romans 6. Well, apply the same to Romans 8! How do you answer someone who says, rightly, that the world will not be completely just and right until the new creation, and who deduces, wrongly, that there is no point trying to bring justice to the world (or for that matter ecological health, another topic for which there is no space here) until that time? Answer, from everything I have said so far: insist on inaugurated eschatology, on a radical transformation of the way we behave as a worldwide community, *anticipating* the eventual time when God will be all in all even though we all agree things won't be complete until then. There is the challenge. The resurrection of Jesus points us to it and gives us the energy for it. Let us overcome our surprise that such a hope should be set before us, and go to the task with prayer and wisdom.

3. Beauty

An apparently quite different theme now emerges as part of the work of mission within a theology of new creation. I believe that taking creation and new creation seriously is the way to understand and revitalize aesthetic awareness and perhaps even creativity among Christians today. Beauty matters, dare I say, almost as much as spirituality and justice.[5] Of course, if you have to choose between beautiful slavery and an ugly Exodus you must go for the Exodus; but, as William Temple said in a different (though related) context, fortunately we don't have to make that choice.

Romans 8, with its rich theology of new creation, offers us a way of appreciating natural beauty. Paul speaks of the creation groaning in travail, waiting to give birth to God's new world. The beauty of the present world, I suggested earlier in the book, has something about it of the beauty of a chalice, beautiful in itself but more hauntingly beautiful in what we know it's meant to be filled with; or that of the violin, beautiful in itself but particularly because we know the music it's capable of. Another example might be the engagement ring, which is meant as it is to delight the eye but which is meant even more to delight the heart because of what it promises. I want now to develop this further in terms of the new creativity to which I believe Christians are called as we find ourselves poised between creation and new creation.

We are moving away, I think, from the old split in which it was expected that good Christians couldn't be artists and good artists couldn't be Christians. We now have, thank God, some wonderful Christian painters, composers, sculptors and even poets who are showing the way forward. We even have some splendid theoreticians, such as Jeremy Begbie and his project, *Theology through the Arts*, which has done so much in this area. I want to offer a proposal about where the artistic endeavour belongs, where what we loosely call human culture belongs, within the discipline of Christian mission, within the map of creation and new creation.

It is, I believe, part of being made in God's image that we are ourselves creators, or at least procreators. The extraordinary ability to bring forth new life, supremely of course through begetting children but in millions of other ways as well, is central to the mandate the human race receives in Genesis 1 and 2. To make sense of and celebrate a beautiful world through the production of artefacts which are themselves beautiful is part of the call to be stewards of creation, as was Adam's naming of the animals. Genuine art is thus itself a response to the beauty of creation, which itself is a pointer to the beauty of God.

But we don't live in the garden of Eden, and art which attempts to do so quickly becomes flaccid and trivial. (The church doesn't have a monopoly on kitsch or sentimentalism, but if you want to find it the church may well be the easiest place to start.) We live in a fallen world, and any attempt to plug in to some kind of pantheism, worshipping the creation as if it were itself divine, always runs up against the problem of evil. At that point, art, like philosophy and politics, often swings round the other way, and determinedly responds to ugliness with more ugliness. (This reflects the supposed swing in Greek tragedy from Sophocles, describing the world as it ought to be, to Euripides, describing the world as it is.) We have a rash of this in the British arts world at the moment, a kind of brutalism that, under the guise of realism, simply expresses futility and boredom. We are back here on the fault line between those who refuse to recognize evil on the one hand and those who see nothing but evil on the other.

This presents a wonderful opportunity for Christians with an integrated worldview, and with a theology of both creation and new creation, to find the way forwards, perhaps to *lead* the way forwards, beyond such a sterile impasse. When we read Romans 8 we find Paul affirming that the whole of creation is groaning in travail as it longs for its redemption. Creation is good, but it is not God. It is beautiful, but its beauty is at present transient. It is in pain, but that pain is taken into the very heart of God and becomes part of the pain of new birth. The beauty of creation, to which art responds and which it tries to express, imitate and highlight, is not simply beauty which it possesses in itself, but the beauty which it possesses in view of what is promised to it: back to the chalice, the violin, the engagement ring. We are committed to describing the world not just as it should be, not just as it is, but as – by God's grace alone! – one day it will be. And we should never forget that when Jesus rose from the dead, as the paradigm, first example and generating power of the whole new creation, the marks of the nails were not only visible on his hands and his feet. They were the way he was to be identified. When art comes to terms with *both* the wounds of the world *and* the promise of resurrection, and learns how to express and respond to both at once, we will be on the way to a fresh vision, a fresh mission.

There is a parody of this in the passionate belief of many artists and writers of the last generation that the only true art is that which is politically committed. At least the Marxists who thought like that had grasped the point that neither sentimentality nor brutalism will do, but only eschatology in the process of being realized. If Christian artists can glimpse the truth of which that Marxist vision is a parody, they may find a way forwards to celebrating beauty without lapsing into pantheism on the one hand or cynicism on the other. This will take serious imagination, imagination fuelled by reflection and prayer at the foot of the cross and before the empty tomb, imagination that will discern the mysteries of God's judgment on evil and God's reaffirmation, through resurrection, of his beautiful creation. Art at its best not only draws attention to the way things are but to the way things will be, when the earth is filled with the knowledge of God as the waters cover the sea. That remains a surprising hope, and perhaps it will be the artists who are best at conveying both the hope and the surprise.

4. Evangelism

If we are engaging in the work of new creation, in seeking to bring advance signs of God's eventual new world into being in the present, in justice and beauty and a million other ways (there is no space for more in this book, and justice and beauty themselves cry out, of course, for fuller treatment), then at the centre of the picture there stands the personal call of the gospel of Jesus to every child, woman and man.

The word 'evangelism' still sends shivers down the spines of many people. There are various reasons for this. Some people have been scared off by frightening or bullying harangues, or tactless and offensive behaviour, or embarrassing and naive presentations of 'the gospel'. Others have never suffered such indignities, but heard or read about them, and are glad to have a good excuse to pour scorn on all evangelism – as though, because some people do it badly, nobody should ever do it at all. And, of course, many in the media still confuse 'evangelist' (one who preaches the gospel) with 'evangelical' (someone who holds certain doctrines in certain particular ways), and hence 'evangelism' (the preaching of the gospel) with 'evangel-icalism' (the broad coalition of 'evangelicals', which cuts across the lines of 'official' denominations). This is not the place to address the many issues of the nature of evangelism itself, or what counts as 'preaching the gospel', or the relation of 'evangelism' to 'mission' as abstract categories – though I hope the present chapter will give food for thought on all these topics. Rather, I simply want to show how the paradigm I have advanced in this book, of the surprising hope we find in the resurrection of Jesus and the New Testament's exploration of its significance, gives a new perspective on what 'evangelism' might be, and hence how one might go about it.

Much 'evangelism' has, of course, consisted of taking the traditional framework of a heaven-and-hell expectation and persuading people that it's time they considered the 'heaven' option and grabbed it while they had the chance. What's stopping them getting there is sin; the solution is provided in Jesus Christ; all they have to do is to accept it! Millions of Christians today are Christians because they heard that mes-sage and responded to it. Am I therefore saying – since plainly I think that way of putting things is at best lopsided – that they have been deceived or mistaken?

No. God gloriously honours all kinds of ways of announ-cing the good news. I do not suppose for a moment that my own way of preaching, or talking to individuals about God, is perfect and without flaws, and yet God (I believe) has graciously honoured some at least of what I do. No doubt he would have been far more honoured if I had done it better and more prayerfully. No doubt the flaws in my own preaching, and the different flaws in other presentations, will eventually show up in the Christian lives of those who come to faith as a result, and no doubt we all ought to polish up and improve what we do for the sake of our hearers and the honour of God. But, as every generation has known, it isn't the quality of the preaching that counts, but the faithfulness of God.

And, of course, the praying that goes with the preaching. The first time I preached a proper sermon, my mentor gave me some good advice: your praying and your preaching should be of the same length. You don't want to find yourself limping, with one leg shorter than the other. God works as a result of prayer and faithfulness, not technique and cleverness.

But none of this is an excuse for not understanding what is going on when we evangelize, or not shaping the way we do it in accordance with the full biblical gospel. So let's start with the latter point, and say clearly at once: 'the gospel', in the New Testament, is the good news that God (the world's creator) is at last becoming king, and that Jesus, whom this God raised from the dead, is the world's true Lord. There are a thousand different ways of saying this, depending on where the audience is starting from and what sort of occasion it is. (Compare the various speeches in Acts!) Some people will know who Jesus is, others will have only a hazy idea about him; some will hear the word 'God' and think of an old man with a white beard, while others will think of a sort of heavenly gas. Almost everyone will need help to understand what the message is about at some point or another.

The power of the gospel lies, not in the offer of a new spirituality or religious experience, not in the threat of hellfire (certainly not in the threat of being 'left behind') which can be removed if only the hearer ticks this box, says this prayer, raises a hand, or whatever . . . but in the powerful announcement that God is God, that Jesus is Lord, that the powers of evil have been defeated, that God's new world has begun. This announcement, stated as a fact about the way the world is rather than as an appeal about the way you might like your life, your emotions or your bank balance to be, is the foundation of everything else. Of course, once the gospel announcement is made, in whatever way, it means instantly that all people everywhere are gladly invited to come in, to join the party, to discover forgiveness for the past, an astonishing destiny in God's future, and a vocation in the present. And in that welcome, and invitation, all the emotions can be, and one hopes will eventually be, fully engaged.

But how can the church announce that God is God, that Jesus is Lord, that the powers of evil, corruption and death itself have been defeated and that God's new world has begun? Doesn't this seem laughable? Well, it would be if it wasn't happening. But if a church is working on the issues we've already looked at – if it's actively involved in seeking justice in the world, both globally and locally, and if it's cheerfully celebrating God's good creation, and its rescue from corruption, in art and music, and if, in addition, its own internal life gives every sign that new creation is indeed happening, generating a new type of community – then suddenly the announcement makes a lot of sense.

So what account can we give, within this theology of new creation, of what happens when the gospel takes root? It happens again and again, thank God: people discover, firing up within themselves, the sense that it does make sense, that they really believe it, that they find it transforming the way they are thinking and feeling about all sorts of other things, that the presence of Jesus is suddenly a reality for them, that reading the Bible becomes exciting, that they can't get enough of Christian worship and fellowship. We use various words for this moment, or this process (with some people it happens in a flash, with others it takes a long time): conversion, which means turning round to travel in the opposite direction; regeneration, which means new birth; 'entering into Christ', which means joining the family which takes its name and its character from Jesus himself. The New Testament speaks of such a person 'dying with Christ' and 'being raised with him' (Romans 6; Colossians 2 and 3), of passing through the water of baptism as the sign and means of leaving behind the old life and beginning the new, of identifying with the death and resurrection of Jesus himself. And, in terms of the big picture of new creation which we have been drawing throughout, what we must say is this. Such a person is a living, breathing little bit of 'new creation' – that new creation which has already begun to happen in Jesus' resurrection, and which will be complete when God finally makes his new heavens and new earth and raises us to share in that new world. Paul puts it like this: 'If anyone is in Christ – new creation!'[6]

Stating the matter like this avoids three problems into which evangelism can often run. First, it makes it clear that to become a Christian is not to say 'no' to the good world which God has made. It is, of course, to turn one's back on all the corruptions into which the world has fallen, and into which each individual has fallen. Sometimes converts will need to say a firm 'no' to things which are not evil in themselves (alcohol, for instance) in order to put a clear space between themselves and habits and patterns of life which had previously held them in their grip. But to think in terms of 'new creation' avoids the problem of supposing for a moment that one could forget earth and concentrate on heaven.

Second, to see evangelism in terms of the announcement of God's kingdom, of Jesus' lordship and of the consequent new creation, avoids from the start any suggestion that the main or central thing that has happened is that the new Christian has entered into a private relationship with God or with Jesus,

and that this relationship is the main or only thing that matters. (Some currently popular Christian songs seem to suggest
this rather too frequently, as though the main thing about the
gospel is that Jesus could take the place of my girlfriend or
boyfriend.) Seeing evangelism and any resulting conversions
in terms of new creation means that the new convert knows
from the start that he or she is part of God's kingdom-project,
which stretches out beyond 'me and my salvation' to embrace,
or rather to be embraced by, God's worldwide purposes. Along
with 'conversion' there will then go, at least in principle, the call
to find out where in the total project one can make one's own
contribution. (The fact that this vocation often takes time to
emerge doesn't mean it isn't something one must expect from
the outset.)

Third, putting evangelism and conversion within the context of new creation means that the convert, who has heard
the message in terms of the sovereign and saving lordship of
Jesus himself, will never be inclined to think that Christian behaviour – saying 'no' to the things which diminish human flourishing and God's glory, and saying 'yes' to the things which
enhance them – is an optional extra, or simply a matter of getting your head round some rather strange rules and regulations.
There have in the past been some kinds of evangelism which
have implied that the main thing is to sign on, to pray a particular prayer which results in the assurance that one is safely
on the way to heaven – and which have failed to mention, to
the frustration of pastors and teachers who then try to look
after such 'converts', the fact that following Jesus means just
that, *following Jesus*, not ticking a box which says 'Jesus' and
then sitting back as though it's all done. To speak, rather, of
Jesus' lordship, and of the new creation which results from his
victory on Calvary and at Easter, implies at once that to con-
fess him as Lord and to believe that God raised him from the
dead is to allow one's entire life to be reshaped by him, knowing that, though this will be painful from time to time, it will

be the way, not to a diminished or cramped human existence, but to genuine human life in the present, and complete, glorious, resurrected human life in the future. As with every other aspect of new creation, there will be surprises on the way. But Christian ethics will only gain from being understood as one expression of Christian hope.

5. Conclusion

The mission of the church must therefore reflect, and be shaped by, the future hope as the New Testament presents it. I believe that if we take these three areas – justice, beauty and evangelism – in terms of the anticipation of God's eventual setting-to-rights of the whole world, we will find that they dovetail together, and in fact that they are all part of the same larger whole, which is the message of hope and new life that comes with the good news of Jesus' resurrection.

This is the foundation, I believe, for the work of hope in the day-to-day life of the church. My own vocation has taken me to an area of my country where, for many people, hope has been in short supply. A nebulous sense of injustice hangs over many a community in the shape of the half-formed belief that the industrial collapse of the late twentieth century must be somebody's fault, and that something should be done about it. This is very different from the sense that the world owes you a living. It is a reflection of the fact that when a large community has been built up over several generations around one or two key industries, and when those industries are then shut down not because they are not productive, or because the workers are incompetent or lazy, but because they do not fit the larger strategic plans of people whose faces are never seen in the area, then there is a quiet anger, a sense that something has gone wrong at a structural level. Human societies should not work like that, and if they do then questions have to be asked. Part of the task of the church must be to take up that sense of injustice, to bring it to speech, to help people both articulate it and, when they are ready to do so, to turn it into prayer (it's surprising, until you find yourself in that position, how many of the Psalms suddenly become relevant!). And the task then continues with the church's work with the whole local community, to foster programmes for better housing, schools and community facilities, to encourage new job opportunities, to campaign and cajole and work with local government and councils and, in short, to foster hope at any and every level. And part of the argument of this book is that, when this is done, this is not something other than the surprising hope of the gospel, the hope for 'life after life after death'. It is the direct result of that: the hope for 'life before death'.

The second feature of many communities both in the post-industrial West and in many of the poorer parts of the world is ugliness. True, some communities manage to sustain levels of art and music, often rooted in folk culture, which bring a richness even to the most poverty-stricken areas. But the shoulder-shrugging functionalism of post-war architecture, coupled with the passivity born of decades of television, have meant that for many people the world appears to offer little but bleak urban landscapes on the one hand and tawdry entertainment on the other. And when people cease to be surrounded by beauty, they cease to hope. They internalize the message of their eyes and ears, the message that whispers that they are not worth very much, that they are, in effect, less than fully human.

To communities in danger of going that route, the message of new creation, of the beauty of the present world taken up and transcended in the beauty of the world that is yet to be – with part of that beauty being precisely the healing of the present anguish – comes as a surprising hope. Part of the role of the church has been in the past, and could and should be again, to foster and sustain lives of beauty and aesthetic meaning at every level, from music-making in the village pub to drama in the local primary school, from artists' and photographers' workshops to still-life painting classes, from symphony concerts (well, they managed them in the concentration camps; how inventive might we be?) to driftwood sculptures. The church, because it is the family that believes in hope for new creation, should stand out in every town and village as the place where new creativity bursts forth for the whole community, pointing to the hope which, like all beauty, always comes as a surprise.

And, of course, evangelism – which will flourish best if the church is giving itself to works of justice (putting things to rights in the community) and works of beauty (highlighting the glory of creation and the glory yet to be revealed) – evangelism will always come as a surprise. You mean there is more? There is a new world, and it has already begun, and it works by healing and forgiveness and new starts and fresh energy? Yes, answers the church; and it comes about as people worship the God in whose image they are made, as they follow the Lord who bore their sins and rose from the dead, as they are indwelt by his Spirit and thereby given new life, a new way of life, a new zest for life. It is often pointed out that some of the places most lacking in hope are not the industrial wastelands or the bleak landscapes shorn of beauty, but the places where there is too much money, too much high culture, too much of everything except faith, hope and love. To such places, and the sad people who live in them, as well as to those who find themselves battered by circumstances beyond their control, the message of Jesus and his death and resurrection comes as good news from a far country, news of surprising hope.

This is the good news – of justice, beauty and above all Jesus – that the church is called upon to live and to speak, to bring into reality, in each place and each generation. What might the life of the church look like if it was shaped, in turn, by this hope-shaped mission?

14

Reshaping the church
for mission (1): biblical roots

1. Introduction

If today's, and tomorrow's, church is to engage in this kind of mission, seeking both to implement the achievement of Jesus and his resurrection and thereby to anticipate the final renewal of all things, it must itself be renewed, resourced and reshaped for this mission. What will this look like?

It is vital that we address this question in terms of the scriptural witness to the resurrection and the way in which, in the Bible itself, this witness is directly translated into mission and the life of the church. The present chapter will therefore examine, briefly, the gospels, Acts and Paul with this in mind, before the final chapter in which we shall apply this to specific issues in the life of the church.[1]

Much of the talk about 'mission-shaped church' in recent days has inevitably, and rightly, been about the practicalities of church life: about restructuring ministry, parishes, ways of working in order the better to facilitate the mission to which we are called. I'm not going to attempt to address that in what follows. Instead, I want to undergird that necessary and vital task by setting out what seem to be the scriptural and spiritual priorities of a church refocused on a hope-shaped mission. Without this, there is always the danger of mere pragmatism. And with pragmatism there often comes opportunism – for the advancing of agendas which are driven, not by the imperative to mission, but by one or other of the old models of church life which are now running out of steam. My task in this chapter and the final one will be, rather, to lay some foundations: first in the Bible and then in key areas of Christian living.

2. The gospels and Acts

The first and perhaps most obvious meaning of the resurrection of Jesus, which emerges strongly in all four gospels, is that God has vindicated the Jesus who proclaimed the kingdom and died as Israel's representative. This may sound obvious, but to judge from the reactions I often get when I say this sort of thing I think it is not sufficiently recognized. In Mark's short and probably truncated account there is no sense of 'Jesus is raised, therefore there really is life after death'; rather, the point is, 'Jesus is raised, therefore you'd better go to Galilee and see him there.' For anyone who has read the whole gospel, the strong implication is, 'Jesus is raised, just as he told you he would be; in other words, all that he said about the coming of the kingdom through his own work, through his death and resurrection, has come true.' The resurrection completes the inauguration of God's kingdom. In Mark's perspective, it is at least part of what Jesus meant when he said that some standing with him would not taste death before they saw the kingdom of God come with power. This points us forward to the more detailed outworking in the other gospels. The resurrection is not an isolated supernatural oddity proving how powerful, if apparently arbitrary, God can be when he wants to. Nor is it at all a way of showing that there is indeed a heaven awaiting us after death. It is the decisive event which means that God's kingdom really has been launched on earth as it is in heaven.

When we turn to Matthew, we find that he takes this further – and it is indeed quite possible that Mark's original text had something like this as well. When the disciples go to Galilee and see Jesus there, they worship him (though some, interestingly, doubt); this is the culmination of the Christology which has been building up throughout the gospel. Jesus is vindicated as the Emmanuel, the man who is God-with-us. But there is no sense either that this is just a nice thing that's happened to him, or that the point of it all is for him to say, 'So if you go on behaving yourselves you'll be able to join me in heaven one day.' On the contrary. Just as Jesus taught his followers to pray that God's kingdom would come on earth as in heaven, so now he claims that all authority in heaven and on earth has been given to him, and on that basis he commands the disciples to go and make it happen, to work, in other words, as agents of that authority. What remains implicit in Mark, at least as we have it, is made explicit in Matthew: resurrection doesn't mean *escaping from* the world, but *mission to* the world based on Jesus' *lordship over* the world.

Already we begin to see how the watershed works. If the resurrection is an event that actually occurred (in some sense) in time and space, as well as in the material reality of Jesus' body, it has implications for other events that must follow. If it's only (what we call) a 'spiritual' event, either involving Jesus being alive now in some heavenly realm, or simply involving a new sense of faith and hope in our minds and hearts, the only events that will follow are various forms of private spirituality. So Matthew gives us the clear message of what the resurrection means: Jesus is now enthroned as the Lord of heaven and earth. His kingdom has been established. And this kingdom is to be put into practice by his followers summoning all nations to obedient allegiance to him, marking them out in baptism. The closing line draws together the major themes of the gospel: the Emmanuel, the God-with-us, is now Jesus-with-us, until the final end of the old age, the time when the new age which has been inaugurated in the resurrection has completed its transforming work in the world.

This brings us to Luke, and in particular to the marvellous story of the two disciples on the road to Emmaus. There is much that could be said about Luke 24, but for the moment I simply draw attention to the answer which this chapter gives to the question, 'So what if Jesus is raised bodily from the dead?'[2] The biggest and most important answer is that with the resurrection of Jesus the entire story of God and Israel, and God and the world, must be told in a new way.

This, again, is watershed stuff. Without the resurrection there is one way of telling the story; with the resurrection there is a whole other way. Without the resurrection, the story is an unfinished and potentially tragic drama, in which Israel can hold on to hope but with an increasing sense that the narrative is spinning out of control. Without the resurrection even the story of Jesus is a tragedy, certainly in first-century Jewish terms, as the two on the road to Emmaus knew very well. But with the resurrection there is a new way of telling the entire story. The resurrection isn't just a surprise happy ending for one person, but is the turning-point for everything else. It is the point at which all the old promises come true at last: the promises of David's unshakeable kingdom; the promises of Israel's return from the greatest exile of them all; and behind that again, quite explicit in Matthew, Luke and John, the promise that all the nations would now be blessed through the seed of Abraham.

If Jesus has not been raised, Luke is saying, all you have is hopes raised once more and dashed once more. They would go on hoping, no doubt, because they were faithful Jews; but if Jesus is not raised, nothing has happened to show that their hopes might after all be fulfilled. But if Jesus has been raised, then this is how the Old Testament has to be read: as a story of suffering and vindication, of exile and restoration, a narrative which reaches its climax not in Israel becoming top nation and beating the rest of the world at its own game, but in the suffering and vindication, the exile and restoration, of the Messiah – not for himself alone, but because he is carrying the saving promises of God. If the messenger bringing vital news falls into the river and is then rescued, he isn't rescued for himself alone, but for the sake of those who are waiting in desperate hope for his life-giving message. If Jesus is raised, Luke is saying, he really was and is the Messiah; but if he's the Messiah, he is God's messenger, God's promise-bearer, carrying the promises made to Abraham, Moses, David and the prophets, promises not only for Israel but for the whole world.

That is why, incidentally, the Old Testament must be seen as part of Christian scripture. I respect those who call the Old Testament 'the Hebrew scriptures' to acknowledge that they are still the scriptures of a living faith community different from Christianity. But Luke insists that, since Jesus really was raised from the dead, the ancient scriptures of Israel must be read as a story which reaches its climax in Jesus and will then produce its proper fruit not only in Israel but in Jesus' followers and, through them, in all the world. That's why, when Jesus appears to the disciples in the upper room in verses 36–49, his opening of their minds to understand the scriptures (vv. 44–46) results directly in the new commission: that 'repentance and forgiveness of sins is to be proclaimed in his name to all nations, beginning from Jerusalem'. This is not something other than the Jewish hope. It is woven into the scriptures from very early on that when God finally does for Israel what he's going to do, then the nations of the world will come to share in the blessing. This, indeed, is one of the central keys to unlocking New Testament theology.

Of course, if Jesus is not raised from the dead, we might recognize two sorts of religion or faith: a Christian faith that believed it gained access to 'the divine' through Jesus, and a Jewish faith that believed it gained access to 'the divine' apart from Jesus (and was perhaps still waiting for another Messiah). But both of these would be very different from real Christianity and real Judaism. If, out of a desire to be fair to Judaism, you turn both Christianity and Judaism into examples of 'a religion', a way of ordering your own spirituality, you may be more politically correct, but you will do violence to both actual households of faith. But if Jesus is raised from the dead, then the scriptures have reached their goal in him, and it's now time for the moment the Psalms and prophets longed to see, when the nations of the earth will bring their treasures in loyalty and obedience to God's anointed king, Israel's Messiah.

The further question, of how Christianity continues to relate to the Judaism that does not recognize Jesus as Messiah, is of course vital. It is addressed in the New Testament, not least by Paul. But we cannot allow our proper sensitivities on this subject to prevent us from speaking of Jesus' resurrection, and from embracing the challenge that comes as a result. For Luke, the point of the resurrection is that the long story of Israel, the great overarching scriptural narrative, has reached its goal and climax, and must now give birth, as it always intended, to the worldwide mission in which the nations are summoned to turn from their idolatry and find forgiveness of sins. And they are to do this, Luke implies, because in Jesus we see the true God in human form, the reality of which all idols are parodies, and the true forgiveness of sins through his cross, the reality before which all sacrifices are types and shadows. The resurrection, in other words, is for Luke neither an odd miracle that happens to have restored Jesus to life but has no other meaning as such, nor a sign that we shall all go to heaven when we die, but the fulfilment of the ancient scriptural promises on the one hand and the beginning of God's worldwide mission on the other.

All these themes reach their fullest statement in the gospel of John, where they are displayed in a sequence of scenes that are as moving as they are masterly.[3] John 20 and 21 present us with two main themes: the new day and the new commission.

John 20 stresses twice (in vv. 1 and 19) that Easter is the first day of the new week. John has so ordered his gospel that the sequence of seven signs, climaxing in the cross of Jesus on the sixth day of the week and his resting in the tomb on the seventh, functions as the week of the old creation; and now Easter functions as the beginning of the new creation. The Word through whom all things were made is now the Word through whom all things are remade. So far from Jesus' resurrection being an odd or isolated 'supernatural' event, breaking in as a sign of what God could do if he chose but normally doesn't, it is to be seen as the beginning of the new world, the first day of the new week, the unveiling of the prototype of what God is now going to accomplish in the rest of the world. Mary supposes Jesus is the gardener; that's the right mistake to make, because like Adam he is charged with bringing God's new world to order. He has come to uproot the thorns and thistles, and to plant myrtle and cypress instead, as Isaiah promised in his great picture of the new creation that would result from the Word of God coming like rain or snow into the world.[4]

This, too, has little to do with the resurrection showing that we 'go to heaven when we die', and a great deal to do with the new commission of the disciples to be for the world what Jesus was for Israel: 'As the father sent me,' he says, 'so I send you.'[5] And, as in Luke, the commission is accompanied by the necessary equipment: to be Jesus' agents in the world, his followers need, and are given, his own Spirit. Easter and Pentecost belong together. Easter commissions Jesus' followers for a task; Pentecost gives them the necessary equipment to accomplish it.

In particular, as we began to see in an earlier chapter, Jesus calls his followers to a new mode of *knowing*.[6] I have written elsewhere about what I have called an epistemology of love. We have traditionally thought of knowing in terms of subject and object, and have struggled to attain objectivity by detaching our subjectivity. It can't be done, and one of the achievements of postmodernity is to demonstrate that. What we are called to, and what in the resurrection we are equipped for, is a knowing in which we are involved as subjects *but as self-giving, not as self-seeking, subjects*: in other words, a knowing which is a form of love. The story of Thomas encapsulates this transformation of knowing. He wants knowledge he can control, objective evidence and all that goes with it. But when Jesus confronts him and offers him the proof he asked for, his blustering turns to belief and confession: 'My Lord,' he says, 'and my God!'[7] The story of Peter in John 21 then opens this up to a different level: the key question, echoing down the centuries in the ears of all who have struggled and failed in their discipleship, is the ultimate one: 'Do you love me?'

This sends us back to Ludwig Wittgenstein, whom we met earlier on in the book, and to his famous saying that 'it is love that believes the resurrection'. Wittgenstein's most famous book, the *Tractatus Logico-Philosophicus*, was first published in 1921, and remains one of the most seminal and provocative texts of philosophy not only of the modern period, but, some would say, ever. Wittgenstein orders his remarks with a severe and logical numbering: 1; 1.1; 1.11; 1.12; 1.13; 1.2; 1.21; then 2; and so on. Number 1 takes only half a page, whereas 2 takes five pages, 3 takes nine, and so on. There are six sections in all, ending with a subsection numbered 6.54. Then, tellingly, section 7 consists of a single sentence: 'What we cannot speak about, we must pass over in silence.'[8]

Wittgenstein, of course, was Jewish, and a man of amazing cultural and aesthetic awareness. He had perfect musical pitch and a perfect architect's eye. He also had a strong mystical streak. I can't claim to understand all the main six sections of the *Tractatus*, but I think I know what Wittgenstein was doing at this point. I think he was consciously modelling Genesis 1: knowledge, like creation, starting small but pregnant, developing in complexity until the full height of the sixth day, the day when humans are created in God's image. Then, on the seventh day, a silence: a rest, a pregnant pause – in other words, a sabbath. Some things, Wittgenstein indicates, go beyond speech and philosophy, and about them one can and must remain silent. What I want to suggest, with great temerity, is that in the resurrection one is given the beginning of a new knowing, a new epistemology, a new coming-to-speech, the Word born afresh after the death of all human knowing and speech, all human hope and love, after the silent rest of the seventh-day sabbatical in the tomb. I don't know if any Christian philosophers have thought of writing a post-Wittgensteinian *Tractatus Resurrectio-Philosophicus*, starting with the number 8; but I suggest that to attempt such a thing would be to take seriously, in terms of the science of knowing itself, what John is saying in chapters 20 and 21.

Coming back to the text from that diversion, we find in John 21 (one of the most moving and profound chapters in the whole Bible) a multi-layered statement of the new commission already announced in 20.19–23. The disciples go fishing, but catch nothing. Jesus then helps them to an enormous catch, but proceeds to commission Peter to be a shepherd rather than a fisherman. There are many things going on simultaneously here, but at the centre is the challenge to a new way of life, a new forgiveness, a new fruitfulness, a new following of Jesus which will be wider and more dangerous than what has gone before. This is a million miles from the hymns which simply speak of Jesus' resurrection in terms of our own assurance of a safe and happy rest in heaven. Quite the contrary. Jesus' resurrection summons us to dangerous and difficult tasks on earth.

In this story, 'fishing' seems to stand for 'what the disciples, like the rest of the world, were doing anyway', whereas 'shepherding' seems to stand for 'the new tasks within the new creation'. To develop that as a metaphor, it seems to me that a good deal of the church's work at the moment is concentrating on fishing, and helping others to fish, rather than on shepherding. Yes, there are tasks to be done in helping the present world to do better what it should be doing. Jesus will help us to do that. We are to be at work in partnership with the wider world. But if we only try to do alongside others what they are doing already we will miss the really significant task. As with Isaiah's vision in the Temple, and many other scenes both biblical and modern, Peter's change from fisherman to shepherd comes through his facing of his own sin and his receiving of forgiveness, as Jesus with his three-times-repeated question goes back to Peter's triple denial and then offers him forgiveness precisely in the form of a transformed and newly commissioned life. Those who don't want to face that searching question and answer may remain content to help the world with its fishing. Those who find the risen Jesus going to the roots of their rebellion, denial and sin, and offering them love and forgiveness, may well also find themselves sent off to be shepherds instead. Let those with ears listen.

All this comes out in a dozen ways in Acts. As Jesus was about to be taken from them for the last time, the disciples were still pressing the point that they thought was the centre of his whole mission in the first place. 'Lord, is this the time when you will restore the kingdom to Israel?'[9] Often enough, when that passage is read, people assume that Jesus' response means, 'No, you've got the wrong end of the stick'; in other words, 'We've left behind the categories of kingdom, Israel and all that; instead, you've got quite a different job to do.' But I suggest that, if we understand what the kingdom and Israel mean, and what Jesus' reply is about, we can see that his answer is actually, 'Yes! – but it won't look like you imagine, but like something very different instead.'

The disciples are assuming that for the kingdom to be restored to Israel will mean some kind of national superiority, perhaps a military defeat of Israel's enemies. But what Jesus has in mind is every bit as much the fulfilment of God's long-delayed plan for Israel and the kingdom. He has now been raised from the dead as Israel's Messiah; and Israel's Messiah, as the Psalms and prophets insist, is the world's true Lord. 'His dominion shall be from one sea to the other, from the River to the ends of the earth.'[10] That, of course, is the true message of the ascension story that follows immediately: as every Roman knew, the one who ascends into heaven is enthroned as the divine Emperor.

And how is this Emperor going to take command of his world-wide empire? His messengers, his emissaries, are to go off into all the territories of which he is already enthroned as Lord, and to bring the good news of his accession and his wise and just rule. 'You are to be my witnesses,' he says, 'in Jerusalem, Judaea, Samaria and to the ends of the earth.'[11] And that is of course exactly the pattern that follows in the whole book of Acts. The apostles are not offering people a new religious experience, though that will come as well. They are not telling them that they can now go to heaven when they die, though they will, if they believe, there to wait until the resurrection itself. Nor are they telling them that God has done an extraordinary miracle which shows how powerful he is, though he has. They are to go and tell the world that Jesus, the Jewish Messiah, is the world's true Lord, and to summon them to believing obedience. And that is exactly what they do.

Notice how the shape of the book of Acts works this out in terms not of what we call religion so much as what we call politics. The first half of Acts, up to chapter 12, has Jesus being announced as the risen Messiah, King of the Jews, under the nose of the Jewish authorities and particularly the Herod family. Finally Herod Agrippa, who had James killed and tried to have Peter killed as well, gets a dose of megalomania and thinks he's become divine, like a Hellenistic princeling or a Roman emperor; and he dies on the spot. (The incident is recorded by Josephus as well, and is clearly grounded in solid history.[12]) Then, in the second half of the book, Paul is always travelling, confronting Caesar's empire with news of its new Lord; and he ends up in Rome, under Caesar's nose, proclaiming God's kingdom, says Luke, and teaching about King Jesus as Lord, openly and without hindrance.[13] There could not be a much clearer statement of intent: the kingdoms of the world are now claimed as the kingdom of Israel's God, and of his Messiah.

And the basis of this announcement is the resurrection of Jesus: not his parables, not his healings, not even his atoning death, important though all of those are and remain. It is the resurrection of Jesus that means he is now enthroned as Lord. (We note in passing that, though this sequence of thought makes perfect though surprising sense within the world of first-century Judaism, the opposite movement doesn't work at all. Some people have suggested that the church first came to believe that Jesus was enthroned as Lord, and then deduced from that that he had been raised from the dead. This would make no sense whatever within that world.) The whole point is that Israel and the world have turned a great corner, and people have to be told about it. In a telling phrase, Luke says that the Sadducees were annoyed because the apostles were 'proclaiming in Jesus the resurrection of the dead'.[14] Many modern translations tone this down to something like 'announcing the resurrection of the dead because of Jesus', implying that the apostles were saying that because of Jesus' resurrection other people could now be raised to life. They may have been saying that too, but that's not the point Luke is getting at. The point is that they were announcing that in Easter 'the resurrection from the dead' had actually begun. Easter was the beginning of God's new world, the long-awaited new age, the resurrection of the dead.

Then, dramatically, Paul stands on the Areopagus in Athens, where, in Aeschylus's play six centuries earlier, Apollo had declared that 'When a man dies, and his blood is shed on the ground, there is no resurrection.' And on that spot, according to Acts 17, Paul declares that the speculations and puzzles of pagan theology and philosophy could now all be put on a different footing, because the one true God had unveiled himself and his plan for the whole world by appointing a man to be judge of the whole world, and had certified this by raising him from the dead.[15] This is what the resurrection does: it opens the new world in which, under the saving and judging lordship of Jesus, the Jewish Messiah, everything else is to be seen in a new light.

All this, naturally and rightly, raises huge questions for us. They are put succinctly in a letter I received a year or two ago, after I had made some protests about the way in which the whole notion of the kingdom of God had been carefully and deliberately screened out – and I mean literally 'screened out'! – from the BBC television series *Son of God*. My correspondent went straight to the point. 'As there is clearly no trace of a new kingdom after 2,000 years,' he wrote, 'perhaps it is kinder to Jesus to leave it out.' Well, it depends what you mean. People tend, in this conversation, to refer to the Crusades and the Spanish Inquisition, and to imply that all the Christian church has ever done can be summed up by those two monstrosities. This is of course ridiculous; but the church has been on the back foot for so long that we've forgotten how to give the right answer. But we might just note two striking lessons from the last twenty-five years of world history.

Granted that Eastern European Communism was going to fall by its own weight sooner or later, it is highly significant that the thing that actually put the crowbar under it and toppled it over was the fearless witness of a Polish pope and those who took courage from his faith and hope. And granted that apartheid could not last for ever, it is highly significant that at the centre of the movement for its peaceful dismantling, instead of the bloodbath all commentators had been expecting and many on the ground were hoping for, was a black African archbishop who spent the first three hours of every day, and repeated moments thereafter, in devout and fervent prayer. Who would have thought, thirty years ago, that we would see a Commission of Truth and Reconciliation set up to bring healing to that troubled country?

Now of course there are still many running sores in the world, many of which, like Northern Ireland, have brought shame on the church. Of course it is open to anyone to give alternative explanations of these and other events, and to ignore evidence which suggests that Jesus is Lord. His lordship is, after all, always exercised through, and visible to, faith. Even the striking occasional miracles that the early apostles performed didn't convince everybody at the time. This isn't just a cop-out. The

difference between the kingdoms of the world and the kingdom of God lies exactly in this, that the kingdom of God comes
through the death and resurrection of his son, not through
naked displays of brute force or wealth. But I rejoice that we
don't just have to talk of St Francis or Mother Teresa, or even
of William Wilberforce, but that we can speak perfectly cred-
ibly in our own day too of the power of the kingdom of the
risen Jesus to overthrow proud and oppressive regimes and to
give hope to the humble and poor, and to do so with remarkable restraint, dignity, justice and peace. And, on a smaller scale,
there are of course hundreds and thousands of things being
done by the church, in the name and power of the risen Jesus,
every day. I was privileged to be in Southwark Cathedral one
Saturday in 2001 to witness Nelson Mandela opening a new
suite of buildings which have dramatically extended the
Cathedral's work with the homeless and with young people,
including a room named after Bishop Desmond Tutu: a striking symbol, at the heart of multiracial South London, of the
power of the resurrection in a community that has often been
troubled and divided.

The gospels and Acts set the scene. But our main spokes-
man for the early church is St Paul; and, as we now move to
consider his writings, we shall see that he not only agrees with
the gospel-writers about the basic significance of the resurrection, but that he turns this into a bracing challenge to Christian living in the present.

3. Paul

We have already studied Paul's robust hope for the resurrection of the body. We have seen, too, that he can speak mov-
ingly of the intermediate state between death and resurrection:
his desire, he says, is 'to depart and be with Christ, which is
far better'.[16] Clearly this belief is based not just on the beliefs

of his Jewish upbringing, important though they were, but on the resurrection of Jesus himself.

But, like the gospel-writers, Paul does not see Jesus' resurrection as simply meaning that we are assured of being with Christ after death, and of final resurrection beyond that. The meaning of Easter, for him, is by no means confined to hope beyond the grave. He, like the gospel-writers, sees Jesus' resurrection as the start of a new world, a new creation, in which Jesus is already ruling and reigning as Lord. Nobody could accuse Paul of being unaware of the paradox of making such claims. Some of his most striking statements of the point are written from prison. And, in that context, it is Paul who articulates most strikingly what the resurrection means not just for the world in particular, vital though that is as the overall context, but for the ordinary life of every Christian, child, woman and man.

We begin with Paul's great statement of the new world in 1 Corinthians 15.12–28. He is battling to get it into the heads of the ex-pagan Corinthians, many of whom clearly hadn't fully grasped that the gospel meant what it said about Jesus' resurrection. The crunch comes in verse 17: if the Messiah isn't raised, then your faith is futile *and you are still in your sins*. In other words, with the resurrection of Jesus a new world has dawned in which forgiveness of sins is not simply a private experience; it is a fact about the cosmos. Sin is the root cause of death; if death has been defeated, it must mean that sin has been dealt with. But if the Messiah has not been raised, we are still in a world where sin reigns supreme and undefeated, so that the foundational Christian belief, that God has dealt with our sins in Christ, is based on thin air, and is reduced to whistling in the dark.

Paul then describes this new world in the striking and seminal passage in verses 20–28. The writing here is typically dense, but the central statements are strong and clear. The Jewish expectation of resurrection – the resurrection of all God's people at the end of time – has been split into two: first an advance foretaste, then the rest to follow. The Messiah has been raised as the start of the general resurrection; those who belong to him will be raised at his final appearing (v. 23). Then, and only then, will he complete the implementation of the victory he won at Calvary and Easter. That is the time when all enemies, including death itself, will be put under his feet, in fulfilment of scriptural promise (vv. 24–26). But notice verse 25a: *he must reign until . . .* ; in other words, he is already reigning, even though we do not yet see the full result of that reign.[17] And if we ask what on earth can possibly justify such an outrageous statement – that Jesus is already king of the world, even though Caesar seems to be, and death itself is still rampant – there can only be one answer: the resurrection.

Paul is thus firmly on the same page as the gospel-writers. The main meaning of the resurrection of Jesus for him is that God's new world has been brought into being through this event, the long-promised new world in which the covenant will be renewed, sins will be forgiven and death itself will be done away with. The resurrection is neither an isolated and out-of-character divine 'miracle', nor simply the promise of eternal life beyond the grave. It is, rather, the decisive start of the world-wide rule of the Jewish Messiah, in which sins are already forgiven and the promise of the eventual new world of justice and incorruptible life are assured.

So what will this mean in practice for us? We may be prepared to grant that the resurrection of Jesus has opened a new era in world history. Even this, however, takes some doing. As we saw a moment ago, the anti-Christian rhetoric of the last two hundred years in the western world has done its best to deny such a thing. Most of us have a Pavlovian reaction to the sort of claim about the present kingdom that the New Testament makes. We instantly want to talk about the ambiguities of the Constantinian settlement, the connivance of many churches in twentieth-century atrocities, and much in between. But we shouldn't let a proper penitence for past wickedness turn into a false humility about the extraordinary achievements of the church in both the past and the present. The Wilberforces and the Tutus are real, and they matter; and so are a million others, less well known but equally signs of the strange lordship of Jesus over the world. We are all called to live within the world where these things are possible, and to be agents of such things in so far as they lie in our calling and sphere. But for Paul the resurrection is not just about large-scale or public work. It is about the personal and intimate life of resurrection to which each of us is called. It is, in other words, about baptism and holiness. This is where his bracing command comes home to us: it's time to wake up.

The first main passage in which this point is made is Romans 6. This chapter follows straight on from one of Paul's majestic overviews of the whole of God's saving purposes: 'As sin reigned through death,' he writes at the end of Romans 5, 'so grace shall reign through righteousness to eternal life through Jesus the Messiah, our Lord.' There is God's new world; and the question is, where do we belong in it?

He faces this question in 6.1: 'What shall we say? Shall we continue in sin, that grace may abound?' Are we just spectators in God's great drama, sitting on the sidelines, unaffected by the big picture? If God delights to bring his grace to sinners, as Christian evangelists have always rightly insisted, should we go on being sinners in order to get more grace?

Paul's answer is clear: certainly not! We are committed, in our baptism, to being resurrection people. Verses 2–4 set out the groundwork: in baptism we died with the Messiah and were raised with him to new life. Then, in typical Pauline style, he explains further what he means in verses 5–7. We were planted with the Messiah in his death, with the result that our old identity, the old self, was crucified with him. And if that's true, it means that sin has no rights over you, no official hold over you. Instead (vv. 8–10), if the Messiah has been raised from the dead, and if you are in the Messiah, by baptism a member of his people, then it means that you too, in him, have been raised from the dead. Many have supposed that Paul meant this in a purely future sense, but the point of verse 11 is that it is also a present experience: you must now calculate, do the sum, reckon it up, 'consider yourself'[18] to be dead to sin and alive to God in the Messiah, Jesus. It is on this basis that he can go on in the following passage to instruct his hearers not to let sin rule in their present bodies.

We can sum this up in the following way. *The revolutionary new world which has begun in the resurrection of Jesus, the world where Jesus reigns as Lord having won the victory over sin and death, has its front-line outposts in those who in baptism have shared his death and resurrection.* The intermediate stage between the resurrection of Jesus himself and the renewal of the whole world is the renewal of human beings – you and me! – in our own lives of obedience here and now.

Before we comment further on this, we note that the same point is underlined in Colossians 2 and 3. We begin with 2.12: 'In baptism – which corresponds to the Jewish circumcision [that is, it is the mark of entry into God's covenant people] – you were buried with the Messiah; and you were also raised with him through faith in the power of God who raised him from the dead.' Paul assumes that baptism is coupled with faith in God's resurrection power, because the basic baptismal confession is 'Jesus is Lord', and the belief which grounds this confession is the gospel message that God raised Jesus from the dead.[19] He then continues to draw out the implications of having died with the Messiah: the Jewish laws and regulations no longer have any hold over you (2.16–23).

But at the start of Colossians 3 he focuses on what it actually means to share, here and now, in the resurrection of the Messiah. Paul insists that if you are already raised with Christ – in other words, if you are, through baptism and faith, a resurrection person, living in the new world which began at Easter, energized by the power which raised Jesus from the dead – then you have a responsibility to share in the present risen life of Jesus. 'If, then, you are risen with the Messiah, seek the things that are above; set your thoughts on things above, not on things of the earth.' It is no use simply saying, 'I've been baptized; therefore God is happy with me the way I am.' Paul's logic is: 'You have been baptized; therefore God is challenging you to die to sin and live the resurrection life.'

At this point we face a problem which had better be dealt with head on. It has two aspects, a street-level one and a more recondite one. To answer them we shall have to think a bit harder about the meaning of the word 'heaven' itself, and similar ideas like 'the things that are above'.

The street-level problem is the old jibe about being 'so heavenly minded that we are no earthly use'. I say it's an old jibe; I haven't heard it so much recently, perhaps because these days many practising Christians bend over backwards in the other direction, and are often so earthly minded, so concerned with practical details and nuts and bolts, that one wonders if they are any longer any *heavenly* use. However, that's not the point. The jibe only works in a world where heaven and earth are supposed to be detached from each other, to have nothing to do with each other. But in the Bible heaven and earth are made for each other. They are the twin interlocking spheres of God's single created reality. You only really understand earth when you are equally familiar with heaven. You only really know God and share his life when you understand that he is the creator and lover of earth just as much as of heaven. And the point of Jesus' resurrection, and the transformed body he now possesses, is that he is equally at home in both earth and heaven, and can pass appropriately between them, slipping through the thin curtain that separates us from God's blinding reality. That, as we saw in Chapter 7, is part of the core meaning of the ascension.

The second-order problem is a kind of grown-up version of the street-level one, and it's this: doesn't this talk of resurrection in the present mean that we are reducing 'resurrection' to a spiritual experience? Isn't that buying into a gnostic system which devalues the physical body, including the risen body of Jesus?

No. Our minds are so conditioned, I'm afraid, by Greek philosophy, whether or not we've ever read any of it, that we think of 'heaven' as by definition non-material, and 'earth' by definition as non-spiritual or non-heavenly. But that won't do. Part of the central achievement of the incarnation, which is then celebrated in the resurrection and ascension, is that heaven and earth are now joined together with an unbreakable bond, and that we, too, are by rights citizens of both together. We can, if we choose, screen out the heavenly dimension and live as flat-landers, materialists. If we do that we will be buying in to a system that will go bad, and will wither and die, because earth gets its vital life from heaven.[20]

But if we focus our attention on the heavenly dimension, all sorts of positive and practical results will follow. In Colossians 3.11 Paul sees the unity of the church, across cultural and ethnic boundaries, as one of the first of these results. In the passage which follows, he lists all kinds of other things which ought to appear in the life of anyone who really sets his or her mind on the world which is now Jesus' primary home, the world which is designed to heal and restore our present one. In each case what he's talking about *is actual current physical reality, shot through now with the life of heaven.* Part of getting used to living in the post-Easter world – part of getting used to letting Easter change your life, your attitudes, your thinking, your behaviour – is getting used to the cosmology which is now unveiled. Heaven and earth (I repeat) are made for each other, and at certain points they intersect and interlock. Jesus is the ultimate such point. *We as Christians are meant to be such points, derived from him.* The Spirit, the sacraments and the scriptures are given so that the double life of Jesus, both heavenly and earthly, can become ours as well, already in the present.

All of which brings us to our last Pauline passage. Ephesians is a companion letter to Colossians, and here we find the bracing instruction, taken perhaps from an early Christian poem or hymn: 'Awake, sleeper, rise from the dead, and the Messiah will give you light!' (5.14).

In other words: it's time to wake up! Living at the level of the non-heavenly world around you is like being asleep; worse, it's like that for which sleep is a metaphor – it's like being dead. Lying, stealing, sexual immorality, bad temper and so on (Paul lists them all in a devastating short passage[21]) are forms of death, both for the person who commits them and for all whose lives are touched by their actions. They are ways of sleeping a deadly sleep. It's time to wake up, he says. Come alive to the real world, the world where Jesus is Lord, the world into which your baptism brings you, the world you claim to belong to when you say in the creed that Jesus is Lord and that God raised him from the dead. What we all need from time to time is for someone (a friend, a spiritual director, a stranger, a sermon, a verse of scripture, or simply the inner prompting of the Spirit) to say, 'It's time to wake up! You've been asleep long enough! The sun is shining and there's a wonderful day out there! Wake up and get a life!'

The message of Easter, then, is neither that God once did a spectacular miracle but then decided not to do too many others, nor that there is a blissful life after death to look forward to. The message of Easter is that God's new world has been unveiled in Jesus Christ and that you're now invited to belong to it. And precisely because the resurrection was and is bodily, albeit with a transformed body, the power of Easter to transform and heal the present world must be put into effect both at the macro-level, in applying the gospel to the major problems of the world – and if Soviet Communism and apartheid don't count on that scale I don't know what will – and to the intimate details of our daily lives. Christian holiness consists not of trying as hard as we can to be good, but of learning to live in the new world created by Easter, the new world which we publicly entered in our baptism. There are many parts of the world we can't do anything about except pray. But there is one part of the world, one part of physical reality, which we can do something about, and that is the creature we each call 'myself'. Personal holiness and global holiness belong together. Those who wake up to the one may well find themselves called to wake up to the other. And that leads us precisely into the next, and final, chapter.

15

Reshaping the church
for mission (2): living the future

1. Introduction: celebrating Easter

So how can we learn to live as wide-awake people, as Easter people? Here I have some bracing suggestions to make. I have come to believe that many churches simply throw Easter away year by year; and I want to plead that we rethink how we do it, so as to help each other, as a church and as individuals, to live what we profess. I am speaking here particularly from, and to, the church I know best. Those who celebrate in other ways will, I think, be able to make appropriate adjustments and take whatever they need to apply to their own situations.

For a start, consider Easter Day itself. It's a great step forward that many churches now hold Easter vigils, as the Orthodox Church has always done; but in many cases they are still too tame by half. Easter is about the wild delight of God's creative power; not very Anglican, perhaps, but at least we ought to shout Alleluias instead of murmuring them, we should light every candle in the building instead of only some, we should give every man, woman, child, cat, dog and mouse in the place a candle to hold, we should have a real bonfire, and we should splash water about as we renew our baptismal vows. Every step back from that is a step towards an ethereal or esoteric Easter experience, and the thing about Easter is that it is neither ethereal or esoteric. It's about the real Jesus coming out of the real tomb and getting God's real new creation under way.

But my biggest problem starts on Easter Monday. I regard it as absurd and unjustifiable that we should spend forty days keeping Lent, pondering what it means, preaching about self-denial, being at least a little gloomy, and then bringing it all to a peak with Holy Week, which in turn climaxes in Maundy Thursday and Good Friday . . . and then, after a rather odd Holy Saturday, we have *a single day* of celebration.

All right, the Sundays after Easter are still within the Easter season. We still have Easter readings and hymns for several weeks. But Easter week itself ought not to be the time when all the clergy sigh with relief and go on holiday. It ought to be an eight-day festival, with champagne served after morning prayer or even before, with lots of Alleluias and extra hymns and spectacular anthems. Is it any wonder people find it hard to believe in the resurrection of Jesus if we don't throw our hats in the air? Is it any wonder we find it hard to *live* the resurrection if we don't do it exuberantly in our liturgies? Is it any wonder the world doesn't take much notice if Easter is celebrated as simply the one-day happy ending tacked on to forty days of fasting and gloom? It's long overdue that we took a hard look at how we keep Easter in church, at home, in our personal lives, right through the system. And if it means rethinking some cherished habits, well, maybe it's time to wake up. That always comes as a surprise.

And while we're about it, we might write some more good Easter hymns, and take care to choose the many good ones already written that celebrate what Easter really is, rather than treating it as simply our ticket to a blissful life hereafter. Interestingly, most of the good Easter hymns turn out to be from the early church, and most of the bad ones from the nineteenth century. But we should be taking steps to celebrate Easter in creative new ways: in art, literature, children's games, poetry, music, dance, festivals, bells, special concerts, anything that comes to mind. This is our greatest festival. Take Christmas away, and in biblical terms you lose two chapters at the front of Matthew and Luke; nothing else. Take Easter away, and you won't have a New Testament; you won't have a Christianity; as

Paul says, you will still be in your sins. We shouldn't allow the secular world, with its schedules and habits and para-religious events, its cute Easter bunnies, to blow us off course. This is our greatest day. We should put the flags out.

In particular, if Lent is a time to give things up, Easter ought to be a time to take things up. Champagne for breakfast, again; well, of course. Christian holiness was never meant to be merely negative. Of course you have to weed the garden from time to time; sometimes the ground-ivy may need serious digging before you can get it out. That's Lent for you. But you don't want just to get the garden back to being simply a neat bed of blank earth. Easter is the time to sow new seeds and to plant out a few cuttings. If Calvary means putting to death things in your life that need killing off if you are to flourish as a Christian and as a truly human being, then Easter should mean planting, watering and training up things in your life (personal and corporate) that ought to be blossoming, filling the garden with colour and perfume, and in due course bearing fruit. The forty days of the Easter season, until the ascension, ought to be a time to balance out Lent by taking something up, some new task or venture, something wholesome and fruitful and outgoing and self-giving. You may only be able to do it for six weeks, just as you may only be able to go without beer or tobacco for the six weeks of Lent. But if you really make a start on it, it might give you a sniff of new possibilities, new hopes, new ventures you never dreamed of. It might bring something of Easter into your innermost life. It might help you wake up in a whole new way. And that's what Easter is all about.

2. Space, time and matter: creation redeemed

At this point we have to face a serious current problem. Many of the places within the western churches where new life has erupted, with young people coming into the church and all kinds of new energy, music and initiative, have also been places where, often enough, people have quite deliberately abandoned most of the traditional practices of the mainstream churches – church buildings, liturgies, formal prayers and even, in some places, the sacraments themselves (except in a rather occasional and half-hearted way). This, I think, has stemmed from a kind of latent Protestantism in western Christian culture, an implicit belief that buildings, liturgies and so on are in their very nature unspiritual, uninspiring and stultifying, and that the less we can have of them the better. Many people in the newer churches that have gone this route, and in the newer expressions of this type within traditional denominations, have indeed found that their traditional churches were fairly lifeless. Such people, discovering the joy of new life in Christ for themselves, have gladly abandoned all that they now regard as boring, staid and even unspiritual. For many people, in fact, 'fresh expressions' of faith means no church buildings, no 'services' as such, certainly no liturgy, no fixed times or days, and no sacraments (at least, no formal eucharist; there will be various kinds of homemade para-sacraments, but that's another story). It may be that some readers, coming at last to a chapter on shaping the church for mission, are expecting that I will agree with this relentless popular-level Protestantism (which is what it is).

If so, I am afraid I am going to disappoint them. Let me be clear. I am all for a 'mixed economy' in worship. We live in a many-sided society both locally and globally, and it would be silly to suppose that any one size or shape will 'fit' all the worshippers who, we hope, might think of joining us. But the logic of new creation compels me to what I hope are some salutary reflections, not to dampen the enthusiasm of new expressions of Christian life, but to remind them that they must not throw the banana away with the skin. There is always the danger, as in one of Jesus' greatest parables, of a plant which grows up energetically but which has no root – just as, of course, there are plants which have very deep roots but allow other things to choke them. In other words, it won't do either to stick slavishly to old forms of church or, equally slavishly, to abandon all traditions and insist on perpetual innovation. We must keep our eyes fixed on the hope that is set before us, and on the resurrection of Jesus which is our launching-pad, and must reorder our worship and our work in the world accordingly.

Let us, then, remind ourselves of the starting point. The created order, which God has begun to redeem in the resurrection of Jesus, is a world in which heaven and earth are designed, not to be separated, but to come together. In that coming together, the 'very good' which God spoke over creation at the beginning will be enhanced, not abolished. The New Testament never imagines that, when the new heavens and new earth arrive, God will say, in effect, 'well, that first creation wasn't so good after all, was it? Aren't you glad we've got rid of all that space, time and matter?' Rather, we must envisage a world in which the present creation, which we think of in those three dimensions, is enhanced, taken up into God's larger purposes no doubt, but certainly not abandoned.

What happens when we think of space, time and matter as being renewed, not abandoned, within the life of the church?

The renewal and reclaiming of *space* has recently involved, among other things, a fresh grasp of the Celtic tradition of 'thin places', places where the curtain between heaven and earth seems almost transparent. This is in fact just one aspect of a much wider 'theology of place' which has been under serious threat in the West since the Enlightenment.[1] We urgently need to recapture this theology before, to use an obvious metaphor, all the ancient trees are cut down to make room for a shopping centre and a car park, just when people are starting to realize how much shade those trees provide in summer, how much fruit they bear in autumn, and how beautiful they look in spring. Jesus does indeed declare that God calls all people everywhere to worship him in spirit and truth, rather than limiting worship to this or that holy mountain.[2] But this doesn't undercut a proper theology of God's reclaiming of the whole world, which is anticipated in the claiming of space for worship and prayer. Church buildings, and other places where, in Eliot's phrase, 'prayer has been valid', *are not a retreat from the world, but a bridgehead into the world*, a way of claiming part of God-given space for his glory, against the day when the whole world will thrill to his praise.

It is nothing short of dualistic folly, then, simply to declare without more ado (as many try to do today, supposedly in the interest of 'mission' but in fact in the interest of dualism – or a quick profit) that old church buildings and the like are irrelevant to the mission of God today and tomorrow. Of course there are plenty of times when a church building has served its purpose and can now be demolished or given over to alternative use. But many are rediscovering in our day that there are indeed such things as places sanctified by long usage for prayer and worship, places where, often without being able to explain it, people of all sorts find that prayer is more natural, that God can be known and felt more readily. We should reflect long and hard on a proper theology of place and space, thought through in terms of God's promise to renew the whole creation, before we abandon geography and territory. Yes, territorial claims can become idolatrous or abusive – as, for instance, when a church which has long since abandoned any pretence at orthodox Christianity tries to use its canonical powers to insist on some kind of 'territorial rights', or when a few people cling on to a building for sentimental reasons long after it has ceased to serve its local community. But the answer to abuse is not dualism but proper use.

The renewal and reclaiming of *time* takes at least three forms.

(1) It was dramatically symbolized in the fourth century when Dionysius the Insignificant constructed a dating scheme for the whole world based on the (supposed) birth-date of Jesus. The fact that this scheme is still in use more or less worldwide, despite

abortive attempts such as that of the French Revolutionaries to supplant it, came briefly to notice a few years ago at the time of the Millennium, but is largely ignored.[3] Like a great church bell ringing out over a sleepy town, every time someone puts a date on something it speaks of the lordship of Jesus, whether people listen or not.

(2) More specifically, though, the *time* of the church, the long story of church history and the 'tradition' that has accrued during it, must be taken seriously in any eschatologically based and mission-shaped view of the church. Once again, we must of course beware of idolatry, the hallowing of things that were once indifferent and are now irrelevant. One must be constantly aware that the church has done and said many foolish and wicked things as well as many wise and godly things. But the story of the church is the story of the ways in which, despite folly, failure and downright sin, God's future has already burst in upon what, for our forebears, was 'the present time', leaving us a legacy of that bit of the 'past' which is full not only of mistakes and culturally conditioned lifestyles, but of patterns of new creation which have already, from our point of view, been woven into history – bits of God's future, so to speak, which are now already bits of our past.

It is of course all-important to discern what, in 'tradition', is to be seen as an example of this, and what is to be seen as an example of the church getting it wrong. But jettisoning tradition just because it is 'tradition' is to capitulate to postmodernity, and to a kind of ultra-Protestantism that cuts the tree off at the root because it believes that trees should be entirely visible and obviously fruitful, not buried in dirty soil.

(3) In particular, the gospels (especially John), and the early practice of the church as in Paul, reflect the very early understanding of the church that *the first day of the week*, the day of Easter, has become a sign within the present world and its temporal sequence that the life of the age to come has already

273

broken in. Sunday, kept as a commemoration of Easter ever since that event itself (a quite remarkable phenomenon, when you come to think about it), is not simply a legacy of Victorian values, but a perpetual sign, joyfully renewed week by week, that all time belongs to God, and stands under the renewing lordship of Jesus Christ.[4]

Of course, worship should be 'seven whole days, not one in seven'. Many Christians will find, for all kinds of reasons, that Sunday is a difficult day to attend long church services. But we should remind ourselves that the earliest Christians lived in a world where Sunday was the first day of the working week, much like our Monday, and that they valued its symbolism so highly that they were prepared to get up extra early both to celebrate Easter once again and to anticipate the final Eighth Day of Creation, the start of the new week, the day when God will renew all things.

The most contentious of the space-time-matter trio is of course *matter* itself, the stuff of which (as the Protestant tradition has always rightly warned) idols are made. Yet again, however, if we are not to collapse into Platonism, denying the goodness of creation, it is crucial to recapture both the bodily incarnation and resurrection of Jesus and the promise that creation itself will be renewed, liberated from death and decay (and therefore presumably, as in C. S. Lewis's remarkable imaginative world in *The Great Divorce*, more solid, more real, than the present one). It is within this framework of thought that the classic Christian sacraments of baptism and eucharist make sense.

Of course, the sacraments can degenerate into mere superstition and idolatry. But we should never forget what happened when the Israelites allowed that to happen with the Ark of the Covenant, treating it simply as a magic talisman to be taken note of only when they were doing badly in battle (1 Samuel 4—5). The Ark was captured, and the Israelites lost the battle. But when the Philistines put the Ark into the temple of Dagon their god, Dagon fell flat on his face before it. Abuse of the sacrament does not nullify the proper use.

Successive Christian generations have struggled to find language to do justice to the reality of what happens in baptism, and of what happens in the eucharist. It is perhaps not surprising that they have largely failed, because in fact the sacraments are designed to be their own language, ultimately untranslatable even though we can describe what is going on from various angles, themselves all inadequate. (Remember the ballerina who, asked to say what a particular dance 'meant', replied, 'If I could have said it, I wouldn't have needed to dance it.') But to reject, marginalize, trivialize or be suspicious of the sacraments (and quasi-sacramental acts such as lighting a candle, bowing, washing feet, raising hands in the air, crossing oneself, etc.) on the grounds that such things *can* be superstitious or idolatrous, or that some people might suppose that by doing them they are putting God in their debt, is like rejecting sexual relations in marriage on the grounds that it's the same act that, in other circumstances, constitutes immorality. I am always amused, on this point, when I visit churches that have carefully abandoned all the signs of professional worship from a former age – robed choirs, processions, organists and the like – and then have invented new forms of worship which demand just as much professionalism in terms of competent people managing sound systems, lighting, overhead projection and PowerPoint, and so on. There is nothing wrong with either. All can and should be done to the glory of God. But the implication that older styles of worship are somehow less 'spiritual' and that modern electronic worship is somehow more worthy is sheer cultural prejudice and should be happily laughed at whenever it emerges.

Try looking at it like this (shortening, for the moment, a much longer case that could be argued). In the eucharist, the bread and the wine come to us as part of God's new creation, the creation in whose reality Jesus already participates through the resurrection. They speak powerfully, as only encoded actions can speak (whether a handshake, a kiss, the tearing up of a contract, or whatever), both of the death he suffered, through which idolatry and sin have been defeated, and of his future Arrival in which creation is to be renewed (1 Corinthians 11.26). We feed on that reality, even though we may find it difficult to conceptualize what *sort* of reality it is. Knowing that we are thereby renewed as the people of Jesus who live and work in the tension between Easter and the final renewal enables us at least to relax and enjoy all that the sacrament has to offer.

If, then, the church is to be renewed in its mission precisely in and for the world of space, time and matter, we cannot ignore or marginalize that same world. We must, rather, claim it for the kingdom of God, for the lordship of Jesus, and in the power of the Spirit, *so that we can then go out and work for that kingdom, announce that lordship, and effect change through that power.* You do not teach people to sing by first carefully throwing away your musical instruments. The mission of the church must therefore include, at a structural level, the recognition that our present space, time and matter are all subject, not to rejection, but to redemption. Living between the resurrection of Jesus and the final coming together of all things in heaven and earth means celebrating God's healing of his world, not his abandoning of it; God's reclaiming of space as heaven and earth intersect once more; God's redeeming of time as years, weeks and days speaks the language of renewal; and God's redeeming of matter itself, in the sacraments which point in turn to the renewal of the lives that are washed in baptism and fed with the eucharist. Despite the tendency in some parts of the 'emerging church' to marginalize space, time and matter, I remain convinced that the way forward is to rediscover a true eschatology, to rediscover a true mission rooted in anticipating that eschatology, and to rediscover forms of church which embody that anticipation.

3. Resurrection and mission

What then will the church look like as it moves from renewed worship into renewed mission?

I hope I have said enough to make it clear that the mission of the church is nothing more nor less than the outworking, in the power of the Spirit, of Jesus' bodily resurrection, and thus the anticipation of the time when God will fill the earth with his glory, transform the old heavens and earth into the new, and raise his children from the dead to populate and rule over the redeemed world he has made.

If that is so, 'mission' must urgently recover from its long-term schizophrenia. As I have said before, the split between 'saving souls' and 'doing good in the world' is a product, not of the Bible or the gospel, but of the cultural captivity of both within the western world. We return to the themes of two chapters ago (justice, beauty, evangelism) with hope renewed, precisely because of the promise of space, time and matter re-newed. Space, time and matter is where real people live; where real communities happen; where difficult decisions are taken, where schools and hospitals bear witness to the 'now, already' of the gospel while police and prisons bear witness to the 'not yet'. Space, time and matter are where parliaments, city coun-cils, Neighbourhood Watch schemes and everything in between are set up and run for the benefit of the wider community, the community where anarchy will mean that bullies (economic or social as well as physical) will always win, where the weak and vulnerable will always need protecting, and where therefore the social and political structures of society are part of the creator's design.

And the church that is renewed by the message of Jesus' resurrection must be the church that goes to work precisely in that space, time and matter, and claims it in advance as the place of God's kingdom, of Jesus' lordship, of the power of the Spirit.

Councils and parliaments can and often do act wisely (the 'already' of the gospel, which the church must seek to foster), though, because they may in turn become agents of bullying and corruption, they will always need scrutiny and accountability (the 'not yet' of the gospel, in which the church must be active and watchful).

Thus the church that takes sacred *space* seriously, not as a retreat from the world but as a bridgehead into it, will go straight from worshipping in the sanctuary into the council chamber – to debate matters of town planning, of harmonizing and humanizing beauty in architecture, in green spaces, in road traffic schemes, and (not least in the rural areas which are every bit as needy) in environmental work, creative and healthy farming methods, and proper use of resources. If it is true, as I have argued, that the whole world is now God's holy land, we must not rest as long as that land is spoiled and defaced. This is not an 'extra' to the church's mission. It is central.

The church that takes seriously the fact that Jesus is Lord of all *time* will not only celebrate quietly every time we write the date on a letter or document, will not only set aside Sunday as far as humanly and socially possible as a celebration of God's new creation (and will point out the human folly of a seven-day working week), will not only seek to order its own life in an appropriate rhythm of worship and work. Such a church will seek to bring wisdom, and freshly humanizing order, to the rhythms of work in offices and shops, in local government, in civic holidays and the shaping of public life. These things cannot be taken for granted. The enormous shifts during my own lifetime, from the whole town observing Good Friday and Easter to those great days being simply more occasions for football matches and yet more televised reruns of old movies (with, often enough, no sign in the television schedules of anything remotely to do with Jesus or the gospel!), are an index of what happens when a society loses its roots and drifts with prevailing social currents. The reclaiming of time as God's good gift (as opposed to time as simply a commodity to be 'spent' for one's own benefit, which often means fresh forms of slavery for others) is not an 'extra' to the church's mission. It is central.

And, of course, the church that takes seriously the fact that in and through Jesus the creator God has grasped the world of *matter* once more and has transformed it by his own person and presence, and will one day fill it with his knowledge and glory as the waters cover the sea, will not only seek to celebrate the coming of God in Christ in and through the sacramental elements, but will go straight from baptism and the eucharist to make God's healing, transforming presence a reality in the physical matter of real life. One of the things I have most enjoyed about being a bishop is watching 'ordinary' Christians (not that there are any 'ordinary' Christians, but you know what I mean) going straight from worshipping Jesus in church to making a radical difference in the material lives of people down the street, by running playgroups for children with single-parent working mums, by organizing credit unions to help people at the bottom of the financial ladder find their way to responsible solvency, by campaigning for better housing, against dangerous roads, for drug rehab centres, for wise laws relating to alcohol, for decent library and sporting facilities, for a thousand other things in which God's sovereign rule extends to hard, concrete reality. Once again, all this is not an 'extra' to the mission of the church. It is central.

It should be clear that this way of coming at the tasks of the church in terms of space, time and matter plays straight into the categories I used before, of justice and beauty. But it also leads directly into evangelism. When the church is seen to move straight from worship of the God we see in Jesus to making a difference and effecting much-needed change in the real world; when it becomes clear that the people who feast at Jesus' table are the ones in the forefront of work to eliminate hunger and famine; when people realize that those who pray for the Spirit to work in and through them are the people who seem to have extra resources of love and patience in caring for those whose lives are damaged, bruised and shamed – then it is not only natural to speak of Jesus himself and to encourage others to worship him for themselves and find out what belonging to his family is all about, but it is natural for people, however 'irreligious' they may think of themselves as being, to recognize that something is going on which they want to be part of. In terms that the author of Acts might have used, when the church is living out the kingdom of God, the word of God will spread powerfully and do its own work.

Of course, no one individual can attempt more than a fraction of this mission. That's why mission is the work of the whole church, the whole time. Some will find God nudging them to work with handicapped children. Some will sense a call to local government. Others will discover a quiet satisfaction in artistic or educational projects. All will need one another for support and encouragement. All will need to be nourished by the central, worshipping life of the church, and that central life will itself be nourished and renewed as the friends of Jesus come back to worship from their mission in the world.[5]

A good deal of this activity will cheerfully and rightly overlap with work being done, and often done very well, by those of other faiths or none. That is what we should expect and welcome, if indeed it is true that (over against all dualisms) the one true God is the creator of all, who has not left himself without witness in the world. Paul's advice to the Philippians – even though he and they knew they were suffering for their faith, and might be tempted to retreat from the world into a dualistic, sectarian mentality – was upbeat. 'These are the things you should think through,' he wrote: 'whatever is true, whatever is holy, whatever is upright, whatever is pure, whatever is attractive, whatever has a good reputation; anything virtuous, anything praiseworthy.'[6] And in thinking through these things, we will discover more and more about the same creator God whom we ourselves know in and through Jesus Christ, and will be better equipped to work effectively, not over against 'the world' but with the grain of all good will, of all that seeks to bring and enhance life.

The same letter, of course, would also urge us not to be naive. There are plenty of places and situations where vested interests, corrupt policies and politicians, tyrants, bullies and communities that have turned in on themselves racially and cul- turally will find the church's witness in any of the ways I have described threatening and offensive. This will be no surprise to those churches who find themselves facing, in today's western world, the 'politically correct' banning of Christian symbols and festivals. Nor will it be a surprise to those who have tried to campaign for better housing, for better conditions for farm or factory workers, and have found implacable anger from those who have been quietly but ruthlessly exploiting others.

But note what such people will then say. They will tell the church, again and again, to get back to its proper business of 'saving souls'. *That radical distortion of Christian hope belongs exactly with a quietism which leaves the world as it is and thus allows evil to proceed unchecked.* This is where the 'surprise' of hope catches people unawares; and they react by telling us Christians what *they* think our 'hope' ought to be – a hope that will cut the nerve of, and the need for, any attempt to make things better in the present world of space, time and matter.

It is at this point that the church must learn the arts of col- laboration without compromise, and of opposition without dualism. There are good things going on in the wider world, and we must join in, while always remaining on the lookout for the point where we will be asked to do something which goes against the grain of the gospel. There are wicked things going on in the wider world, and we must stand out against them, while always remaining on the lookout for the point where we become mere dualists, retreating from the world which is already charged with the grandeur of God. All this is difficult enough at the best of times, and all the more so now because we in the West have simply not thought in these terms for a couple of hundred years. Once again, William Wilberforce and others like him would have something to teach us. And suddenly all those shrewd remarks of Jesus come home to roost. It is time to figure out what it will mean, in the real world of the twenty-first century, to be wise as serpents and innocent as doves.

I have argued that a 'mission-shaped church' must have its mission shaped by its hope; that the genuine Christian hope, rooted in Jesus' resurrection, is the hope for God's renewal of all things, for his overcoming of corruption, decay and death, for his filling of the whole cosmos with his love and grace, his power and glory. I have argued that, to be truly effective in this kind of mission, one must be genuinely and cheerfully rooted in God's renewal of space, time and matter within the life of the church. There is no use (to re-adapt, once more, a metaphor I have already used more than once) trying to get fruit from a tree whose roots you have systematically dug up.

I am not, of course, saying, 'Do "traditional church" well and mission will follow.' Far too much 'traditional church' has been too much tradition and not enough church. What I am saying is, think through the hope that is ours in the gospel; recognize the renewal of creation as both the goal of all things in Christ and the achievement that has already been accomplished in the resurrection; and go to the work of justice, beauty, evangelism, the renewal of space, time and matter, as the anticipation of the eventual goal and the implementation of what Jesus achieved in his death and resurrection. That is the way both to the genuine mission of God and to the shaping of the church by and for that mission.

All of this means, of course, that the people who work at and for this mission in the wider world must themselves be living, modelling and experiencing the same thing in their own lives. There is, ultimately, no justification for a private piety that doesn't work out in actual mission, just as there is ultimately no justification for people who use their activism in the social, cultural or political sphere as a screen to prevent them facing the same challenges within their own lives – the challenge, that is, of God's kingdom, of Jesus' lordship, and of the Spirit's empowering. If the gospel isn't transforming you, how do you know that it will transform anything else?

From one point of view, this might seem to lead back to some rather 'ordinary' topics. But I now want to suggest, in the final section of this concluding chapter, that the basic disciplines of Christian spirituality, the disciplines through which the church is nourished for this space-time-matter mission of justice, beauty and evangelism, are themselves best understood in the context of the surprising hope, the hope that is rooted in Jesus' resurrection and that reaches out to anticipate God's new creation in all its fullness.

4. Resurrection and spirituality

Space forbids more than a brief outline of six central aspects of Christian spirituality which appear in a new light when we see them as part of God's surprising hope, the Easter call to us to wake up and come alive within his new world.

a. New birth and baptism

One of the most striking mentions of the new birth is found in the great opening of 1 Peter. God, in his great mercy, has given us a new birth to a living hope by the resurrection of Jesus Christ from the dead.[7] Jesus' resurrection is directly instrumental in bringing about this new birth and its consequences. It is all because of what happened at Easter: a new reality has opened up in the world, a new kind of life both inward and, importantly, outward, in holiness and in the hope of our own resurrection. The preaching for, and experience of, the new birth has of course been central to some movements within

Christianity, notably evangelicalism, down the years. Though often mocked and caricatured (one recalls the snide remarks journalists used to make about President Jimmy Carter 'having been born a bit too often'), it rightfully retains that place.

But what has proved much harder to do, in those movements that have stressed the new birth as a vital spiritual experience, is to articulate a theology of baptism which goes with it, as it obviously does in the New Testament. Evangelicalism's inability to do this left the door wide open to the various theologies of Spirit-baptism which have characterized Pentecostalism, but that's another story. Baptism too, of course, is closely allied with the resurrection of Jesus, in two passages in particular: Romans 6 and Colossians 2.

In order to understand baptism, here and elsewhere, we have to say something about sacramental theology. I have come to believe that the sacraments are best understood within the theology of creation and new creation, and of the overlapping of heaven and earth, which I have been exploring throughout this book. The resurrection of Jesus has brought about a new state of affairs in cosmic history and reality. God's future has burst into the present, and (as happens sometimes in dreams, when the words we are saying or the music we are hearing are also *happening* in the events in which we are taking part) somehow the sacraments are not just signs of the reality of new creation but actually part of it. Thus the event of baptism – the action, the water, the going down and the coming up again, the new clothes – is not just a signpost to the reality of the new birth, the membership (as all birth gives membership) in the new family. It really is the gateway to that membership.

Of course, as all pastors in all traditions know only too well, there are many who have shared in baptism who now seem to want nothing to do with the new family, or the new life, to which it should have introduced them. But this is not an argument against Paul's very realistic language about baptism. (Nor is it an argument against baptizing young children; the problem of people 'falling away' is just as real with adult baptisms too.) In fact, Paul himself seems to have faced the same problem in 1 Corinthians 10, where some who had been baptized were refusing to live in the appropriate way. In addressing this problem, he doesn't deny the validity of their entry into the people of God, but rather presupposes it. The consequence is a severe warning: God will judge those who presume upon his kindness, upon their privilege of membership.

The important thing, then, is that in the simple but powerful action of plunging someone into the water in the name of the triune God, there is a real dying to the old creation and a real rising into the new – with all the dangerous privileges and responsibilities that then accompany the new life as it sets out in the as-yet-unredeemed world. Baptism is not magic, a conjuring trick with water. But nor is it simply a visual aid. It is one of the points, established by Jesus himself, where heaven and earth interlock, where new creation, resurrection life, appears within the midst of the old. The idea of associating baptism with Easter always was, and still is, a proper Christian instinct. Just as for many Christians the truth of Easter is something they glimpse occasionally rather than grasp and act on, so, for many, baptism remains in the background, out of sight, whereas it should be the foundational event for all serious Christian living, all dying to sin and coming alive with Christ.

b. Eucharist

From baptism we move naturally to the eucharist. Let me sketch three views of the eucharist, and show how the theology of new creation, coming forwards to meet us in the present, enables us to see more clearly what's going on.

For many Christians, the sacraments have been all too close to the performance of sympathetic magic. A holy person, a shaman-like figure, mumbles the magic words and does the magic deeds; a wonderful conjuring trick is performed in which ordinary food is turned into the actual body and blood of Jesus

Christ; once again evil is warded off, atonement is made, God is appeased, prayers are offered with special efficacy, social power and control are reinforced, everyone is happy. A caricature, of course, of what any real theologians actually believed; but this is how things have often appeared to many ordinary folk. And, at that level, the church's sacraments are little better than pagan ritual.

Until, of course, the Reformation, at which point the entire system was challenged. One extreme of Reformation theology, determined to resist anything that smacked of magic or paganism, or that confirmed the power of the priestly class, insisted on denying everything that Rome taught. Thus the radical Swiss Reformers regarded the eucharist as a bare sign, a simple reminder, of the historic fact that Christ had died for our sins. Meditate on that fact, they said, and you would get just as much spiritual benefit as you would from eating the bread – indeed, much more than if you ate it without such meditation.

In between the quasi-magic ritual on the one hand and the bare memory on the other, a more historically grounded view would remind us of how the Jewish sacred meals (not least the Passover from which the eucharist takes its point of origin) were thought to function. To this day, when Jews celebrate Passover, they don't suppose they are essentially doing something *different from* the original event. 'This is the night', they say, 'when God brought us out of Egypt.' The people sitting round the table become, not the distant heirs of the wilderness generation, but the same people. Time and space telescope together. Within the sacramental world, past and present are one. Together, they point forwards to the still-future liberation.

What happens in the eucharist is that, through the death and resurrection of Jesus Christ, this future dimension is brought sharply into play. We break this bread to share in the body of Christ; we do it in remembrance of him; we become, for a moment, the disciples sitting around the table at the Last Supper. Yet if we stop there we've only said the half of it. To make any headway in understanding the eucharist, we must see it just as much in terms of the arrival of God's future in the present, not just the extension of God's past (or of Jesus' past) into our present. We do not simply remember a long-since-dead Jesus; we celebrate the presence of the living Lord. And he lives, through the resurrection, precisely as the one who has gone on ahead *into the new creation*, the transformed new world, as the one who is himself its prototype. The Jesus who gives himself to us as food and drink is himself the beginning of God's new world. At communion we are like the children of Israel in the wilderness, tasting fruit plucked from the promised land. It is the future coming to meet us in the present.

This perspective is a far more helpful way to talk about the presence of Christ in the eucharist than any amount of re-definitions of the old language of transubstantiation. The problem with that was not that it was the wrong answer, but that it was the right answer to the wrong question. It was right to insist on the true presence of Christ, but wrong to explain that presence in terms of the philosophies of the time, the Aristotelian distinction between substance and accident, and the supposed power of the priest to alter the 'substance' (the inner, invisible reality of an object like a piece of bread) while leaving the 'accidents' (its outward properties like weight, colour, chemical make-up) apparently untouched. That was one way of saying what needed to be said in language that some people in the Middle Ages could understand, but it has produced all kinds of misunderstandings and abuses.

A far better way forward is provided by the New Testament's language about new creation. Take Romans 8 as a good starting point: creation is groaning in travail, as it waits for redemption. But one part of the old creation has already been transformed, is already liberated from bondage to decay, namely, the body of Christ, the body which died on the cross and is now alive with a life that death can't touch. Jesus has gone ahead into God's new creation, and as we look back to his death through the lens he himself provided – that is, the meal he shared on the night he was betrayed – we find that he comes to meet us in and through the symbols of creation, the bread and the wine, which are thus taken up into the Christ-story, the event of new creation itself, and become vessels, carriers, of God's new world and the saving events which enable us to share it.

Within this framework, that of a true Easter understanding of creation and new creation, we can understand the eucharist most fully as the anticipation of the banquet when heaven and earth are made new, the marriage supper of the Lamb. (Some liturgies have tried to express this, but sadly have often collapsed back into mere talk of 'heaven', which is precisely not the point.) It is the breaking in of God's future, the Advent future, into our present time. Every eucharist is a little Christmas as well as a little Easter.

This is not magic. Magic seeks to gain by cunning, and for personal power or pleasure, what God gives by grace, to faith, to promote holiness and love. The resurrection of Jesus, and the promise of a world made new, provide the ontological, epistemological and above all eschatological framework within which we can understand the eucharist afresh. Let us not rob ourselves of the hope that comes forward from God's future to sustain us in the present. God's new world has begun. If we don't see it breaking into the present world we are denying the energizing foundation of Christian life.

c. Prayer

The third area is prayer. There is something about prayer which says: we are open to someone, something, beyond; we are, at least in principle, aware of a power beyond our own power, a presence, perhaps even a person, beyond and probably higher than our own person. All prayer is like that. It is at least a start.

But, because of the death and resurrection of Jesus and the bursting into our present world of God's future reality, the

New Testament writers do not want to leave our praying in the rather crude, vague and unformed state implied by that lowest-common-denominator description. We may again outline three different ways of looking at prayer, and then show how an authentically Christian view retains the strong point of each while going beyond, called by the God of the future who has burst into the present.[8]

The first way of understanding prayer is as a kind of nature mysticism: being open to the beauty, joy and power of the world around us. It is what happens, unaided and unbidden, as we gasp at a vision of snow-capped mountains, or as we stand on a summer's night away from the city lights and are overwhelmed with awe at the starry heavens. It's what happens when we fall deeply in love and discover a previously unimagined wholeness, a fulfilment of self in giving self away. Each of these is, as people often say, a profoundly 'religious' experience. Each of them, if we hold them in our minds and hearts, can be described as a sort of prayer, celebrating something beyond ourselves and feeling part of it, caught up in it, in a kind of union way beyond humdrum daily life. Such a sense of nature mysticism can be extremely powerful and moving, indeed life-changing. Some people describe such experiences glowingly and expect the church to approve. But this is not, yet, what the New Testament understands by Christian prayer.

At the other extreme we find that kind of prayer, common in ancient paganism to look no further, which sees it as the making of petitions to a deity or deities who are distant, not well known, certainly capricious, and possibly malevolent. Here is a sailor going off to sea. He visits Poseidon's temple and offers a sacrifice to pray for a safe voyage. He is still secretly afraid that someone else may have bribed Poseidon, more successfully, to create a wind going in the wrong direction. Or he may have got some of the magic formulae wrong. Or the sacrifice may be blemished in some way, despite his best efforts. Many people approach prayer like that, even in church: a distant appeal to a faceless bureaucrat who may or may not be interested or kindly disposed.

In between the two, with elements of both but going way beyond, we find the prayer life of ancient Israel. Though the Psalms do have some pagan parallels here and there, there is nothing like this collection anywhere else. It celebrates the goodness of creation ('The earth is the Lord's, and all that therein is') and recognizes that the heavens declare the glory of God. Yet the Psalms celebrate their intimate union, not with creation as such, but with the creator God whose love and power are made known in creation. The Psalmists often feel that God has become distant and remote, perhaps even that he has turned to fight against them. Yet they refuse to believe, when they call and nothing happens, that the boss has gone fishing or is away playing golf. They go on battering on his door until they can remind him of his personal promises, his great acts of old on Israel's behalf, and above all his personal love. And even when they find no way to turn the corner towards resolution (Psalms 88 and 89), they are eventually if sorrowfully content to leave the dire situation in front of God's door. '*You* have put lover and friend away from me.' Like Job, though God should slay them, yet will they trust in him.[9] And of course, along with the Psalms, the thrice-daily prayer of the Jew from early times to the present was and is the great shema prayer: 'Hear, O Israel: the Lord our God, the Lord is One. There is one God, and he is *our* God.' Transcendence; intimacy; celebration; covenant. Those are the roots of biblical prayer.

Now notice what happens when we move into the New Testament, particularly in the light of Jesus' death and resurrection. We find, as with everything else, that the Jewish theory and practice of prayer has been refocused and drawn further forwards by the climactic and decisive events concerning Jesus. And, through this, the twin poles of nature mysticism and petitionary prayer, particularly prayer in trouble or danger, are drawn together into a new configuration.

Among the great passages on prayer, the Farewell Discourses of John 13—17 stand out, culminating of course in Jesus' own astonishing prayer to the father. There is much to ponder here for which there isn't space, but I want to note that in these chapters Jesus speaks repeatedly of the new relationship that the disciples will have with the father as a result of his own 'going away' – which is more or less a shorthand for his death and resurrection – and as a result of his sending of the Spirit, his own Spirit, to be with them and in them. In this intimacy of relationship they are encouraged to ask for whatever they want – anything at all – in Jesus' name. 'The father himself loves you,' explains Jesus.[10]

Gradually we realize what is happening. The extraordinary, unique, intimate relationship which Jesus himself had enjoyed with the father is now open to all his followers. John finally explains why and how this comes about, in the first of his resurrection chapters. The risen Jesus tells Mary Magdalene to go and say to 'my brothers', 'I am going up to my father *and your father*, to my God *and your God*.'[11] Jesus, as himself the fulfilment and goal of Israel's vocation to be God's son, his beloved one, now shares this status, and its benefits, with all his followers. God's intention for the end, to draw humans freely into intimate fellowship with himself, has come forward to meet us in Jesus of Nazareth. This is yet one more meaning of the resurrection.

But if this new intimacy stands at the heart of the New Testament's view of prayer, this doesn't mean that we've left behind that sense of oneness with the created order which we find in so many religions and indeed in our own experience. The great heavenly scene of Revelation 4 and 5 stands out as a moment when the church is gathering up the praises of all creation and presenting them before God's throne. But within these chapters, again, the central problem of nature mysticism is named and dealt with. The world is out of joint. If we bring ourselves simply into harmony with the created order as it is

at present, we are embracing death: not only nature red in tooth
and claw, but the cosmos running down into the cold night of
entropy. Yes, says Revelation 5: the problem with the good creation is, how can God's purposes for it be fulfilled? How can
the scroll of God's will be unrolled and read so that it comes
to pass? No one is worthy to do it. The answer, through which
the prayer and worship of the church and creation is taken
through into a new dimension, is that the Lion who is also the
Lamb has conquered, and through him God's purposes are
going forwards. And, with that, prayer and worship break out
in a new way. Heaven and earth come together in a new way.
Future and present are joined in a new way. In the death and
resurrection of Jesus the new creation has begun, and with it
the new song, 'Worthy is the Lamb', the song that lies at the
heart of Christian adoration.[12]

Nor have we thereby abandoned the Psalmist's sense of
frustration, of battering at God's door. Paul, at one of the most
climactic moments in all his writings (Romans 8), pauses to
comment that we Christians are caught in between creation and
new creation, and this shows in how we pray and what we pray
for. Or rather, in the fact that for much of the time we don't
know what to pray for. We have glimpsed in Jesus the new creation coming to birth. We have felt something of its power, by
the Spirit, in our own lives. But this hasn't given us a simplis-
tic, easy answer to the puzzles and problems of prayer. Rather,
it has given us the immense privilege of sharing the intimate
life of the triune God himself. The Spirit calls from deep within us, calls to the father, calls from the pain of the world, the
pain of the church, the pain of our hearts. And with that call,
and with the answering love of the father, we are, as Paul says,
conformed to the image of the Messiah, God's son (Romans
8.26–30), the one who shared the suffering of the world so that
he might be the true intercessor for the world. The connections
between Romans 8 and the Johannine Farewell Discourses are
many and deep, and never more so than when they speak of

the way in which the inner life of God himself, Father, Son and Spirit, comes to meet us, comes forwards from God's future to where we are in the present.

Notice what happens with all this. If we were to say, 'Well, that's all a bit complex and high-flown; I'm not sure I really grasp it; I'll rest content to feel a oneness with the sea and the sky, the leaves and the loves of this world, and that will be enough to keep me from collapsing into a one-dimensional secular world' – if we were to say any such thing, the New Testament writers would be horrified. 'What,' they'd say, 'God's future has come forward to meet you in the present, to transform your present muddled praying into the sharing of his own intimate life, and you're going to be happy with living in the unredeemed world, untouched by the future which burst into our world at Easter?'

It will, of course, be costly. You don't get to share God's life and escape without wounds. Look what happened to Jesus himself. But see what happens when the central Jewish prayer, the shema, comes forward into Christianity, and turns into the Lord's Prayer. Thy kingdom come *on earth as in heaven*. Is that not what we've been talking about throughout this book? Are we going to refuse, at the final hurdle, to finish the course and translate our theology into prayer?

d. Scripture

Fourth, scripture. This may seem a strange topic to bring in as a way of reflecting on how the themes of resurrection and new creation are reflected in Christian spirituality and practice, and of how our future hope, which shapes our mission, must also shape our common Christian life. But I am convinced that unless we think something like this we will misunderstand scripture and perhaps also misuse it.[13]

Scripture – the Old and New Testaments – is the story of creation and new creation. Within that, it is the story of covenant and new covenant. When we read scripture as Christians, we read it precisely as people of the new covenant and of the new creation. We do not read it, in other words, as a flat, uniform list of regulations or doctrines. We read it as the narrative in which we ourselves are now called to take part. We read it to discover 'the story so far', and also 'how it's supposed to end'. To put it another way, we live somewhere between the end of Acts and the closing scene of Revelation. If we want to understand scripture, and find it doing its proper work in and through us, we must learn to read and understand it in the light of that overall story.

As we do this – as groups, churches and individuals – we must allow the power of God's promised future to have its way with us. As we read the gospels, we must remind ourselves again and again – because the pull of prevailing western culture is so strong that if we don't it will suck us back down into dualism – that this is the story of how God's kingdom was established on earth as in heaven in and through the work of Jesus, fulfilling Israel's great story, defeating the power of evil, and launching God's new world. As we read the letters, we must remind ourselves that these are the documents designed to shape and direct the community of the new covenant, the people who were called to take forward the work of new creation. As we read Revelation, we must not allow the wonderful heavenly vision in chapters 4 and 5 to lull us into imagining that this is the *final* scene in the story, as though the narrative were simply to conclude (as in Charles Wesley's hymn) with the redeemed casting their crowns before the throne. This is a vision of *present* reality, seen in its heavenly dimension. We must read on to the end, to the final vision of Revelation 21 and 22, the chapters which give final meaning to all that has gone before, and indeed to the entire canon.

Likewise, when we read the Old Testament, we must read it – as it manifestly asks to be read – as the long and winding story of how God chose a people to take forward his plan to rescue his creation, not the story of how God had a shot at calling a people whom he would save from the world, and how this was aborted, forcing him to try something else (a caricature, I know, but one many will recognize). And this means that, though the Old Testament must be read as part of 'our story' as Christians, we must not imagine that we are still living within that moment in the story. The story itself points beyond itself, like a set of parallel lines meeting in the infinitely rich narrative of the gospels and the sudden outburst of new life in Acts and the letters.[14]

The Bible as a whole thus does what it does best when read from the perspective of new creation. And it is designed, itself, not only to tell us *about* that work of new creation, as though from a detached perspective, not only to provide us with true information about God's fresh, resurrection life, but actually to *foster* that work of new creation in the churches, groups and individuals who read it, who define themselves in terms of the Jesus they meet in it, who allow it to shape their lives. The Bible is thus the *story of* creation and new creation, and it is itself, through the continuing work of the Spirit who inspired it, an *instrument of* new creation in human lives and communities.

The Bible is not, in other words, simply a list of true doctrines, or a collection of proper moral commands – though it includes plenty of both. The Bible is not simply the record of what various people thought as they struggled to know God and follow him, though it is that as well. It is not simply the record of past revelations, as though what mattered were to study such things in the hopes that one might have one for oneself. It is the book whose whole narrative is about new creation, that is, about resurrection, so that when the gospels each end with the raising of Jesus from the dead, and when Revelation ends with new heavens and new earth populated by God's people risen from the dead, this should not come as a surprise, but as the ultimate fulfilment of what the story had been about all along. (This, by the way, is the deep-level reason why the 'other gospels' were not included in the canon.

It isn't that they were the really exciting or subversive bits that the early church excluded in the interests of power and control. They were the books that had stopped talking about new creation and were offering a private, detached spirituality instead. The sudden enthusiasm for these 'other gospels' in certain quarters of the western world in our own day is a token, not of the rediscovery of genuine Christianity, but of the desperate attempts to avoid it. New creation is far more demanding – though ultimately of course far more exhilarating – than gnostic escapism.)

Thus, just as the proclamation of Jesus as Lord results in men, women and children coming to trust and obey him in the power of the Spirit, and to find their lives transformed by his saving lordship, so the telling of the story of creation and new creation, of covenant and new covenant, doesn't just *inform* the hearers *about* this narrative. It *invites them into it*, enfolds them within it, assures them of their membership in it, and equips them for their tasks in pursuit of its goal.

All of which leads us to one of the greatest challenges of our day.

e. Holiness

Fifth, holiness. This is what Paul hammers away at in the early chapters of 1 Corinthians, and it's because they don't understand the resurrection that the Corinthians are having difficulty with it. What you do with your body in the present matters, he insists, because God raised the Lord and will also raise us by his power. Glorify God in your body, because one day God will glorify the body itself. What is to be true in the future must begin to be true in the present, or it will be called into question whether you are really on track in the first place. Here we are building once more on passages like Romans 6 and Colossians 3, and working out what it means to live as part of God's new creation.

It is Romans that provides the key to so much of this, the key which seems to have been thrown away in some recent debates. The letter works in a complex but coherent symphonic development. It is not simply a string of points, one after another, with some doctrines here and some ethics there. In particular, the analysis of the human plight in 1.18—2.16 is not at all meant as a throwaway bit of polemic against rent-a-crowd stage villains, as is often suggested. It is carefully calibrated and integrated into the flow of the letter. When Paul reflects on the behaviour that had become standard among pagans, he speaks of God 'giving them up' to an unfit *mind*, and the worst thing he can say about pagan immorality in chapter 1 is the last verse, that 'they not only do such things, but approve those who practise them'.[15] It's one thing to be lured into sin, quite another to change the moral compass and call good evil and evil good. And this cast of the mind links directly to the major command of 12.1: do not be conformed to this world, but be transformed by the renewal of your minds. This is inaugurated eschatology; this is what the resurrection looks like when it comes forward into the moral life of the person of faith. For Paul, holiness is never a matter of simply finding out the way you seem to be made and trusting that that's the way God intends you to remain. Nor is it a matter of blind obedience to arbitrary and out-of-date rules. It's a matter of *transformation*, starting with the mind.

That is why, to return to 1 Corinthians, it is the resurrection – both that of Jesus, and that of ourselves – which provides, in passages like chapters 5 and 6, the ultimate rationale for Christian behaviour. It isn't the case that 'Christian ethics' consists of a few odd regulations and restrictions which Christians are supposed to follow while still living in exactly the same world as everyone else, just as it isn't the case that the resurrection of Jesus was simply a very strange 'miracle' within the world of old creation. The resurrection was the full bursting in to this world of the life of God's new creation; 'Christian ethics' is the lifestyle that celebrates and embodies that new creation. Living out a life of Christian holiness makes sense, perfect sense, *within God's new world*, the world into which we are brought at baptism, the world where we are nourished by the eucharist. Of course, if you try to live a Christian lifestyle outside this framework, you will find it as difficult, indeed nonsensical, as it would be for an orchestral performer to play his or her part, separated from the rest of the players, amid the crashes and metallic screeching of an automobile factory. Not that we aren't called, of course, to practise our discipleship in the hard, outside world which rumbles on as though Easter had never happened. But if we are to be true to our risen Lord we will need, again and again, to retune our instruments and practise once more alongside our fellow musicians.

All of which brings us, in Paul's words, to the most excellent way of all.

f. Love

Finally, and climactically, we come to love. Think of the wonderful poem which we call 1 Corinthians 13, which looks forward to the exposition of the resurrection in 1 Corinthians 15. The poem itself is complete, and exquisite. But it speaks of something which is incomplete, frustratingly so:

> Our knowledge is incomplete; our prophecy is incomplete; but when completion arrives, the incomplete is done away. When I was a child, I spoke as a child, I thought as a child, I reasoned like a child; but when I became a man, I put away childish things. For now we see in a mirror, dimly, but then face to face; now I know in part, but then shall I know, even as also I am known.[16]

This passage is the bit we don't expect in this wonderful chapter. The poem doesn't just celebrate the fact that love is the greatest thing in God's world. It doesn't just explain what love will mean in hard-edged practice (patient, kind, not jealous or boastful, and so on). It isn't, in other words, a poetic way of giving us simply a rule of life, another goal in the struggle for obedience or even Christlikeness. The poem does much, much more: it yearns over the fact that our experience of love, as of everything else that matters, is decidedly incomplete. The way we are now, seen against the way we shall be in God's design, is only partly what it is meant to be, and is emphatically partly not what it is meant to be. But Paul is urging that *we should live in the present as people who are to be made complete in the future*. And the sign of that completeness, that future wholeness, the bridge from one reality to the other, is love.

Remember what the letter as a whole is about. The young church was in a mess. They were ridden with personality cults. They were socially divided, rich against poor. They were spiritually divided, jealous of one another's gifts. They tolerated immorality. Their worship was chaotic; their grasp on the gospel was shaky. Oh, they had an energy, a drive; they were going somewhere, even if they weren't sure in which direction. I'd rather have a live church with problems than a dead church offering the spurious peace of the tombstone, though let me quickly add that I'd rather not have all the problems of Corinth at once, thank you very much.

Paul goes through the problems one by one, almost as though they form a kind of shopping list. Great discussions, each one hammered out on the anvil of scripture and serious Christian thinking. And then, in the middle of it all, like Mozart's *Ave Verum* making its way through the noise of a factory until the machinery falls silent, is the still music of chapter 13. Listen to it in the old language of the King James version:

> Though I speak with the tongues of men and of angels, and have not charity, I am become as sounding brass, or a tinkling cymbal. And though I have the gift of prophecy, and understand all mysteries, and all knowledge; and though I have all faith, so that I could remove mountains, and have not charity, I am nothing . . .

Charity suffereth long, and is kind; charity envieth not; charity vaunteth not itself, is not puffed up, doth not behave itself unseemly, seeketh not her own, is not easily provoked, thinketh no evil; rejoiceth not in iniquity, but rejoiceth in the truth; beareth all things, believeth all things, hopeth all things, endureth all things . . .

. . . For now we see through a glass darkly; but then face to face: now I know in part; but then shall I know even as also I am known. And now abideth faith, hope, charity, these three; but the greatest of these is charity.

This isn't simply a wonderful poem stuck in to the letter at this point to change the mood. This poem, both in tone and content, is the still, quietly beating heart that makes sense of everything else. Everything Paul says in the rest of the letter is drawn together at this point.

But he's not done yet. That last stanza of the poem, insisting on the incompleteness of our present experience, points on to the final great discussion of the letter, namely chapter 15, in which Paul gives the fullest exposition in all early Christian writing of Jesus' resurrection and what it means. It means that a new world order has opened up in the midst of the present one. God's future has arrived in the present in the person of the risen Jesus, summoning everybody to become people of the future, people in Christ, people remade in the present to share the life of God's future. Our present experience, even our present Christian experience, is incomplete. But in Christ we have heard the complete tune; we know now what it sounds like and that we shall one day sing it in tune with him. Our present experience, with all its incompleteness, is meant to point us to the fact that we will one day wake up and arise from sleep. That, after all, is what resurrection is all about.

It is this future emphasis, the stress that what we are at the moment is incomplete, which turns Paul's poem on love away from being mere moralism ('please try harder to behave like this!') and into something altogether stranger and more powerful. We all know that it's no good simply telling people to love one another. One more exhortation to love, to patience, to forgiveness, may remind us of our duty. But as long as we think of it as duty we aren't very likely to do it.

The point of 1 Corinthians 13 is that love is not our duty; it is our *destiny*. It is the language Jesus spoke, and we are called to speak it so that we can converse with him. It is the food they eat in God's new world, and we must acquire the taste for it here and now. It is the music God has written for all his creatures to sing, and we are called to learn it and practise it now so as to be ready when the conductor brings down his baton. It is the resurrection life, and the resurrected Jesus calls us to begin living it with him and for him right now. Love is at the very heart of the surprise of hope: people who truly hope as the resurrection encourages us to hope will be people enabled to love in a new way. Conversely, people who are living by this rule of love will be people who are learning more deeply how to hope.

This is the message that underlies the gospel command to forgiveness – which is also, of course, the command to remit debts, about which I spoke earlier. But forgiveness is not a 'moral rule' which comes with sanctions attached. God doesn't deal with us on the basis of abstract codes and rules like that. Forgiveness is a way of life, God's way of life, God's way *to* life; and if you close your heart to forgiveness – why, then you close your heart to forgiveness. That is the point of the terrifying parable in Matthew 18, about the slave who had been forgiven millions but then dragged a colleague into court to settle a debt of a few pence. If you lock up the piano because you don't want to play to somebody else, how can God play to you?

That is why we pray 'forgive us our trespasses, *as we forgive those who trespass against us*'. That isn't a bargain we make with God. It's a fact of human life. Not to forgive is to shut down a faculty in the innermost person, which happens to be the same faculty that can receive God's forgiveness. It also happens to be the same faculty that can experience real joy and real grief. Love bears all things, believes all things, hopes all things, endures all things.

Of course, in our incomplete world, God's gentle offer and demand press upon us as fearful things, almost threatening. But God's offer and demand are neither fearful nor threatening. God in his gentle love longs to set us free from the prison we have stumbled into – the loveless prison where we refuse both the offer and the demand of forgiveness. We are like a frightened bird before him, shrinking away lest this demand crush us completely. But when we eventually yield – when he corners us, and finally takes us in his hand – we find to our astonishment that he is infinitely gentle, and that his only aim is to release us from our prison, to set us free to be the people he made us to be. But when we fly out into the sunshine, how can we not then offer the same gentle gift of freedom, of forgiveness, to those around us? That is the truth of the resurrection, turned into prayer, turned into forgiveness and re-mission of debts, turned into love. It is constantly surprising, constantly full of hope, constantly coming to us from God's future to shape us into the people through whom God can carry out his work in the world.

Tailpiece: two Easter sermons[1]

If I were a betting man, I would lay good money on two basic messages going out from pulpits this Easter.

Pastor Frank Gospelman believes passionately in the bodily resurrection of Jesus, the empty tomb, the angels, the whole supernatural shebang. Every Easter he denounces the wicked liberals, not least the Reverend Jeremy Smoothtongue up the road, for their unwillingness to acknowledge that the Bible is true, that God really does do miracles, and that – as the demonstration of those two points – Jesus really did rise again. Pastor Gospelman may try a few stunts to show that eyewitnesses can tell strange stories and still be speaking the truth: watch him eat a daffodil in the pulpit. He may quote the old chorus: 'You ask me how I know he lives? He lives within my heart!' Yes, Jesus is risen from the dead, and he is therefore alive and we can get to know him for ourselves.

When it comes to the 'so what', the Pastor is equally emphatic. There really is a life after death! Jesus has gone to prepare a place for us in heaven! Salvation awaits, in a glorious, blissful world beyond this one. We are, after all, 'citizens of heaven', as Paul says, so when we're done with this wicked world our souls will be snatched away to be there for ever. We shall be reunited with our loved ones (don't you wish there was a better phrase, even a better cliché, for saying that?). We shall share the life of the new Jerusalem. 'Here for a season, then above, O Lamb of God I come.' 'Till we cast our crowns before thee, lost in wonder, love and praise.'

Alas: Pastor Gospelman has missed the point. Much of what he says is true, but most of it isn't the truth that the Easter stories were written to convey.

Down the road, fortified by champagne in the Rectory after the midnight Easter vigil (why not break the Lenten fast in style, even if your fasting had itself been, well, somewhat sporadic), Mr Smoothtongue is in full flow. We know of course that the crude, surface meaning of the story can't be what the writers really meant. Modern science has shown that miracles don't happen, that dead people don't rise. Anyway, what kind of a God would break into history just this once, to rescue one favoured person, while standing back and doing nothing during the Holocaust? To believe in something so obvious, so blatant, so . . . *unspiritual* as the empty tomb and the bodily resurrection – it's offensive to all one's finer instincts. In particular, it might be taken to mean (as his good friend Pastor Gospelman up the road would no doubt imagine, bless his fundamentalist socks) that Christianity is therefore superior to all other faiths, whereas we know that God is radically inclusive and that all religions, all faiths, all worldviews can be equally valid Pathways to the Divine.

So . . . the stories of the empty tomb were probably made up many years later. The learned Rector wants to make this quite clear: they are a re-mythologization of the primal eschatological drama, which caught up the disciples in a moment of sociomorphic, possibly even sociopathic, empathy with the apocalyptic denouement of the Beatific Vision. Hmm. No, the congregation didn't quite get that either. But then they, too, had ended the Lenten fast in style.

When it comes to the 'so what', Mr Smoothtongue is emphatic. Now that we've got away from that crude supernatural nonsense, the way is clear to 'True Resurrection'. This, it turns out, is a new way of construing the human project, breaking through the old taboos (he has traditional sexual ethics in mind, but is much too delicate to mention it) and discovering a new kind of life: a welcoming, yes, 'inclusive' approach. The 'stone' of legalism has been rolled away, and the 'risen body', the true spark of life and identity hidden inside each of us, can burst forth. And – well, of course, this new life must now infect all our relationships. All our social policies. Resurrection must become, not a one-off event, imagined by pre-modern minds and insisted on by backward-looking conservatives, but an ongoing event in the liberation of humans and the world.

Mr Smoothtongue is on to something here at last, but he doesn't know what it is. Or why.

What Pastor Gospelman never notices is that the resurrection stories in the gospels *aren't about going to heaven when you die.* In fact, there is almost nothing about 'going to heaven when you die' in the whole New Testament. Being 'citizens of heaven' (Philippians 3.20) doesn't mean you're supposed to end up there. Many of the Philippians were Roman citizens, but Rome didn't want them back when they retired. Their job was to bring Roman culture to Philippi.

That's the point which all the gospels make, in their own ways. Jesus is risen, therefore God's new world has begun. Jesus is risen, therefore Israel and the world have been redeemed. Jesus is risen, therefore his followers have a new job to do.

And what is that new job? To bring the life of heaven to birth in actual, physical, earthly reality. This is what Pastor Gospelman never imagines (though his preaching does, accidentally, often have this result). The bodily resurrection of Jesus is more than a proof that God performs miracles or that the Bible is true. It is more than the Christians' knowing of Jesus in our own experience (that is the truth of Pentecost, not of Easter). It is much, much more than the assurance of heaven after death (Paul speaks of 'going away and being with Christ', but his main emphasis is on *coming back again* in a risen body, to live in God's new-born creation). Jesus' resurrection is the beginning of God's new project, not to snatch people away from earth to heaven, but to colonize earth with the life of heaven. That, after all, is what the Lord's Prayer is about.

That's why Mr Smoothtongue's final point has a grain of truth in it, though all his previous denials make it impossible for him to see why it's true or what its proper shape is. The resurrection is indeed the foundation for a renewed way of life in and for the world. But to get that social, political and cultural result you really do need the bodily resurrection, not just a 'spiritual' event that might have happened to Jesus or perhaps simply to the disciples. And his insistence on 'modern science' (not that he's read any physics recently) is pure Enlightenment rhetoric. We didn't need Galileo and Einstein to tell us that dead people don't come back to life.

When Paul wrote his great resurrection chapter, 1 Corinthians 15, he didn't end by saying 'So let's celebrate the great future life that awaits us.' He ended by saying 'So get on with your work, because you know that in the Lord it won't go to waste.' When the final resurrection occurs, as the centrepiece of God's new creation, we will discover that everything done in the present world in the power of Jesus' own resurrection will be celebrated and included, appropriately transformed.

Of course, when the muddled Rector tries to make Easter mean 'liberation from moral constraint', and 'discovering the true spark within each of us', he is standing genuine Christianity on its head and making it perform tricks like a circus lion, turning it into just another form of gnosticism. Easter is about new creation, a huge and stunning fresh gift of transforming grace, not about discovering that the old world has been misunderstood and needs simply to be allowed to be truly itself. Romans 6, 1 Corinthians 6 and Colossians 3 stand firmly in his way at this point.

Hands up all those who have heard one or other of those sermons. Thank you. How much did I win?

Now hands up those who have heard a sermon which reflects what Paul is talking about in Romans 8, or the evangelists in their final chapters, or John the Seer in Revelation 21 and 22: that, with Easter, God's new creation is launched upon a surprised world, pointing ahead to the renewal, the redemption, the rebirth of the entire creation. Hands up those who have heard the message that every act of love, every deed done in Christ and by the Spirit, every work of true creativity – every time justice is done, peace is made, families are healed, temptation is resisted, true freedom is sought and won – that this very earthly event takes its place within a long history of things which *implement* Jesus' own resurrection and *anticipate* the final new creation, and act as signposts of hope, pointing back to the first and on to the second . . .

I thought so. Thank you.

Notes

Preface

1 See, in particular, *The New Testament and the People of God* (1992); *Jesus and the Victory of God* (1996); *The Resurrection of the Son of God* (2003) and *Paul: Fresh Perspectives* (2005), the first three forming part of the series Christian Origins and the Question of God. All are published by SPCK in London and Fortress Press in Minneapolis; the US title given to the last is *Paul in Fresh Perspective*. In subsequent references these works are referred to as *NTPG*, *JVG*, *RSG* and *Paul*.

1 All dressed up and no place to go?

1 See *The Cross and the Colliery* (London: SPCK, 2007).

2 David Edwards describes a modern version of this in his *After Death? Past Beliefs and Real Possibilities* (London: Cassell, 1999), 101f.

3 Nigel Barley, *Grave Matters: A Lively History of Death around the World* (New York: Holt, 1997; formerly published as *Dancing on the Grave*: Abacus, 1995), 97.

4 'Crossing the Bar' in *The Works of Alfred Lord Tennyson* (London: Macmillan, 1898), 894.

5 'When Earth's Last Picture is Painted' in Rudyard Kipling's *Verse: Inclusive Edition 1885–1926* (London: Hodder & Stoughton, 1927), 223f.

6 A fascinating sidelight on the crisis of faith, and almost equally (though not so widely hailed) the crisis of doubt, is provided by Timothy Larsen, *Crisis of Doubt: Honest Faith in Nineteenth-Century England* (Oxford: Oxford University Press, 2007). Anthony Kenny summarizes the thesis fascinatingly (in the *Times Literary Supplement*, 1 June 2007, 33): 'The plebeian radicals caught the disease [of doubt] at an early stage: a striking number of them recovered after a longer or shorter illness and ended their lives as champions of Christianity. Members of the social elite, on the other hand, were infected at a later stage with a more

virulent form of Victorian doubt, and never grew out of it in their lifetimes.'

7 *Measure for Measure*, Act 3, Scene 1. Shakespeare's most famous treatments of this theme are found in the two famous soliloquies: 'O that this too too solid flesh would melt' and 'To be or not to be', in *Hamlet* (Act 1 Scene 2; Act 3 Scene 1).

8 P. B. Shelley, 'Adonais', st. 39, 42–3, 55.

9 Rupert Brooke, 'The Soldier' (1914).

10 Quoted in Edwards, *After Death?*, 44.

11 M. Edson, *Wit: A Play* (London: Faber and Faber, 1999).

12 See the comments of Pat Jalland, 'Victorian Death and its Decline: 1850–1918' in P. C. Jupp and C. Gittings (eds), *Death in England: An Illustrated History* (New Brunswick, NJ: Rutgers University Press, 1999), 230–55, here at 245, referring to Thomas Huxley.

13 Dylan Thomas, 'Do not go gentle into that good night' (1952) in *The New Oxford Book of English Verse*, chosen and edited by Helen Gardner (Oxford: Oxford University Press, 1972), 942. Reproduced by permission of David Higham Associates.

14 Will Self, *How the Dead Live* (London: Bloomsbury, 2000); e.g., 390.

15 The poem is often attributed to Mary Elizabeth Frye (1904–2004), but its origin is sometimes disputed.

16 Quoted in Ted Harrison, *Beyond Dying: The Mystery of Eternity* (Oxford: Lion, 2000), 68, 72.

17 Philip Pullman, *His Dark Materials*, a trilogy consisting of *Northern Lights*, *The Subtle Knife* and *The Amber Spyglass* (London: Scholastic, 1997, 2000).

18 Nick Hornby, *Fever Pitch* (London: Penguin, 2000 [1992]), 63.

19 Hornby, *Fever Pitch*, 64. Highbury was, until recently, Arsenal's home ground.

20 See, e.g., Harrison, *Beyond Dying*, 17.

21 Barley, *Grave Matters*, 84.

2 Puzzled about paradise?

1 Henry Scott Holland, 'The King of Terrors' in *Facts of the Faith: Being a Collection of Sermons Not Hitherto Published in Book Form*, ed. Christopher Cheshire (London: Longmans, Green & Co., 1919), 125–34.

2 'Death, be not proud' in Helen Gardner (ed.), *The New Oxford Book of English Verse* (Oxford: Oxford University Press, 1972), 197. The punctuation of the last line becomes a major theme in Edson's play *Wit* (see above, 13f.).

3 Compare Donne's famous prayer, 'Bring us, O Lord, at our last awakening, into the house and gate of heaven.' We might want to clarify the use of 'heaven' for the risen life, as we shall see, but the point I am making is that Donne was clear about a two-stage post-mortem existence, with the relation between the first and second stages being conceived in terms of sleeping and waking.

4 That is why I find it extraordinary that so good a scholar as Douglas J. Davies can say that 'Christianity glorified death', and that 'the very existence of Easter' led people 'to speak of human life as a journey through life to the heavenly city': *A Brief History of Death* (Oxford: Blackwell, 2005), 7. Davies's book is remarkable for the way it either marginalizes resurrection altogether or collapses it into a heavenly life after death.

5 Brian Innes, *Death and the Afterlife* (New York: St Martin's Press, 1999).

6 Shakespeare, *Hamlet*, Act 3, Scene 1.

7 Maria Shriver, *What's Heaven?* (New York: St Martin's Press, 1999).

8 The pages are not numbered; these extracts comprise the main message of the whole, short, book.

9 A healthy corrective to all this sort of thing is found in a series of books by Randy Alcorn, principally *Heaven* (Carol Stream, IL: Tyndale House, 2004). Alcorn comes from a tradition that might easily have lapsed into Shriver-type platitudes, but his study of scripture has led him to a far more robust and biblical view – even though he still uses the word 'heaven' when what he emphatically talks about throughout is the new heavens and new earth.

10 I have set this out at length in *Jesus and the Victory of God* (London: SPCK; Minneapolis: Fortress Press, 1996) and *The Challenge of Jesus* (London: SPCK; Downers Grove, IL: InterVarsity Press, 2000).

11 'Till we cast our crowns before thee/ Lost in wonder, love and praise', from 'Love divine, all loves excelling'.

12 It is fascinating to see how, even when faced with the clear and unambiguous teaching of Revelation 21 about 'new heavens and

new earth' and about the new Jerusalem coming down from heaven, some writers continue to refer to all this as simply 'heaven': e.g., Roland Chia, *Hope for the World: A Christian Vision of the Last Things* (Downers Grove, IL: InterVarsity Press, 2005), 102, contrasted with his later brief treatment at 129–33.

13 Cf., e.g., Peter Stanford, *Heaven: A Traveller's Guide to the Undiscovered Country* (London: HarperCollins, 2003); and even Alister E. McGrath, *A Brief History of Heaven* (Oxford: Blackwell, 2003). Considerably more thorough and nuanced, but with several of the same weaknesses, are Colleen McDannell and Bernhard Lang, *Heaven: A History* (New Haven and London: Yale University Press, 2nd edn, 2001 [1988]) and Jeffrey Burton Russell, *A History of Heaven* (Princeton, NJ: Princeton University Press, 1997). Ulrich Simon's older work, *Heaven in the Christian Tradition* (London: Rockliff, 1958), does its best to combine traditional visions of heaven with the solidity of the resurrection ('The Bible views Heaven and Earth as one world. If the earth is spatial, so is Heaven', p. 126), but, though pregnant and thoughtful, the book never quite resolves matters in the way the New Testament itself does.

14 See the remarkable statement of this in David Edwards, *After Death? Past Beliefs and Real Possibilities* (London: Cassell, 1999), 78. For fuller discussion of this point, see Chapter 8 below.

15 A classic statement of this position is found in John Hick, *Evil and the God of Love* (London: Fontana, 1974).

16 John Keble, 'Sun of my soul, thou Saviour dear'.

17 J. H. Newman, 'Lead, kindly Light'.

18 I am grateful to the Revd Peter Tyreus for pointing out to me the difference between the hymn as English-speakers know it and the original Swedish.

19 This point seems to be missed by Stephen Smalley, *Hope for Ever: The Christian View of Life and Death* (Milton Keynes: Paternoster Press, 2005), 79, who treats the 'rest' and the 'calm' as part of an undifferentiated final heavenly state. This is consonant with his view that a 'spiritual resurrection' awaits us after death (17, 78); cf. 65: resurrection will be 'spiritual and relational, rather than physical'.

20 See my *For All the Saints? Remembering the Christian Departed* (London: SPCK; Harrisburg, PA: Morehouse Publishing, 2003).

21 R. Anne Horton, *Using Common Worship Funerals: A Practical Guide to the New Services* (London: Church House Publishing, 2000). To be fair, the word 'resurrection' does occur once or twice, but only in quotations from actual services; it is not discussed in the 'theological introduction', nor is it in the index – despite the assertion that 'great care has been taken to honour the breadth of theological understanding that is held within the Church of England' (61).

22 *Common Worship: Funeral* (London: Church House Publishing, 2000), 6 (260 in the full *Common Worship* book).

23 *Common Worship: Funeral*, 39f. (373f. in the full *Common Worship*).

24 *Common Worship: Funeral*, 51 (330 in the full *Common Worship*). True, the words of 'committal' which precede these prayers do use the phrase 'sure and certain hope of the resurrection to eternal life'. My contention is that the framework and general thrust of these services is such as to encourage people to treat that traditional phrase simply as a metaphor for 'going to heaven when you die'.

25 See, e.g., D. G. Rowell, *The Liturgy of Christian Burial* (London: Alcuin/SPCK, 1997); P. C. Jupp and A. Rogers (eds), *Interpreting Death: Christian Theology and Pastoral Practice* (London: Cassell, 1997); Paul P. J. Sheppy, *Death, Liturgy and Ritual: Vol. I, Pastoral and Liturgical Theology; Vol. II, A Commentary on Liturgical Texts* (London: Ashgate, 2003) and *In Sure and Certain Hope: Liturgies, Prayers and Readings for Funerals and Memorials* (Norwich: Canterbury Press, 2003).

26 Sheppy, *In Sure and Certain Hope*, 26. The theological basis for this collapsing of categories is clear in Sheppy's *Death, Liturgy and Ritual*, 81f., where the bodily resurrection is dismissed as irrelevant, despite Sheppy's insistence on abandoning body/soul dualism: 'the resurrection of the body means that out of death we are incorporated finally into God, and into the Christ.' To this the only possible answer is that, no, that is not what 'the resurrection of the body' means.

27 See my book *Scripture and the Authority of God* (London: SPCK, 2005; US title, *The Last Word*, San Francisco: HarperSanFrancisco, 2005).

28 Wright, *For All the Saints?*

3 Early Christian hope in its historical setting

1 K. R. Popper, *The Open Society and its Enemies* (Princeton, NJ: Princeton University Press, rev. edn, 1971 [1945]).
2 David Edmonds and John Eidinow, *Wittgenstein's Poker: The Story of a Ten-Minute Argument between Two Great Philosophers* (London: Faber and Faber, 2001).
3 For all this, and much besides, see my *The Resurrection of the Son of God* (London: SPCK; Minneapolis: Fortress Press, 2003). The speculation by Herod Antipas that Jesus might be John the Baptist risen from the dead (Mark 6.16) is an exception that proves the rule.
4 Mark 6.14–16 and parallels.
5 John. 11.24.
6 On this whole area, see now the important study of J. D. Levenson, *Resurrection and the Restoration of Israel: The Ultimate Victory of the God of Life* (New Haven and London: Yale University Press, 2006).
7 Mark 12.18–27; Matt. 22.23–33; Luke 20.27–40.
8 Mark 9.10; interestingly, reported in Mark only.
9 Nor did anybody say of Jesus what Johanan ben Zakkai is reported to have said about the destruction of the Temple in AD 70: don't worry about its destruction, we've got something just as good – Torah!
10 David Lawrence, *Heaven: It's Not the End of the World! The Biblical Promise of a New Earth* (London: Scripture Union, 1995).
11 Luke 23.43; John 14.2; Phil. 1.23 with 3.9–11, 20–21.
12 1 Cor. 15.12.
13 2 Tim. 2.18.
14 See Wright, *RSG*, 534–51.
15 Stephen Patterson, in his review of *RSG* in the *Journal of Religion*, 84 (2004), 636f., suggests that this is a 'novel view' of 1 Cor. 15.44. It isn't; and the argument I presented on pp. 347–60 ought to demonstrate it beyond cavil.
16 Matt. 13.43.
17 Phil. 2.15.
18 Gen. 5.25; 2 Kings 2.11–12.
19 Note the way Jesus can speak of 'in the resurrection', parallel to 'in the new world': Matt. 19.28; 22.30.

20 Acts 1.6; see too Rom. 11.15.
21 Josephus, *Antiquities* 20.200–3, on which see my *The New Testament and the People of God* (London: SPCK; Minneapolis: Fortress Press, 1992), 353f. For the various resistance movements, see *NTPG*, 170–81.
22 See Josephus, *Jewish War* 7.153–7.
23 See my *Paul: Fresh Perspectives* (London: SPCK, 2005; US title, *Paul in Fresh Perspective*, Minneapolis: Fortress Press, 2005), ch. 4.
24 See my *Judas and the Gospel of Jesus* (London: SPCK; Grand Rapids, MI: Baker, 2006), esp. ch. 5. Note particularly the rationale given by the pagans for the persecutions at Lyons in AD 177. Note, too, the way in which 'resurrection' is diminished in importance during the medieval period as the church itself becomes increasingly imperial.

4 The strange story of Easter

1 I leave out of consideration the very different account in the so-called *Gospel of Peter*: see N. T. Wright, *The Resurrection of the Son of God* (London: SPCK; Minneapolis: Fortress Press, 2003), 592–6.
2 I here summarize *RSG*, 599–608.
3 One reviewer of *RSG* suggested that I had not sufficiently demonstrated that the four narratives are independent. Close study of the Greek text should make the point well enough: even when the writers are telling the same story, they manage to find quite different phraseology.
4 'Docetism' comes from the Greek word for 'seem' or 'appear'.
5 On all this, see *RSG*, 697–701.
6 On this, see *RSG*, 701–6.
7 John Updike, 'Seven Stanzas at Easter' in *Telephone Poles and Other Poems* (New York: Alfred A. Knopf, 1964), 72f.
8 This argument, which will appear ridiculous even to many sceptics, has been seriously proposed by S. J. Patterson, *The God of Jesus: The Historical Jesus and the Search for Meaning* (Harrisburg PA: Trinity Press International, 1998), ch. 7. Patterson repeats it in his review in the *Journal of Religion*, 84 (2004), 637: 'Those who did accept Jesus' resurrection as a fact might well

have done so out of sheer devotion to their slain martyr and the conviction held by many pious Jews, that God in his righteousness would not give the enemy the final word.' The short answer to this is that we know of a good many pious Jews who were faced with just this kind of situation, and that in no other case did they ever say that their slain, righteous martyr had already been raised from the dead.

9 Cf. Acts 12.15, with *RSG*, 134.

10 Two writers who have devoted a great deal of attention to these questions, and whose numerous works have done a great deal to advance the apologetic argument, are William Lane Craig (e.g., *Assessing the New Testament Evidence for the Historicity of the Resurrection of Jesus* (New York: Edwin Mellen Press, 1989)) and Gary Habermas (e.g., *The Case for the Resurrection of Jesus* (Grand Rapids, MI: Kregel Publications, 2004)). I regret that I did not cite Craig or Habermas in *RSG*.

11 I did once watch the sun set twice in a day; one winter's afternoon I took off from Aberdeen shortly after sunset, and the sun rose again, in the west, as we climbed, only then to set, gloriously, a second time shortly afterwards. That was, of course, cheating.

12 So e.g., Lesslie Newbigin, *Living Hope in a Changing World* (London: Alpha International, 2003), 36.

13 Though some have gone that route and have found their way thereby to full faith: e.g., Frank Morison, *Who Moved the Stone?* (London: Faber and Faber, 1930 and frequently reprinted).

14 *Easter Oratorio*, music by Paul Spicer, words by Tom Wright, is recorded by the Birmingham Bach Choir and available from Farringdon Records: see <www.easteroratorio.com>.

15 See particularly Gerald O'Collins, *Easter Faith: Believing in the Risen Jesus* (London: Darton, Longman & Todd, 2003), 32f., 106f.

16 L. Wittgenstein, *Culture and Value: A Selection from the Posthumous Remains*, ed. G. H. von Wright *et al.*, tr. Peter Winch (Oxford: Blackwell, 1998), 39. The whole passage is truly remarkable and deserves close attention.

17 Once more, Wittgenstein has some extremely suggestive reflections on this whole issue. See, e.g., L. Wittgenstein, *Lectures and Conversations on Aesthetics, Psychology and Religious Belief*, ed.

C. Barrett (Berkeley and Los Angeles: University of California Press, no date).

18 Patterson, in his review already referred to (*Journal of Religion*, 84, 637), suggests that this line of thought is ironic, meaning presumably that it is my own view that is trying to bully opponents into submission. Those who have chafed under the tyranny of being told that because we are children of the Enlightenment we cannot believe in these ancient superstitions will understand what I am talking about.

19 Oscar Wilde, *Salome* in *Complete Works of Oscar Wilde* (London and Glasgow: Collins, 1966 [1948]), 565.

5 Cosmic future: progress or despair?

1 Theologians will recognize that I am in implicit dialogue throughout this Part of the book with two of the great German theologians of the last generation: Wolfhart Pannenberg (see, e.g., his *Systematic Theology*, vol. 3 (Grand Rapids, MI: Eerdmans; Edinburgh: T. & T. Clark, 1993), ch. 15 and many other places; and Jürgen Moltmann, e.g., *Theology of Hope* (London: SCM Press, 1967) and *The Coming of God: Christian Eschatology* (Minneapolis: Fortress Press, 1996). There is an entire book to be written as part of this ongoing conversation, but this is not it. On Moltmann, see particularly R. J. Bauckham, *God Will Be All In All: The Eschatology of Jürgen Moltmann* (Edinburgh: T. & T. Clark, 2005 [1999]).

2 Sources I have found helpful in these chapters include John Polkinghorne and Michael Welker (eds), *The End of the World and the Ends of God: Science and Theology on Eschatology* (Harrisburg, PA: Trinity Press International, 2000); John Colwell (ed.), *Called to One Hope: Perspectives on Life to Come* (Carlisle: Paternoster Press, 2000). The latter includes my lecture, 'New Heavens, New Earth', originally given in 1993, which anticipates several aspects of the present book, not least these chapters. See too my *The Myth of the Millennium* (London: SPCK, 1999), published in the USA as *The Millennium Myth* (Louisville, KY: Westminster John Knox Press). Among other recent writers, Richard Bauckham is prolific and, in my view, largely on the right lines: see, e.g., his book with Trevor Hart, *Hope against Hope: Christian Eschatology in Contemporary Context* (Grand Rapids, MI: Eerdmans, 1999).

3 See Bauckham in Colwell (ed.), *Called to One Hope*, 240–51.

4 On the reasons for the uncritical acceptance of Darwin, see interestingly L. Wittgenstein, *Lectures and Conversations on Aesthetics, Psychology and Religious Belief*, ed. C. Barrett (Berkeley and Los Angeles: University of California Press, no date), 26f.

5 Ursula King, 'Teilhard de Chardin, Pierre' in *The Oxford Companion to Christian Thought*, ed. A. Hastings (Oxford: Oxford University Press, 2000), 694–6, at 695.

6 King, 'Teilhard de Chardin', 696.

7 The prayer (which begins 'O God of unchangeable power and eternal light . . .') appears to originate in the 1912 Scottish Book of Common Prayer.

8 See my *Evil and the Justice of God* (London: SPCK; Downers Grove, IL: InterVarsity Press, 2006).

9 On all this, see Polkinghorne and Welker, *End of the World*, 1–13; W. R. Stoeger in *End of the World*, ch. 1 (19–28); and Polkinghorne in *End of the World*, ch. 2 (29–41). Polkinghorne begins his chapter by questioning the 'scientific' side of Teilhard de Chardin's theory.

10 See, too, my *Judas and the Gospel of Jesus* (London: SPCK; Grand Rapids, MI: Baker, 2006) and other works referred to there.

11 Joni Mitchell, 'Woodstock' (1970).

12 See Stuart Holroyd, *The Elements of Gnosticism* (Shaftesbury: Element, 1994), esp. chs 1 and 7.

13 On Phil. 3.20f.; 1 Pet. 1; etc., cf. 111f., 145, 163f. below.

6 What the whole world's waiting for

1 See Hag. 2.6f.; cp. Rom. 8.18–26.

2 On Col. 1, cf. my *The Climax of the Covenant* (Edinburgh: T. & T. Clark; Minneapolis: Fortress Press, 1992), ch. 5. The relevant passage is set out in full at the end of the present chapter (p. 118).

3 1 Cor. 15.20, 23; cf. Rom. 8.23; 11.16; 16.5; 1 Cor. 16.15; 2 Thess. 2.13; Jas 1.18.

4 There are attempts from time to time to imply that even Jesus' resurrection might be evidence of a new strand in some sort of evolutionary process: Jesus had 'developed' further than the rest of us, so that he was able, by 'natural' means, to pass through death and on into a new life: e.g., Stephen Holt in S. E. Porter, M. A.

Hayes and D. Tombs (eds), *Resurrection,* JSNT Supplement Series 186 (Sheffield: Sheffield Academic Press, 1999), 11.

5 Contra Kathryn Tanner in John Polkinghorne and Michael Welker (eds), *The End of the World and the Ends of God: Science and Theology on Eschatology* (Harrisburg, PA: Trinity Press International, 2000), 232.

6 This is taken for granted by, e.g., Alister E. McGrath, *A Brief History of Heaven* (Oxford: Blackwell, 2003), 12f. McGrath goes so far as to suggest that this (mis)interpretation is 'one of the leading themes of Paul's theology'.

7 On Phil. 3.20f., see my *The Resurrection of the Son of God* (London: SPCK; Minneapolis: Fortress Press, 2003), 229–36.

8 See, e.g., Jürgen Moltmann, *God in Creation: An Ecological Doctrine of Creation* (London: SCM Press, 1985), 86–93.

9 Isa. 11.9; Hab. 2.14.

10 Paul of course also knows this idea: Gal. 4.26. Cf. too Heb. 12.22–24.

11 This translation is taken from my *Paul for Everyone: The Prison Letters* (London: SPCK; Louisville, KY: Westminster John Knox Press, 2002), 148.

7 Jesus, heaven and new creation

1 Ps. 110.1, a favourite text of the early Christians: cf. Matt. 22.44 and parallels; Mark 16.19 (in the 'longer ending', of course); Acts 2.34f.; Eph. 1.20; Col. 3.1; Heb. 1.13; 10.12; 1 Pet. 3.22; Rev. 3.21; cf. Luke 19.27; 1 Cor. 15.25.

2 E.g., Rom. 8.34; Eph. 1.20; 2.6.

3 Douglas Farrow, *Ascension and Ecclesia: On the Significance of the Doctrine of the Ascension for Ecclesiology and Christian Cosmology* (Grand Rapids, MI: Eerdmans, 1999). See too G. S. Dawson, *Jesus Ascended: The Meaning of Christ's Continuing Incarnation* (London: T. & T. Clark International, 2004).

4 See particularly T. F. Torrance, *Space, Time and Resurrection* (Edinburgh: Handsel Press, 1976), 110, 123–6; also his *Space, Time and Incarnation* (London: Oxford University Press, 1969).

5 Matt. 28.19.

6 2 Cor. 4.5.

7 On the continuing human work of Jesus, see particularly, of course, the letter to the Hebrews (e.g., 7.25; 9.24); and cf., e.g., Torrance, *Space, Time and Resurrection*, 130, 133.

8 Farrow, *Ascension and Ecclesia*, 130–2, 153f. More detail in J. Pelikan, *The Christian Tradition: A History of the Development of Doctrine*, 5 vols (Chicago and London: University of Chicago Press, 1971–89), 3.160ff.

9 Likewise, finally, only when we grasp that Jesus is already Lord of the world on the one hand, and that at his final appearing every knee will eventually bow to him, do we realize that the proper feast of Christ the King is either Ascension Day itself or Advent Sunday, and to have a feast by that name at any other time is not just a category mistake but indicative of muddled, and actually damaging, theological thinking. Jesus does not become king of the world gradually; and his kingdom can never be identified, one for one, with the extension of the church's witness and influence, as is all too easily implied by the very recent innovation, in Roman Catholic and Anglican circles, of having such a 'feast' on the last Sunday before Advent. See my *For All the Saints? Remembering the Christian Departed* (London: SPCK; Harrisburg, PA: Morehouse Publishing, 2003), 63–70.

10 See again Torrance, *Space, Time and Resurrection*, 133f.

11 Hal Lindsey, *The Late Great Planet Earth* (Grand Rapids, MI: Zondervan, 1971).

12 A very helpful summary and critique of the whole movement is one of the many virtues of Craig C. Hill's book *In God's Time: The Bible and the Future* (Grand Rapids, MI: Eerdmans, 2002), 199–209.

13 See, not least, Psalms 96 and 98.

14 See my *Simply Christian* (London: SPCK; San Francisco: HarperSanFrancisco, 2005), ch. 2.

15 For a full discussion, see my *The New Testament and the People of God* (London: SPCK; Minneapolis: Fortress Press, 1992), ch. 10; and esp. *Jesus and the Victory of God* (London: SPCK; Minneapolis: Fortress Press, 1996), 207–9. A radically different usage, and historical proposal, can be found in J. D. Crossan, *The Birth of Christianity* (San Francisco: HarperSanFrancisco, 1998), esp. chs 15–18. A very helpful study can be found in Richard

Bauckham's article in A. Hastings (ed.), *The Oxford Companion to Christian Thought* (Oxford: Oxford University Press, 2000), 206–9.

8 When he appears

1   And another thing, while we're deconstructing that lovely hymn: neither in the Bible nor Christian tradition (Heb. 2.13, quoting Isa. 8.18, is the only possible exception) are Jesus' followers described as his children. 'His brethren' would be better; perhaps in this politically sensitive age 'his siblings'. This is, perhaps, the implicit docetism of the hymn peeping through, not for the only time, collapsing the vital distinction between Jesus and the father.

2   See my *Jesus and the Victory of God* (London: SPCK; Minneapolis: Fortress Press, 1996), chs 8, 13; *The Challenge of Jesus* (London: SPCK; Downers Grove, IL: InterVarsity Press, 2000), chs 2, 5.

3   Mark 13.26; 14.62 (and parallels).

4   E.g., Matt. 25.14–30; Luke 19.11–27; and the small scenarios in 12.35–48 and elsewhere. On these, see *JVG*, 632–9.

5   E.g., Mal. 3.1; cf. Zech. 14.5; other texts in *JVG*, 615–24.

6   Acts 1.11.

7   See esp., e.g., Acts 3.19–21.

8   See especially *Paul: Fresh Perspectives* (London: SPCK, 2005; US title, *Paul in Fresh Perspective*, Minneapolis: Fortress Press, 2005), ch. 7.

9   See, e.g., Josephus, *Antiquities* 3.80, 203.

10   1 Thess. 5.2; 1 Cor. 1.8; 5.5; 2 Cor. 1.14; Phil. 1.6, 10; 2.16; 2 Pet. 3.10.

11   See C. J. Setzer in J. T. Carroll (ed.), *The Return of Jesus in Early Christianity* (Peabody, MA: Hendrickson, 2000), 169–83.

12   See further, *Paul*, ch. 4, and other material referred to there.

13   For the persecution of the Thessalonians, cf., e.g., 1.6; 2.14; 3.3f.

14   1 Cor. 16.22.

15   Col. 3.4.

16   Rev. 1.7; 2.25; 3.11; 16.15; 22.7, 12, 20.

17   Jas 5.7–8 is important, as is Heb. 9.28. 1 Pet. 1.20f. and 5.4 use the word 'appear' both for the first and the second coming of Jesus.

18   See C. H. Talbert in *Vigilae Christianae*, 20 (1966), 142 (quoted by J. S. Siker, 'The Parousia of Jesus in Second and Third Cen-

tury Christianity' in Carroll (ed.), *The Return of Jesus*, 148). And all these passages, see the relevant places in my *The Resurrection of the Son of God* (London: SPCK; Minneapolis: Fortress Press, 2003), in particular, for 2 Pet. 3.5–13, *RSG*, 462f.

19 See Siker in Carroll (ed.) *The Return of Jesus*; and esp. my *The New Testament and the People of God* (London: SPCK; Minneapolis: Fortress Press, 1992), 459–64.

9 Jesus the coming judge

1 Ps. 98.8; the whole Psalm is relevant, as are several others in that section of the Psalter.

2 See particularly Miroslav Volf, *Exclusion and Embrace: A Theological Exploration of Identity, Otherness and Reconciliation* (Nashville, TN: Abingdon Press, 1994).

3 Acts 17.31; cf. 10.42.

4 On all this, see my *What Saint Paul Really Said* (Grand Rapids, MI: Eerdmans, 1997; Oxford: Lion, 2003), ch. 7, and *Paul: Fresh Perspectives* (London: SPCK, 2005; US title, *Paul in Fresh Perspective*, Minneapolis: Fortress Press, 2005), ch. 6. See also 'Redemption from the New Perspective' in S. T. Davis, D. Kendall, G. O'Collins (eds), *Redemption* (Oxford: Oxford University Press, 2004), 69–100; '4QMMT and Paul: Justification, "Works," and Eschatology' in Sang-Won (Aaron) Son (ed.), *History and Exegesis: New Testament Essays in Honor of Dr E. Earle Ellis for his 80th Birthday* (New York and London: T. & T. Clark, 2006), 104–32; and 'New Perspectives on Paul' in Bruce L. McCormack (ed.), *Justification in Perspective: Historical Developments and Contemporary Challenges* (Grand Rapids, MI: Baker Academic, 2006), 243–64.

5 See my *Romans* in the *New Interpreter's Bible*, vol. X (Nashville, TN: Abingdon Press, 2002), 393–770; the various volumes of *Paul for Everyone* (London: SPCK; Louisville, KY: Westminster John Knox Press: *Galatians and Thessalonians*, 2002; *The Prison Letters*, 2002; *1 Corinthians* and *2 Corinthians*, both 2003; *Romans* (2 vols), 2004); and *The Climax of the Covenant* (Edinburgh: T. & T. Clark; Minneapolis: Fortress Press, 1992), esp. chs 7, 8, 10 and 13.

6 Cf., e.g., 2 Tim. 4.1; 1 Pet. 4.5.

7 John 5.22–30.

8 E.g., John 16.8–11, about which there is no space to say more at this point.

9 See Douglas Farrow, *Ascension and Ecclesia: On the Significance of the Doctrine of the Ascension for Ecclesiology and Christian Cosmology* (Grand Rapids, MI: Eerdmans, 1999), 271.

10 1 Cor. 11.27–34.

11 See esp. T. F. Torrance, *Space, Time and Resurrection* (Edinburgh: Handsel Press, 1976), 158.

12 2 Cor. 4.5.

13 This is the logic behind, e.g., 1 Cor. 15.58; see my *The Way of the Lord: Christian Pilgrimage in the Holy Land and Beyond* (London: SPCK; Grand Rapids, MI: Eerdmans, 1999), ch. 9, and below, Chapter 13.

10 The redemption of our bodies

1 See, obviously, my *The Resurrection of the Son of God* (London: SPCK; Minneapolis: Fortress Press, 2003).

2 1 John 3.1f.

3 John 5.25–29.

4 John 14.2.

5 Luke 23.43.

6 Those interested in exploring the background to the word 'paradise' will find a detailed and fascinating account in J. N. Bremmer, *The Rise and Fall of the Afterlife* (London and New York: Routledge, 2002), 109–27. I regret that this work appeared too late for me to interact with it in *RSG*.

7 Phil. 1.23.

8 Matt. 6.20; 19.21; Luke 12.21; cf. 1 Tim. 6.19.

9 1 Pet. 1.3.

10 Cf. *RSG*, chs 6 and 7.

11 Cf. 2 Cor. 5.17.

12 From 'Light's abode, celestial Salem', attributed to Thomas à Kempis, tr. J. M Neale. (Unfortunately Neale published this in a collection called *The Celestial Country: Hymns on the Joys and Glories of Paradise* (London: Seeley & Co., 1866), which our earlier argument shows to be a typically misleading nineteenth-century way of putting it.)

13 1 Cor. 15.44.

14 1 Cor. 15.50. See, e.g., Irenaeus, *Against Heresies* 5.9.1–4, discussed in *RSG*, 515.

15 Details in *RSG*, ch. 11.

16 C. S. Lewis, *Miracles* (London: Fontana, 1960 [1947]), 155. Lewis's chapter on 'Miracles of the New Creation', from which this is taken, remains one of the clearest succinct statements of the biblical picture.

17 Jeffrey Burton Russell, *A History of Heaven* (Princeton, NJ: Princeton University Press, new edn, 1998), 119f.

18 C. S. Lewis, *The Great Divorce* (London: Macmillan, 1946, frequently republished).

19 1 Tim. 6.16.

20 E.g., Rom. 5.17; 1 Cor. 6.2, 3; 2 Tim. 2.12; Rev. 1.6; 5.10; 20.4; 22.5. Perhaps also (depending on its interpretation) Luke 19.17, 19.

21 This seems to be the position of, e.g., D. J. Davies, *Death, Ritual and Belief: The Rhetoric of Funerary Rites* (New York: Continuum, 2002 [1997]), 128: 'For Christians, resurrection would be the mode of entry into a heavenly domain where salvation would be fully known.' This combines several misunderstandings.

22 Rev. 6.9–11.

23 To be fair, the song in question ('When the trumpet of the Lord shall sound', by James M. Black (1893)) deconstructs its own incipient Platonism with the next line: 'And the morning breaks eternal, bright and fair'. If there is a morning breaking, it can hardly be true that time has stopped.

24 Lewis, *Miracles*, 153.

25 See the whole discussion in J. Polkinghorne, *The God of Hope and the End of the World* (London: SPCK, 2002), esp. 107–12.

11 Purgatory, paradise, hell

1 1 Tim. 1.18; 6.12; see, too, 2 Tim. 4.7.

2 The best and most fascinating treatment I have come across of this whole development is in Stephen Greenblatt, *Hamlet in Purgatory* (Princeton: Princeton University Press, 2001), esp. ch. 2. Greenblatt's eventual thesis – that *Hamlet* has as its subtext an implicitly Protestant son (Hamlet has been studying at Wittenberg) confronted by an implicitly Catholic paternal ghost, still suffering post-mortem anguish – is spectacular, but so,

equally, is his historical and cultural treatment of the rise and development of purgatory and its hold on late-medieval culture. See also the very helpful study of J. N. Bremmer, *The Rise and Fall of the Afterlife* (London and New York: Routledge, 2002), ch. 5.

3 See K. Rahner, *On the Theology of Death* (ET, New York: Herder & Herder, 1961). Rahner's teaching is helpfully summarized in William J. La Due, *The Trinity Guide to Eschatology* (New York and London: Continuum, 2004), 51–7.

4 See Joseph Ratzinger, *Eschatology: Death and Eternal Life* (vol. 9 of Johann Auer and Joseph Ratzinger, *Dogmatic Theology*) (ET, Washington: Catholic University of America Press, 1988), 218–33. See too, e.g., the wise exposition of Dermot A. Lane, *Keeping Hope Alive: Stirrings in Christian Theology* (Eugene, OR: Wipf & Stock, 2005 [originally pub. Paulist Press, 1996]), 143–8. Lane describes a shift among theologians 'from seeing Purgatory as a place to a moment of personal and transforming encounter with the love of God' (148).

5 It seems that this was the preferred option in the famous sermon by Scott Holland we discussed in Chapter 2 above.

6 Phil. 1.26.

7 Rom. 8.1.

8 Rom. 8.38f.

9 Luke 13.3, 5. On the whole topic, cf. my *Jesus and the Victory of God* (London: SPCK; Minneapolis: Fortress Press, 1996), ch. 8.

10 Luke 12.35–59; 16.19–31.

11 Matt. 25.31–46.

12 Miroslav Volf, *Exclusion and Embrace: A Theological Exploration of Identity, Otherness and Reconciliation* (Nashville, TN: Abingdon Press, 1994); Desmond Tutu, *No Future Without Forgiveness: A Personal Overview of South Africa's Truth and Reconciliation Commission* (London: Rider, 2000).

13 See 1 Tim. 6.16.

14 Rom. 2.8; 11.31.

12 Rethinking salvation: heaven, earth and the kingdom of God

1 For my recent debates with J. D. Crossan, see particularly Robert B. Stewart (ed.), *The Resurrection of Jesus: John Dominic Crossan*

and N. T. Wright in Dialogue (Minneapolis: Fortress Press, 2006).

2 A good deal of what follows is in parallel to the work of Richard Bauckham and Trevor Hart, *Hope against Hope: Christian Eschatology at the Turn of the Millennium* (Grand Rapids, MI: Eerdmans, 1999), though it was developed independently. The work of Bauckham here and in many other places (e.g., *Bible and Mission: Christian Witness in a Postmodern World* (Grand Rapids, MI: Baker Academic, 2004)) remains powerful and seminal.

3 1 Cor. 15.19.

4 *Mission-Shaped Church* (London: Church House Publishing, 2004).

5 Adrian Plass, *Bacon Sandwiches and Salvation: An A–Z of the Christian Life* (London: Authentic Media, 2007).

6 Plass, *Bacon Sandwiches*, p. 163.

7 Plass, *Bacon Sandwiches*, pp. 164f., emphasis added.

8 Mark 5.23, 28, 34.

9 Matt. 9.22.

10 There is abundant material to follow up this point: see, e.g., Matt. 8.25; 14.30; Mark 6.56; 10.52; Luke 8.36; 8.50; 17.19; 18.42; Acts 4.9; 14.9; 16.30, 31; 23.24; 27.20, 31, 34, 43, 44; 28.1, 4.

11 See, for a start, my *Evil and the Justice of God* (London: SPCK; Downers Grove, IL: InterVarsity Press, 2006), ch. 3.

12 Rom. 8.19.

13 Matt. 28.18; Rev. 11.15.

14 I have explored this most fully in *Jesus and the Victory of God* (London: SPCK; Minneapolis: Fortress Press, 1996).

15 See particularly *Paul: Fresh Perspectives* (London: SPCK, 2005; US title, *Paul in Fresh Perspective*, Minneapolis: Fortress Press, 2005), ch. 2.

16 See, e.g., my *Evil and the Justice of God*, ch. 3; *The Challenge of Jesus* (London: SPCK; Downers Grove, IL: InterVarsity Press, 2000), ch. 4; *JVG*, ch. 12; *The Meaning of Jesus: Two Visions* (with Marcus Borg, London: SPCK; San Francisco: HarperSanFrancisco, 1999), ch. 6.

17 The so-called 'other gospels' – *Thomas* and the rest – are distinguished by this, that they neither want to see God's kingdom inaugurated on earth as in heaven nor want to know anything about Jesus' saving death. That is why they are so attractive to those

who today prefer, as some did at the time they were written, an escapist philosophy and a spirituality of self-discovery. On all this, see now, e.g., Nicholas Perrin, *Thomas: The Other Gospel* (London: SPCK, 2007); Darrell L. Bock, *The Missing Gospels: Unearthing the Truth Behind Alternative Christianities* (Nashville, TN: Thomas Nelson, 2006).

13 Building for the kingdom

1 Mark 12.18–27 and parallels, referring to Exod. 3.6; see my *The Resurrection of the Son of God* (London: SPCK; Minneapolis: Fortress Press, 2003), 416–29.

2 See now Eric Metaxas, *Amazing Grace: William Wilberforce and the Heroic Campaign to End Slavery* (San Francisco: HarperOne, 2007).

3 E.g., F. A. Hayek, *The Road to Serfdom: Text and Documents*, ed. Bruce Caldwell (Chicago: University of Chicago Press, 2007).

4 On the use of 'Sadducee' as a title for an intellectual movement within the German Enlightenment, following the line of Spinoza into an atheism which left the way clear for humans to do what they liked, see Jonathan I. Israel, *Radical Enlightenment, Philosophy and the Making of Modernity 1650–1750* (Oxford: Oxford University Press, 2001), 154, 367 and elsewhere.

5 On this theme, see my *Simply Christian* (London: SPCK; San Francisco: HarperSanFrancisco, 2005), Part I.

6 2 Cor. 5.17.

14 Reshaping the church for mission (1): biblical roots

1 This chapter was drafted before I read C. J. H. Wright, *The Mission of God: Unlocking the Bible's Grand Narrative* (Downers Grove, IL: InterVarsity Press, 2006). With this work, Christopher Wright (no relation) has continued to establish himself as one of the leading biblical missiologists in the world today.

2 For other reflections on Luke 24, see, e.g., my *The Challenge of Jesus* (London: SPCK; Downers Grove, IL: InterVarsity Press, 2000), ch. 7.

3 For more detail here, see my *Challenge*, ch. 8; *The Resurrection of the Son of God* (London: SPCK; Minneapolis: Fortress Press, 2003), ch. 17; and, in a different genre, *Easter Oratorio*, music by

Paul Spicer, words by Tom Wright, recorded by the Birmingham Bach Choir and available from Farringdon Records: see <www.easteroratorio.com>.

4 Isa. 55.11–13.

5 John 20.21.

6 For an interesting statement of a similar set of questions, see J. L. Martyn, 'Epistemology at the Turn of the Ages' in W. R. Farmer, C. F. D. Moule and R. R. Niebuhr (eds), *Christian History and Interpretation: Studies Presented to John Knox* (Cambridge: Cambridge University Press, 1967) 269–87.

7 John 20.28.

8 Ludwig Wittgenstein, *Tractatus Logico-Philosophicus* (London: Routledge & Kegan Paul, 1974), 74.

9 Acts 1.6. On Acts, see now my *Acts for Everyone* (London: SPCK; Louisville, KY: Westminster John Knox Press, 2008).

10 Ps. 72.8; cf. the visions of worldwide Davidic kingship in, e.g., Isa. 9; 11; 42; etc.

11 Acts 1.8.

12 Josephus, *Antiquities* 19.434–50.

13 Acts 28.31.

14 Acts 4.2.

15 Acts 17.31. See Aeschylus, *Eumenides* 647f. (discussed in *RSG*, 32).

16 Phil. 1.23.

17 Cp. Heb. 2.8f., also using Ps. 8.

18 NRSV; but this could sound as though it's just an opinion which might yet be false, whereas Paul intends it emphatically to be seen as something which is necessarily true of all those in Christ. It needs 'calculating' because it is not an obvious truth; but, once the sum has been reckoned up, it will be recognized to be certainly true.

19 Cf. Rom. 10.9–10.

20 Col. 3.5–9.

21 Eph. 4.21–5.20.

15 Reshaping the church for mission (2): living the future

1 See particularly John Inge, *A Christian Theology of Place* (London: Ashgate, 2003).

2 John 4.24.
3 See my book *The Myth of the Millennium* (London: SPCK, 1999; US title, *The Millennium Myth*, Louisville, KY: Westminster John Knox Press, 1999).
4 See John 20.1, 19; 1 Cor. 16.2.
5 A spectacular and deeply moving account of Christian life in these terms is offered by Samuel Wells, *God's Companions: Reimagining Christian Ethics* (Malden, MA and Oxford: Blackwell, 2006).
6 Phil. 4.8.
7 1 Pet. 1.3.
8 I am here following through some of the lines I began to explore in *Simply Christian* (London: SPCK; San Francisco: HarperSanFrancisco, 2005), ch. 12.
9 Job 13.15.
10 John 16.27.
11 John 20.17.
12 Rev. 5.12.
13 See my *Scripture and the Authority of God* (London: SPCK, 2005; US title, *The Last Word*, San Francsco: HarperSanFrancisco, 2005).
14 After writing this I came across the verdict of Wittgenstein (himself, of course, a Jew): 'The Old Testament [should be] seen as the body without its head; the New T[estament]: the head; the Epistles of the Apostles: the crown on the head. If I think of the Jewish Bible, the Old Testament on its own, I should like to say: the head is (still) missing from this body. The solution to these problems is missing. The fulfilment of these hopes is missing. But I do not necessarily think of a head as having a crown.' *Culture and Value: A Selection from the Posthumous Remains*, ed. G. H. von Wright *et al.*, tr. Peter Winch (Oxford: Blackwell, 1998), 40e.
15 Rom. 1.32.
16 1 Cor. 13.9–12.

Tailpiece: two Easter sermons

1 Slightly adapted from the original, published at Easter 2003 on the 'Ship of Fools' website: <www.shipoffools.com/Features/frameit.htm?0403/wright_wrong.html>

Index of biblical references

Index of biblical references

Index of names

Index of names

Vaughan, H. 28
Volf, M. 191, 321, 324
von Wright, G. H. 315, 328

Watts, Isaac 28
Welker, M. 316–17, 318
Wells, Samuel 327–8
Wesley, Charles 26, 128, 294
Wilberforce, W. 38, 228–9, 258

Wilde, Oscar 87, 316
Winch, P. 315, 328
Wittgenstein, L. 42–6, 64, 84, 252–3, 315, 317, 327, 328
Woolman, John 229
Wright, C. J. H. 326

Yeats, W. B. 102

Index of topics